A Pocket Guide to Ibsen, Chekhov and Strindberg

Michael Pennington has been a leading British actor for 30 years, playing a wide variety of roles in London's West End, for the Royal Shakespeare Company, the Royal National Theatre and the English Shakespeare Company, which he co-founded in 1986. He has appeared in film and on television, and has also directed in England, Japan and the United States. His other books include *Rossya – A Journey Through Siberia*, *The English Shakespeare Company – The Wars of the Roses*, *Hamlet: A User's Guide*, *Twelfth Night: A User's Guide* and his account of his one-man show on Chekhov: *Are You There, Crocodile?*

Stephen Unwin, Artistic Director of English Touring Theatre, has directed more than fifty professional theatre and opera productions, including five highly regarded productions of Ibsen. He co-wrote *A Pocket Guide to Shakespeare's Plays* and *A Pocket Guide to 20th Century Drama*.

A POCKET GUIDE TO
Ibsen, Chekhov and Strindberg

Michael Pennington and
Stephen Unwin

faber and faber

First published in 2004
by Faber and Faber Limited
3 Queen Square London WC1N 3AU

Published in the United States by Faber and Faber Inc.
an affiliate of Farrar, Straus and Giroux LLC, New York

Typeset by Faber and Faber Limited
Printed in England by Bookmarque Ltd, Croydon

A CIP record for this book
is available from the British Library

ISBN 0–571–21475–4

10 9 8 7 6 5 4 3 2 1

Thanks to Kate Wild for her help with Strindberg

Contents

Introduction

The half-century leading up to the outbreak of the First World War in 1914 was a period of unprecedented stability and prosperity in Europe. This briefest of historical outlines emphasizes a flowering in science and the arts as well as great advances in the quality and comfort of middle-class life. It also highlights the emergence of many of the radical new ideas about society which would make the twentieth century so turbulent. Such was the background for the mature work of three of the world's greatest dramatists: Henrik Ibsen (1828–1906), Anton Chekhov (1860–1904) and August Strindberg (1848–1912).

Nations and Empire

By 1900 the world was dominated by Europe to an extent almost inconceivable a century later. The British Empire was the largest in history (ruling nearly a quarter of the world's population); Germany, France, Italy, Spain, Portugal and Belgium also controlled enormous territories, which – like Britain – they managed with a combination of enlightenment, brutality, idealism and greed. What had started as a network of trading stations were now huge zones of influence, each with its codes, rituals and personalities, and each driven by a conviction of Europe's role as the natural ruler and educator of mankind.

The 'bourgeois revolutions' of 1848 had put an end to sixty years of unrest triggered by the French Revolution of 1789; and by 1870 all such upheavals seemed to have subsided for good, as Europe dedicated itself to the serious business of nation-building and making money. Then the shock defeat of imperial France in the Franco-Prussian War marked the arrival of Germany as a power capable of dominating continental Europe. In the face of this, Britain beat her Imperial drum ever more loudly; however, by the death of Queen

Victoria in 1901, confidence had been undermined by further challenges abroad, a decline in industrial output at home and social fragmentation. The balance of power within Europe was increasingly unstable, as August 1914 was to prove.

Throughout, the twin attractions of industrialization and national identity had proved irresistible. Italy had been unified in 1861 and was pressing for recognition as a major European power. Although the Hapsburg Empire was decaying, her capital cities – Vienna and Budapest – were flourishing. The Balkans, caught between the Austro-Hungarian and Ottoman Empires, were dense with nationalist intrigue. In Scandinavia there had been widespread poverty and mass emigration, but when industrialization finally arrived, the result was rapid economic progress and democratic reform; Norway, the poorest region, would eventually gain her independence from Sweden, the largest and most powerful, in 1905.

Elsewhere, the victory of the North in the American Civil War (1865) had given the United States a chance to realize her extraordinary potential: by 1890 she was responsible for nearly a third of the world's industrial output, and by 1901 led the world in the production of coal, steel and crude oil. By 1914 her industrial supremacy was assured. More than thirty million Europeans ('the huddled masses') had emigrated to America and the Statue of Liberty had been erected in New York Harbour in 1886 as an emblem of her appeal.

In Russia, however, the period had a more tragic flavour. The emancipation of more than forty million serfs in 1861 resulted from the reforming instincts of Tsar Alexander II, but it also cut some of the ties which had kept Russia's fragile social order together. Landowners accustomed to depending on serf labour were ill-equipped for self-government; the serfs soon found themselves not so much enfranchised as unprotected, and poverty and illness multiplied. Disillusion on both sides left the field open for violent revolution – Alexander himself was assassinated in 1881 and was succeeded by the reactionary Alexander III, who undid much of his work. The brutal suppression of the Workers' Uprisings in St Petersburg in 1905 accelerated the 1917 Revolution, in which the entire social system of Tsarist Russia was swept away.

The big cities

The boom in the European economy after the Napoleonic Wars turned to bust in the early 1870s. But recovery came in the mid-1890s, and the age of 'high capitalism' dawned, with a huge surge in consumption; large companies now made increasingly advanced products, employing new industrial techniques. The 'second railway age' saw an unprecedented expansion in track and rolling-stock, while demand for steel, coal and other staples soared. Assembly-line mass-production was mastered and by 1913 total world output was five times greater than it had been in 1870.

The agricultural depression of the 1870s had led to rural depopulation, and by 1890 nearly half the people of northern Europe lived in the cities, particularly the capitals. These new centres naturally required workers of all kinds, skilled and unskilled, for manufacturing and service industries alike; the resulting proletariat typically lived in vast working-class quarters, some in reasonable comfort, others in abject poverty. Despite fairly consistent wage increases throughout the period, the relationship between capital and labour was frequently brutal. Gradually, however, the middle classes began to notice the living conditions of the urban poor, and wealthy philanthropists became concerned to better them. Governments, too – first in Germany, then in Britain, France and Scandinavia – turned their attention to improving welfare, housing and education for working people.

The increased involvement of the state in economic and industrial affairs, as well as welfare, called for public officials of all kinds. New economic structures demanded new levels of capital investment: financial services flourished, with the large banks employing armies of managers, tellers and clerks. The new city-dwellers required the services of a whole range of professionals – doctors, lawyers, teachers, journalists – and the modern bourgeoisie was born. White-collar office workers, on good salaries in secure jobs, were eager for new commodities, with familiar results: shopping boulevards, brand names, department stores, mail-order catalogues and billboard advertising. Local authorities built monuments and parks, restaurants and cafés were opened, astonishing buildings such as the Eiffel Tower in Paris and the first steel-frame skyscraper in Chicago were constructed, while large new suburbs sprang up, served by commuter railways such as the London Underground, the New York subway and the Paris Métro. The cities became increasingly congested; modern urban life in all its complexity had begun.

A space of just thirty years (1879–1909) saw an astonishing range of inventions and technological advances. Alexander Bell invented the telephone and Thomas Edison the lightbulb. Heinrich Hertz discovered radio waves, the Lumière brothers created the cinematograph, Marconi invented wireless telegraphy, Daimler and Benz built the car engine, pneumatic tyres were developed, refrigerated transport was pioneered and, on 17 December 1903, Wilbur and Orville Wright's first powered plane took off from Kitty Hawk in North Carolina. Meanwhile, laboratory scientists made a number of significant medical breakthroughs, including the discovery of the cause of tuberculosis and the invention of the X-ray.

The chief beneficiaries of all this were the new middle classes, some of whom, perhaps understandably, came to believe that they were an unquestionable force for good, capable of anything, and that the world they had created was uniquely well-organized. This assumption of moral superiority – symbolized by the values of hard work and family life, patriotism and religious devotion – thinly disguised less attractive phenomena: jingoism, deep racial and social division, prostitution and child labour. But in contrast to the brutality ahead, the period leading up to the First World War was one in which European civilization enjoyed some of its greatest and most peaceful achievements.

La belle époque

Probably the most important art form of this period was the novel. An enormous growth in literacy, and mass education for girls as well as boys, was transforming society. It prepared readers for the novels of Émile Zola, Gustave Flaubert, Leo Tolstoy, Fyodor Dostoevsky, Henry James, Joseph Conrad and Thomas Hardy. These masters observed the complex late-nineteenth-century world with psychological acuity and moral seriousness. They were themselves surrounded by writers as diverse as Theodor Fontane, Knut Hamsun, Hugo von Hofmannstahl, Rudyard Kipling, André Gide, George Gissing, Edmund Gosse, H. G. Wells and Thomas Mann, all producing novels, literary essays and short stories of great value.

Fine art bloomed. The eight Impressionist exhibitions in Paris between 1874 and 1886 introduced the work of Pierre-Auguste Renoir, Edgar Dégas, Claude Monet, Paul Cézanne and Edouard Manet. Their paintings had been inspired by the earlier realism of Gustave Courbet, and they concentrated on the revealing surfaces of everyday life, from railway stations to mountains, cafés to water-lilies, cathedrals to ballet dancers. With the mid-1880s came a reaction, in the form of Post-Impressionism, with Georges Seurat's mathematical pointillism, Vincent van Gogh's swirling landscapes and still lifes, Paul Gauguin's primitivism and Henri de Toulouse-Lautrec's posters of absinthe-soaked Parisian low life. At the turn of the century another wave began, led by Wassily Kandinsky, Henri Matisse, Georges Braque, Edvard Munch and Pablo Picasso, all interested in a more expressive, fragmented view of the world. A confusing range of 'isms' – 'symbolism', 'futurism', 'cubism' and 'fauvism' – denoted the variety of styles.

Music saw similar shifts from realism into modernism. Many opera houses were built (the Bayreuth Festival opened in 1876 with the first complete performance of Wagner's *Ring* cycle), all designed for the new middle classes to enjoy this most sumptuous of art forms. Giuseppe Verdi's late masterpieces, *Otello* (1887) and *Falstaff* (1893), and Giacomo

Puccini's hugely popular *La Bohème* (1896), *Tosca* (1900) and *Madama Butterfly* (1904), marked a high point in operatic 'verisimo'. French grand opera and operetta were at their most luscious in the work of Hector Berlioz, Jules Massenet, Georges Bizet and Jacques Offenbach. Pyotr Tchaikovsky's *Eugene Onegin* was premièred in Moscow in 1879 and Central European composers such as Leos Janáček and Bedrich Smetana produced important operas on national themes.

Johannes Brahms, Gustav Mahler and Anton Bruckner, meanwhile, were writing symphonies for large orchestras, while Claude Débussy's *La Mer* (1905), Gabriel Fauré's *Requiem* (1889) and Edward Elgar's oratorio *Dream of Gerontius* (1900) were premièred. A number of radical composers in the smaller European nations worked in a nationalist folk idiom – among them Antonin Dvořák in Czechoslovakia, Jean Sibelius in Finland and Edvard Grieg in Norway – while in Vienna the early, difficult work of Arnold Schoenberg was heard for the first time.

With the turn of the century came the cinema, recorded music, a boom in the decorative arts and a rapid growth in the mass media. But the optimism of the nineteenth century was giving way to a *fin de siècle* fatalism which sensed impending catastrophe: the world that produced the *belle époque* would soon be buried for ever in the mud and carnage of the First World War.

New Ideas

For all the complacency induced by material comforts, this period also produced a range of philosophers, scientists and intellectuals whose radical, and frequently atheistic, ideas were to change the world.

The first Socialist International had taken place in 1864, but it was the establishment – and violent destruction – of the Paris Commune in 1871 that introduced Europe to class struggle. Then, in 1872, Friedrich Engels and Karl Marx published *The Communist Manifesto*, and Marx's *Das Kapital* appeared in three volumes during the 1880s. The first May Day celebrations took place in 1890 and throughout the period there were continuous – and eventually successful – calls for universal (male) suffrage. The formation of Germany's Social Democratic Party in 1869 was a first step towards the representation of working people in national parliaments, and Britain's Labour Party was founded in 1900. Nevertheless, a conviction was growing that revolutionary violence might be necessary to change society.

In the world of natural science, the controversial conclusions of *The Origins Of Species* (1859) by Charles Darwin, particularly regarding evolution and natural selection, rocked long-held assumptions about the central position of man in creation. They were accepted surprisingly quickly by the educated middle classes in Northern Europe, who saw them as progressive; among their less attractive advocates elsewhere were the Social Darwinists, whose phrase 'the survival of the fittest' was invented to justify the appetites of cultural and social élites.

The German philosopher Friedrich Nietzsche was as influential as he was misinterpreted. In his two most famous works, *Beyond Good And Evil* (1886) and *Thus Spake Zarathustra* (1891), he declared that God was dead and condemned Christian compassion as meaningless. His form of 'aristocratic radicalism' argued for a breed of superman capable of breaking through bourgeois falsity. Although Nietzsche's writing offered intellectual credibility to dubious racial theories, his emphasis on the fulfilment of the individual influences many of today's liberal beliefs.

In Vienna, Sigmund Freud invented psychoanalysis. His three key works – *Studies in Hysteria* (1893–5), *The Interpretation of Dreams* (1900) and *The Psychopathology of Everyday Life* (1901) – probed the complex workings of the subconscious. His emphasis on the central role of sexuality – echoed by the work of Havelock Ellis and Leopold von Sacher-Masoch – cast doubt on some of the nineteenth century's most cherished beliefs. By 1900, Freud's understanding of the workings of the mind was influencing artists and intellectuals.

An early form of feminism was emerging. The figure of the 'New Woman' (much influenced by Nora in Ibsen's play *A Doll's House*) was widely discussed, particularly in the Protestant north. But although the cause of women's suffrage advanced through the 1880s and 1890s, it was not until 1906, when Emmeline Pankhurst started the Women's Social and Political Union, that the overall campaign for women's rights gained any real momentum. And in fact, married women over thirty were not given the vote in Britain until after the 1918 General Election.

In the realm of pure science, breakthroughs in post-Newtonian physics were made by Max Planck in his *Quantum Theory* (1900), by Albert Einstein in *The Theory of Relativity* (1905) and in Nils Bohr's and Ernest Rutherford's analysis of the structure of the atom (1913). The full impact of these was not immediately felt, but they introduced a sceptical relativism important in twentieth-century thinking.

Reactions to the Dreyfus Affair of 1894 (in which a Jewish army officer was framed as a spy) showed that an effective opposition to institutional anti-Semitism was possible, and the first International Zionist Conference was held in 1897. An instinct for pacifism was expressed, and international peace conferences were held in 1899 and 1907. There was also a renewed interest in the ancient world – Heinrich Schliemann discovered and excavated the ruins of Troy in 1872 – accompanied by a fascination with mysticism and the occult. Museums and educational institutions multiplied, and in 1896, in a gesture symbolizing Europe's cultural and social Renaissance, the first modern Olympic Games were staged in Athens.

A theatre for the modern world

By 1870 it had become apparent to many Europeans that a previous generation of Romantic writers had left behind them a drama incapable of expressing the realities of modern life. The heroic *Sturm und Drang* of Friedrich von Schiller, the philosophical ruminations of J. W. Goethe and the theatrical grandeur of Victor Hugo all seemed overblown now, belonging to a more heroic 'age of revolution'.

In Britain, the commercial theatre, however, was thriving. It was dominated by melodrama, spectacle and revivals of Shakespeare, but latterly it produced two comic geniuses: Arthur Wing Pinero and Oscar Wilde, whose *Importance Of Being Earnest* (1895) is one of the masterpieces of *fin de siècle* drama. The Paris theatre, meanwhile, had produced two great *farceurs*, Eugène Labiche and Georges Feydeau, as well as the romantic, historical 'well-made plays' of Eugène Scribe, Alexandre Dumas, Victorien Sardou and Edmond de Rostand, which captured the imagination of a middle-class audience. The German commercial theatre, slavishly following the British and French example, was producing little of originality. These plays were performed in the proscenium-arch theatres which had risen in the capitals and, in imitation, in numerous smaller cities.

Sparkling and well-constructed as much 'boulevard' drama was, it increasingly seemed as irrelevant as the Romantic drama which preceded it. The novelist Émile Zola argued for a new kind of play which would achieve scrupulous objectivity and reflect real life. His essay *Naturalism in the Theatre* (1881) contained a now famous call to arms:

> There is more poetry in the little apartment of a bourgeois than in all the empty, worm-eaten palaces of history.

However, Zola was not quite as innovative as he thought. The Russian theatre had already produced plays on social themes such as Alexander Griboyedov's *Woe from Wit* (1831), Nikolai Gogol's satirical comedy *The Government Inspector* (1836), Ivan Turgenev's *A Month in the Country* (1850) and Alexander Ostrovsky's masterpiece *The Storm* (1860). In Germany, Friedrich Hebbel had written *Maria Magdalena* (1844), a naturalistic play about the middle class, and in

Britain T. W. Robertson had produced 'cup and saucer' dramas such as *Society* (1865), *Ours* (1866) and *Caste* (1867). The radical element in Zola's thinking lay in the exposure of the bourgeoisie's double standards. The Danish critic Georg Brandes got to the heart of the matter in 1871: 'What shows a literature to be a living thing today is the fact of it subjecting problems to debate.'

It is important to set the giant figures of Chekhov, Ibsen and Strindberg against a background of like minded contemporaries. These included Ibsen's fellow Norwegian Bjørnstjerne Bjørnson, the French playwright Henri Becque, the German realist Gerhart Hauptmann, Ibsen's champion George Bernard Shaw, the Viennese satirist Arthur Schnitzler, Chekhov's friend Maxim Gorky, the French anarchist Alfred Jarry, the German expressionist Frank Wedekind, the Belgian symbolist Maurice Maeterlinck and the two most significant Irish dramatists, W. B. Yeats and J. M. Synge. The best of these were creating a new kind of drama, uncompromising in its subject-matter and radical in its form.

Such work called for new approaches, and many original companies were founded by visionary figures – the first modern theatre directors, in fact. The Duke of Saxe-Meiningen set up the highly influential Meiningen Players in 1874 and his meticulously crafted productions toured all over Europe. André Antoine founded the Théâtre Libre in Paris, dedicated to naturalism, in 1887, and premièred Ibsen's *Ghosts* in 1890. Otto Brahm opened the Freie Bühne in Berlin in 1889 as a socialist co-operative and Jack Thomas Grein formed the Independent Theatre Group in London in 1891, both of them influenced by the Théâtre Libre. Aurélian-François Lugné-Poe took over Paul Fort's Théâtre Mixte (renamed the Théâtre de l'Oeuvre in 1893) and dedicated it to the new 'symbolist' drama. Konstantin Stanislavsky and Vladimir Nemirovich-Danchenko founded the Moscow Art Theatre in 1898, and one of their first productions was Chekhov's *The Seagull*. William Archer premièred many of Ibsen's plays in London and the Barker–Vedrenne Management ran important seasons at the Royal Court Theatre in London from 1904 to 1907. Strindberg founded his own Intimate Theatre with 160 seats in Stockholm in 1907 and wrote four extra-ordinary plays specially for it.

All this new work was made possible by technical advances. Since naturalism is not an absolute, its nineteenth-century version would probably strike modern theatre-goers as highly artificial, relying as it did on the primitive scenic techniques. But Antoine's Théâtre Libre invented the notion of the 'fourth wall' – the actors looking out not at the audience but at the fourth wall of an imaginary room – and used real materials in their productions: furniture, food and even fountains. Real doors and windows were constructed, and then set into painted canvas scenery. The invention of electric lighting in the 1880s further transformed what was possible – the advantage over gas lights was that lamps could be dimmed and focused. Despite the invention of magnetic recording, sound remained primitive and was always created live. Costumes increasingly came to be seen as a way of reflecting 'character'. However, in contemporary plays many actors took to wearing their own clothes on stage and the results were sometimes untheatrical. Make-up had to be adjusted to the new lighting techniques, and some of the melodramatic excesses of face-painting began to go out of fashion. The hardest struggle faced by the new directors was to change the prevailing acting style. This was somewhat stentorian and declamatory, favouring washes of strong emotion rather than the fine detail that the new theatre demanded. Stanislavsky was soon to invent his famous System in an attempt to provide a scientific basis for the craft of acting; already such artists were campaigning for a style of performance rooted more deeply in observable reality.

Three different dramatists

The aim of this guide is to give readers and theatre-goers a brief introduction to the most important plays of the three most significant dramatists of the time: Anton Chekhov, Henrik Ibsen and August Strindberg. We have provided a cast list, a synopsis, a short essay and a historical summary of the plays in performance. We have also suggested the influence they exerted on the future. Scholarly studies and learned biographies abound. Our aim is more modest: a practical guide to reading and seeing the plays for the first time.

We have put the three of them in one book because, living at the same time, they were involved in many similar challenges; but of course they were quite distinct. They never met, and were often suspicious of each other's work. As a young man, the tortured Strindberg was implicitly involved in an Oedipal struggle with the older and more successful Ibsen, describing him as 'the fanatical sceptic . . . so impressive and terrifying, so repellent, so attractive'. The warmhearted and fastidious Chekhov had ambivalent feelings about Ibsen: 'Listen – Ibsen is no playwright', he once said. Ibsen himself left no record of his opinion of Chekhov, although he was familiar with his early work. He regarded Strindberg with a mixture of admiration and suspicion; in Christiania he hung a portrait of him on the wall of his study and wrote: 'I am now not able to write a word without having that madman staring down at me.'

Our experience of these writers is primarily as actor and director; we have found working on their plays astonishingly rewarding, comparable only to Shakespeare. The aim of all three was both ambitious and simple: to dramatize in realistic, human ways the complex world in which they lived; and they did it with supreme tact, skill and artistry. Together, they created a new theatre for a new world, and their plays speak as clearly a century later as they did to their contemporaries.

Michael Pennington and Stephen Unwin
December 2003

HENRIK IBSEN
1828–1906

Ibsen's life

Henrik Johan Ibsen was born on 20 March 1828 in the small town of Skien in south-east Norway. His mother came from a wealthy family and his early life was comfortable. However, when he was seven his father went bankrupt and Ibsen spent the rest of his childhood living on a farm in Venstøp in poverty.

In 1844, Ibsen was apprenticed to an apothecary in Grimstad, where he fathered an illegitimate son. In 1849 he wrote his first play, a five-act verse tragedy called *Catiline*, which was published in 1850 under the pseudonym Brynjolf Bjarme. His one-act play *The Burial Mound* was performed in 1850, the first of his works to be staged. He moved to Christiania (now Oslo) in 1850, but failed to secure a place at the university, where he planned to study medicine. Instead he published a weekly magazine called *Andhrimner*, consisting largely of social criticism and satire.

In 1851, at the age of twenty-three, Ibsen was appointed playwright-in-residence and resident stage director of the newly established National Theatre in Bergen. There he wrote four plays: *St. John's Night* (1852), *Lady Inger of Østeraad* (1854), *The Feast At Solhoug* (1855) and *Olaf Liljekrans* (1856). In 1852 he went on a four-month study tour to Hamburg, Copenhagen and Dresden, and in 1857 became Artistic Director of the Norwegian Theatre in Christiania, where he wrote *The Vikings At Helgeland* (1858), *Love's Comedy* (1862) and *The Pretenders* (1863).

In 1858 Ibsen married Suzannah Thoresen, and in 1859 their son Sigurd was born. In 1859 he founded, with his friend and rival playwright Bjørnstjerne Bjørnson, *The Norwegian Company* – a magazine dedicated to Norwegian art and culture. In 1862 he travelled throughout western Norway, collecting

Scandinavian folk-songs and folk-tales. The plays from this period tended to be historical dramas, inspired by folklore and Norwegian history and concerned with questions of national identity, and are written in verse as well as prose.

The years in Christiania were difficult and frustrating for Ibsen, and both the press and the theatre's board felt that he did not fulfil his duties properly. He lost his full-time job in 1862 when the Christiania Theatre went bankrupt, but soon took a new post as a 'consultant'. In 1864 (at the age of thirty-six) he was given a small government grant to travel to Italy, which marked the beginning of his twenty-seven years of life abroad. In 1864 he began to write a play about Julian, a character from antiquity, but did not finish it until 1873, when it was published as *Emperor and Galilean*. In 1866 Ibsen wrote the dramatic poem *Brand*, his first real success as a writer. *Peer Gynt* appeared in 1867: with its focus on the dissolution of an individual's personality, it marks the key breakthrough in his early work.

Ibsen moved from Italy to Dresden in 1868, to Munich in 1875, to Rome in 1878 and back to Munich in 1885. He travelled to Egypt in 1869 to witness the opening of the Suez Canal, and spent several summers in Gossensaß in the Tyrol. With his move to Germany came a change in writing style, as he turned his attention to the lives of the contemporary bourgoisie, and started his great cycle of realistic dramas. *The League of Youth* appeared in 1869 and *Pillars of Society* in 1877. He wrote *A Doll's House* in 1879, *Ghosts* in 1881 and *An Enemy of the People* in 1882. In 1884 he wrote *The Wild Duck*, followed in 1886 by *Rosmersholm* and *The Lady from the Sea* in 1888. In 1889 he met two young women – Emilie Bardach and Helene Raff – and his 'platonic' relationships with them affected his subsequent work. It was during this period that his plays began to be performed throughout Europe and in America. In 1890 he wrote his most famous work, *Hedda Gabler*, the last play he wrote in exile.

In July 1891, aged sixty-three, Ibsen decided to move back to Norway and settled in Christiania, where he wrote *The*

Master Builder (1892), *Little Eyolf* (1894), *John Gabriel Borkman* (1896) and the dramatic epilogue *When We Dead Awaken* (1899). These late, great masterpieces focus on the complex relationships between old age and youth, art and life, and face up to the inevitability of death with great honesty. In the last years of his life Ibsen was an international figure, much fêted and honoured, both in Norway and abroad. In 1900 he suffered the first of a series of strokes that prevented him from writing, and he died in Christiania on 23 May 1906.

Ibsen's theatre

Ibsen's mother was interested in art and theatre, and as a boy Ibsen had a room where he locked himself away with his dolls and paints and staged plays in a puppet theatre. He loved painting and drawing, and his early written work tended to be rather satirical – and sketchy – in quality. However, his father was brutal and domineering, even by the standards of the time, and all accounts of the young Ibsen hint at a rather withdrawn, shy character, but with a deep sense of comic mischief.

Ibsen's formal education was limited, and as an assistant pharmacist he had no opportunities to go to the theatre. However, he read a great deal – Shakespeare, Schiller, the Danish dramatists Ludwig Holberg and Adam Oehlenschlager, as well as the Icelandic sagas, Scandinavian folk mythology, the Greek and Latin classics and, of course, the Bible. All this had a profound impact on his later work.

When Ibsen was coming of age in the 1840s, there were no permanent professional theatres in Norway, only Danish touring companies, and the Norwegian theatre was a pale reflection of Danish taste and tradition. However, this was the great period of European nationalism, especially in the smaller states, and a new National Theatre in Bergen, and the Norwegian Theatre in Christiania, were both set up to create an indigenous theatre. Despite the attempts by the young

Ibsen and others to write 'nationalist' poetic drama which could give Norway its answer to Shakespeare, the repertoire of these new theatres was almost entirely foreign, dominated by French commercial drama and its German and Danish imitations. The key figures were the commercial French dramatists Eugène Scribe and his successor Victorien Sardou, who mastered the art of *la pièce bien fait* (the 'well-made play'), glossy and superficial dramas, written in prose and driven by logical development in plotting and motivation. It is telling that the great plays of Ibsen's maturity avoid 'nationalist' poetic themes entirely, but do employ some of the techniques of the 'well-made play'.

Ibsen's time in Bergen and Christiania was to have a decisive influence on his later development and it is useful to see the young Ibsen as a practical man of the theatre – like Shakespeare and Molière before him. He directed a large number of productions, worked with many actors and actresses, and watched hundreds of performances. He became very familiar with the everyday challenges, both managerial and artistic, of working in the theatre and putting on plays. In other words, by the time Ibsen had decided what he wanted to say and how he wanted to say it, he had acquired a thorough knowledge of the means at his disposal.

Within the space of two years came the two key moments in Ibsen's development. The first was his departure from Norway for southern Europe in 1866 which 'left its mark on all my later work, even though not everything there was beautiful . . . [it was like] a feeling of being released from darkness into the light, escaping through a tunnel from mists into sunshine'. Nine of Ibsen's greatest plays were written in southern Europe and Ibsen's highly ambivalent attitude to his native land runs right through them.

The second decisive event was Ibsen's renunciation of poetic, nationalist drama and his decisive turn towards prosaic naturalism. This work absorbed all the lessons of the 'well-made play' but took it to a new pitch of psychological intensity. It also – in Georg Brandes's term – 'subjected problems to debate'. *A Doll's House* was the decisive moment, as Ibsen recalled in a letter in 1883:

> Verse has done the art of drama immeasurable harm. An artist of the theatre, with a repertoire of contemporary dramatic work, should not willingly speak a line of verse. Verse will scarcely find any application worth mentioning in the drama of the near future . . . In the last seven or eight years I have hardly written a single line of verse; instead I have exclusively studied the incomparably more difficult art of writing in the straightforward honest language of reality.

It is important to stress that Ibsen's naturalism is in no way slavish. Instead, naturalistic dramatic actions are laced with symbolism (a tendency which becomes increasingly marked in the later plays) and, although the language is simple and the living-rooms are real, it is more appropriate to think of Ibsen as writing 'poetic naturalism'. Furthermore, beneath the apparently naturalistic surface lurk a whole catalogue of jostling theatrical and literary genres: Greek tragedy, the Bible, folk art, Shakespeare, Scandinavian mythology and the eighteenth-century comedy of manners. In brief, Ibsen's plays are intense works of art, not mere exercises in verisimilitude.

As was common practice at the time, Ibsen's plays were published before they were performed, and were written to be read as well as to be seen. One of the consequences of this was that he wrote extensive and detailed stage directions, which describe very precisely what he imagined taking place on the stage. Ibsen's acute sense of theatrical poetry and practical knowledge of what works means that when staging his plays modern actors and directors do well to pay heed to this very precise theatrical imagination. Meaning is exacted from as simple and realistic an action as an oil lamp being brought on stage by a maid, or shutters being opened to let in the sun.

In all of Ibsen's great plays, his central subject is the same: the painful struggle for the truth to be spoken. In a letter, he wrote that 'I believe that none of us can do anything other or anything better than realize ourselves in spirit and in truth'. This struggle exists in many areas, personal as well as social, and takes place between the individual on his (or her) path to self-realization on the one hand and the claims of society, with its emphasis on duty to others, on the other. Ibsen never loses touch with the pain that is caused by self-realization, and the destruction that is its inevitable consequence. At times, particularly in the later plays, it is almost as if he is warning us against it. However, with a powerful instinct for tragedy, Ibsen shows that this process of self-realization is inevitable if society and the individual are to be reformed. To think of Ibsen as a mere moralizer is simplistic: his vision is much tougher, and more austere. He is the great dramatist of the modern world and takes his readers and audiences to the fundamental modern question: how do you live in a world without God?

Translations and further reading

George Bernard Shaw's *Quintessence of Ibsenism* (1891) is an excellent introduction to the plays, although it tends to see them as 'Shavian' plays of ideas. Raymond Williams's *Drama from Ibsen to Brecht* (1969) provides a good introduction, if from an explicitly political point of view. *The Cambridge Companion to Ibsen* (1994) brings together a number of fine scholars on various aspects of Ibsen studies, and Joan Templeton's *Ibsen's Women* (1997) is an outstanding study of the major plays from a sophisticated feminist perspective. Frederick J. Marker and Lise-Lone Marker's *Ibsen's Lively Art* (1989) examines the plays as pieces for the theatre. There are two major biographies of Ibsen in English: Michael Meyer's definitive *Ibsen* (1971) and Robert Ferguson's fascinating *New Biography of Ibsen* (1996).

Writing in a small and largely unknown language, Ibsen's work has always relied on its translators. The best are those who have heeded Ibsen's stipulation that the plays be translated into the everyday language of ordinary people. There are several major editions in English: William Archer's *Collected Works* (1906–12), which is no longer in print; the authoritative *Oxford Ibsen* (1960–77) with its excellent notes and appendices (parts of which are still available in paperback); the straightforward, if rather stuffy, Penguin translations by Peter Watts and Una Ellis Fermor; and Michael Meyer's popular but occasionally over-inventive versions for Methuen. Perhaps the best of all are Kenneth McLeish's outstanding translations of several of the plays for Nick Hern Books.

Peer Gynt
(Peer Gynt)

A Dramatic Poem

1867

✑ Characters

Åse, *a farmer's widow*
Peer Gynt, *her son*
Aslak, *a blacksmith*
Mads Moen, *the bridegroom*
Mads Moen's Father and Mother
Young Man at wedding
Solveig, *a farmer's daughter*
Her Father and Mother
Ingrid, *the bride*
Her Father
Woman in Green
Old Man of the Mountains
Troll Chamberlain
Helga, *Solveig's sister*
Kari, *Åse's neighbour*
Troll Child
Trumpetblast, *a Swedish businessman*
Cotton, *an American businessman*
Ballon, *a French businessman*
Eberkopf, *a German businessman*
Anitra, *a desert maiden*
Statue of Memnon
Begriffenfeld, *keeper of the Cairo madhouse*
Schlingenberg, Fuchs, Schafman, and Mikkel, *warders*
Hussein
Ship's Captain and Cook
Strange Passenger
Priest

Button Moulder
Thin Person
Stewards, Thieves, Herdgirls, Egyptians, Villagers,
Wedding Guests, Trolls, the Bøyg, Slaves, Desert Maidens,
Lunatics and Ship's Crew

➣ The story

Act One is set in the wilds of the Gudbrandsal in Norway.
The young Peer Gynt is boasting to his mother, Åse, that he
rode on the back of an enormous buck the length of a per-
ilous ridge, and killed him with a knife. Åse is astonished, but
then suddenly realizes that he is just retelling a popular tale.
She is 'a poor widow' and thinks he should be doing more to
help her. He could have married Ingrid, but she is marrying
someone else. Peer lifts Åse up, puts her on the roof of the
hut and runs off to the wedding. There he joins the party, gets
drunk, is bewitched by the beautiful Solveig and disappears
with Ingrid, the bride.

Act Two takes place in the high mountains. Peer is in exile
from society. He has seduced Ingrid but is now abandoning
her, despite her offers of land and money, and curses all
women – 'all but one'. Meanwhile, Åse is desperately looking
for her 'little Peer'. She is joined by Solveig, who wants to
know everything about him. Peer meets three cattle girls who
lead him off seductively to their hut. But Peer sees his mission
in life ('You have sprung from greatness / and to greatness
you shall attain!') and breaks free. He meets the Woman in
Green and is taken off to meet her father, the Troll King himself, in the Royal Palace. Amidst 'a great crowd of troll
courtiers, gnomes and goblins', Peer is told all about the
peculiarities of the troll way of life. He declares that he wants
to marry the King's daughter (and enjoy her dowry) but will
not accept the conditions (becoming a troll – complete with
tail and three heads). The scene ends in uproar with Peer
running off to avoid a forced marriage. Outside, Peer meets
the Great Bøyg, an enormous, slippery monster whom he

cannot pass. The act ends with Peer outside his mother's hut, exhausted but roused by a glimpse of Solveig.

Act Three opens with Peer as an 'outlaw . . . forced to hide in the forest'. He is building himself a hut when he sees a young boy cut off his finger so as to avoid having to go to war. Meanwhile, Åse has lost her farm and land and, while going through Peer's possessions, finds his old casting-ladle (for buttons). Peer has built his hut with a bolt on the door 'against trolls. Against men and women too'. Solveig arrives, saying that she has left her father and mother in order to be with Peer. Soon, an 'old looking woman' and an 'ugly boy' appear: the Troll King's Daughter and Peer's piglike son. When they have gone, Peer recalls the words of the Bøyg – 'go round about'. When Solveig calls for him from inside the hut, he asks her to be patient and disappears 'down the forest path'. He goes to see his mother, who is dying in poverty, and tries to comfort her. They remember the old days together and, with Peer sitting at the end of his mother's deathbed, act out a sleigh ride, all the way up to the gates of heaven, where Peer tells Saint Peter: 'You're to let Mother Åse come in!' He looks around and sees that she is dead, and leaves for the coast, giving instructions to 'see my mother decently buried'.

Act Four shifts to the 'south-western coast of Morocco' and the millionaire Peer Gynt is 'now a handsome middle-aged man with gold-rimmed spectacles'. His yacht is moored nearby and he is giving a party for four businesmen, his guests on a cruise. They sing his praises and encourage him to recount his adventures, achievements and philosophy. It soon emerges that he earned his fortune shipping 'Negro slaves to Carolina / and heathen images to China' (but he says that he operated ethically). He declares that his ambition is to become 'Emperor . . . of all the world!' He shocks them by saying that he will lend money to the Turks in their war against the Greeks. Soon the businessmen steal his money, but later that night he sees them sailing away on his yacht and begs God to punish their 'treachery'. Amazingly, the yacht explodes. Peer realizes that he will have to fend for himself in the desert and

will have to 'rely on the Lord'. Soon, he finds himself up a tree
fighting off a swarm of apes: 'it doesn't make sense / that man,
who's supposed to be the Lord of Creation / should have to
endure'. He is struck by how animals are content just to 'be',
and is amazed by the desert wastes. This contemplation does
not last long and he fantasizes about a horse, which promptly
appears and carries him off. He is soon surrounded by a chorus of maidens who, to his delight, hail him as a prophet. He
is especially struck by Anitra, and says he wants to give her his
soul. He sings to her and tells her 'what life consists of' – but
she snores, wants his money, notices that he is old and abandons him. Back in European clothes, he declares that he will
'sever completely, from start to finish, the ties that bind one to
home and to friends . . . and all to solve the riddle of Truth!'
Soon, he is walking through the ruins of Ancient Egypt. At the
Great Sphinx, he meets Professor Begriffenfeldt, who says the
riddle of the Sphinx is that 'he is Himself'. At the Cairo
Lunatic Asylum ('Absolute Reason / dropped dead here last
night at 11 p.m.') he meets the inmates. Eventually he collapses and Begriffenfeldt places a wreath on his head, shouting
'Long live . . . the Emperor of the Self'.

Act Five opens with Peer, 'a vigorous old man with steel-
grey hair and beard', on board a ship off the Norwegian coast.
A storm blows up and he encounters a Strange Passenger,
whose macabre talk leads inevitably to the ship sinking on the
rocks. He clambers aboard the keel of a boat but is astonished
to meet the Strange Passenger again, who comforts him by
telling him that 'one doesn't die / right in the middle of Act
Five'. Once ashore, Peer observes a funeral and is struck by
the Priest's sermon. His attempt to auction off his belongings
and his soul is met by laughter. Then, in a clearing in the forest,
he peels an onion to find its centre: 'there's nothing but layers
– smaller and smaller'. He stumbles on Solveig's hut and hears
her singing. He decides to build his own hut on a burned
heath, but is hindered by the sound of leaves sighing and dew-
drops singing at him. His dead mother's voice drives Peer
away. He meets a Button Moulder who cheerfully tells him

that his time is up and that he is going to be 'melted down', but eventually lets him go: 'We'll meet at the next crossroads.' Peer comes across a very old man – the Troll King – and asks him to testify that he refused to be turned into a troll: the Troll King says Peer obeyed the troll motto, 'To thyself be – enough!', and has newspapers to prove it. After another encounter with the Button Moulder, Peer meets a Thin Man, who turns out to be the Devil. Peer begs him to take him off to Hell – but his sins are not big enough. Left alone in the mist, Peer says he will climb the mountain and let the 'snow drift over me'. As church-goers arrive for matins, he meets the Button Moulder a third time, and is reunited with Solveig, who sings a lullaby to Peer, lying in her lap:

> I will cradle you, I will guard you;
> Sleep and dream, dearest son of mine.

ᴄᴏ About the play

Ibsen created his great epic while in Italy, but was so immersed in his Scandinavian material that he wrote 'These days I'm continuously having to pinch my arm to remind myself that I'm not back in Norway'. In 1872 he said that he could only dare to write like this 'far away from home'.

As a young man, Ibsen had steeped himself in Scandinavian myths and legends, both through reading and on research trips. In 1867 he wrote:

> In case it should interest you, Peer Gynt was a real person who lived in Gudbrandsal, probably at the end of the last century or the beginning of this. His name is still famous among the people up there, but not much more is known about his life than what is to be found in Asbjørnsen's *Norwegian Fairy-tales*.

However, Ibsen felt ambivalent towards his source material (which he freely adapted), and the play is much more satirical than celebratory: the trolls are an attack on unthinking nationalism and the peasants are hard-drinking, highly sexed and brutal. The 1860s was a period of Scandinavian self-questioning and *Peer Gynt* was Ibsen's challenge to Norway to discover her true soul and not rely on folksy sentimentality.

The deeper meaning of *Peer Gynt* lies in the journey of its central character, and it is the exploration of Ibsen's extraordinary hero which is the play's *raison d'être*. Peer Gynt is a boaster and a liar, driven by extraordinary energy and a voracious sexual appetite. He is by turns imaginative and irrepressible, philosophical and witty, inarticulate and depressive. He undergoes a whole range of emotions – ecstasy and despair, vision and blindness, wealth and desolation – but is constantly involved in the relentless and all-important pursuit of his own self. If, at the end, Peer can stand alone, independent, true and free, he can avoid both the terrible compromises of the trolls and the terrifying indifference of the casting ladle. His only refuge is in Solveig's lap ('My mother – my wife'), perhaps the only place where he can find his soul.

In 1866, Ibsen had enjoyed his first success with *Brand*, his first 'dramatic poem'; *Peer Gynt*, he declared, 'was the antithesis'. He had been writing poetry since he was a teenager in Grimstad and, in the 1860s it was his poems which had given him his greatest critical successes. Ibsen was later to announce that 'verse is the enemy of drama'; in *Peer Gynt*, he almost proves his point and at times its theatricality can feel overloaded. The verse is freewheeling and imaginative, diverse and fantastical, raw and magnificent:

> Yes, a lie can be refurbished,
> tricked out with boasts and bragging,
> dressed up in a brand new skin
> to disguise its scrawny carcass

If *Peer Gynt* is more of a poetic than a dramatic triumph, lacking the tightness of dramatic construction that was to become such a hallmark of Ibsen's later work, it has a relentless energy all of its own. Like Goethe's *Faust* or Mozart's *Don Giovanni*, it is nothing less than a dramatized modern myth. Like them, it is frivolous and profound, exotic and satirical, controlled yet apparently free: Ibsen at his wildest. The Irish poet and playwright Frank McGuinness captures this quality brilliantly:

> that formidable energy of Ibsen . . . driving all before it, rampaging forward, taking the classic five-act form and inflating it beyond repair, planting dynamite beneath the unities of time and place, risking artistic suicide so that the theatre might never be the same place again. The excitement of it can only be compared to discovering Shakespeare.

With its madmen and its millionaires, its desert maidens and its ship's cooks, its peasants and its trolls, the play's kaleidoscopic quality can feel lurid. However, like Shakespeare, *Peer Gynt* is inhabited by characters of such energy, vividness and three-dimensionality that we are swept along by them and by the end feel that we have met all the world.

Peer Gynt was followed by Ibsen's decision to take naturalism as his means and the apartments of the Norwegian bourgeoisie as his locales – one of the key decisions in the development of world drama. But it was in *Peer Gynt* that he first explored his theme – how to be true to yourself – and without it his great cycle of twelve realistic dramas would not have been possible. As such, it is one of the defining works of modern literature.

ᘔ In performance

On its publication in 1867, *Peer Gynt* met with widespread critical hostility. Even Ibsen's friend Georg Brandes called it 'thankless stuff'. Ibsen's response was stoical, however:

> I am glad that this injustice has been flung at me; it is a sign of divine aid and dispensation; anger increases my strength.

Ibsen described *Peer Gynt* as a 'dramatic poem' and did not intend it to be staged. Indeed some still think that it is 'unstageable' ('The ideal play for radio' as Willy Russell calls it in *Educating Rita*). The first performance took place in Christiania in February 1876 and the next one ten years later in Copenhagen. Ibsen asked the Norwegian composer Edvard Grieg to write music for the piece and his *Peer Gynt Suite* (1888) is one of his most famous works.

Ibsen knew that Norwegian mythology was not appealing to all ('of all my books, I regard *Peer Gynt* as the least likely to be understood outside Scandinavia'), so perhaps he would not have been surprised that it took so many years for the piece to be widely accepted. The Paris première was in 1896 and the American one in 1906. The London première took place on 26 February 1911 at the Rehearsal Theatre and was an entirely experimental event (with a woman playing Peer). The first major London performance was not until 6 March 1922 at the Old Vic. Ralph Richardson played Peer at the New Theatre in 1944, in a production directed by Tyrone Guthrie.

Perhaps the most astonishing *Peer Gynt* of modern times was Peter Stein's famous production at the Schaubühne in Berlin 1971 – with six different Peers and perfomed over two evenings – which presented the play as a deconstruction of the bourgeois personality. Ingmar Bergman's shorter, more purist production in Stockholm in 1991 was devised partly in reaction to Stein's.

Peer Gynt's startling verse is almost impossible to translate. Some have put it into poetry throughout (Peter Watts), some into prose (Frank McGuinness) and some have mixed the two (Kenneth McLeish); none have been entirely successful. Modern British productions include Michael Elliott's with Leo McKern at the Old Vic (1962), the RSC's with Derek Jacobi (1983), Patrick Mason's at the Gate Theatre, Dublin (1988), Declan Donnellan's at the National Theatre (1990) and the Manchester Royal Exchange's production with David Threlfall (1999).

Translated by Michael Meyer, Methuen, 1973

Pillars of Society
(Samfundets støtter)
1877

⌘ Characters

Karsten Bernick, *a consul*
Betty, *his wife*
Olaf, *their son, thirteen*
Martha, *Karsten's sister*
Johan Tönnesen, *Betty's younger brother*
Lona Hessel, *Betty's elder stepsister*
Hilmar Tönnesen, *Betty's cousin*
Rörlund, *a schoolmaster*
Rummel, *a business man*
Vigeland, *a trader*
Sandstad, *a trader*
Dina Dorf, *a young girl living with the Bernicks*
Krap, *chief clerk*
Aune, *shipyard foreman*
Mrs Rummel
Mrs Holt, *the postmaster's wife*
Mrs Lynge, *the doctor's wife*
Miss Rummel
Miss Holt
Townspeople, foreign sailors, passengers, and so on

The action takes place in the garden room of Karsten
Bernick's house in a small Norwegian seaport

⌘ The story

It is a summer's day and a group of seven women are making
clothes for their 'fallen sisters'. The schoolmaster Rörlund
has been reading an 'instructive story' and tells the women he

is concerned about the moral corruption of the wider world. The women speak of how the town has changed: there used to be dances and visits by touring theatre companies, but now 'everything turns on petty, material considerations'. We are told that Betty Bernick's younger brother Johan Tönneson was caught sleeping with an actor's wife and, when it was discovered that he had stolen money, fled to America, where he was joined by Lona Hessel, Betty's half-sister. We hear that after the scandal Bernick adopted the actor's daughter Dina, and that Rörlund now wants to marry her. Lona had been in love with Bernick, but at the last minute he changed his mind and married Betty instead. Bernick emerges, having agreed to help fund the construction of a new railway to the town. He brushes off Rörlund's objections and speaks of how 'the family is the kernel of the community'. A telegram from New York arrives, wanting the ship The Indian Girl sent with 'the least possible repairs'. Bernick knows that 'she'll go to the bottom like a stone if anything happens' and is considering what to do when his son Olaf announces that he has seen 'a whole circus company come ashore'. Suddenly, to everyone's surprise, a 'strange woman' walks in – Lona is back from America. She declares that she is 'used to the air of the prairies' and, when asked what she is going to do, says that she is 'going to let in some fresh air'.

By Act Two, the Bernicks are anxious about what will happen following Lona's return. Aune is worried about getting The Indian Girl seaworthy by the 'day after tomorrow' but relents when Bernick threatens him with dismissal. Lona and Johan have been seen walking through the town with Dina. They arrive and Lona congratulates Bernick on his many achievements, but also boasts of what she achieved in America. Johan offers to take Dina back to America with them. Bernick thanks Johan for taking the blame for his own indiscretion and for saving his engagement to Betty. Johan admits that he has told Lona everything but says she 'won't give anything away'. Bernick's sister Martha criticizes Johan for his past, but Lona is determined to marry Johan off to

Dina. Betty is convinced that this is motivated by revenge against Bernick for having rejected her. Bernick begs Lona for forgiveness, and declares that he 'loved her once'. It soon comes clear that by marrying Betty he 'saved the House of Bernick at a woman's expense'. When Lona asks him whether he is happy, he says he is, adding that Betty has changed. Lona warns him that 'a moment may come, a word may be spoken, and you and all your glory will go to the bottom, unless you save yourself in time'. He is convinced she wants revenge but says she will never succeed. Bernick is summoned to 'a meeting about the railway' and Rörlund asks him whether it is 'with your consent that the young girl who has found shelter under your roof shows herself in the open street with . . . the man from whom, of all men on earth, she should be kept farthest away'. When Johan and Dina arrive, Rörlund announces that Johan stole 'widow Bernick's money'. Johan is appalled and Bernick goes – 'like an automaton . . . to the rescue of society'.

Act Three opens with Bernick furious at his son for having stayed out all night at sea in a small boat. Krap tells Bernick that Aune has sabotaged *The Indian Girl* and that 'she'll go to the bottom like a cracked pot'. Hilmar tells Bernick that the papers are trying to kill off his railway venture. Bernick admits to Lona that no money was stolen and that he allowed a false rumour to be spread: 'Here are you', she says, 'the first man in the town, living in splendour and happiness, in power and honour – you, who have branded an honest man a criminal.' Johan arrives, announcing that 'Dina shall be my wife, and here, here in this town, I mean to live with her and build up a life with her.' This alarms Bernick, who says that he has secretly purchased all the land the railway is going to be built on – with the other town leaders, the 'Pillars of Society' – and is set to make a million. He is desperate that nothing should come out about his former conduct. Johan announces that he is going to leave on *The Indian Girl* and return in two months so that 'the man who is to blame shall take the blame'. Bernick tells his men that the ship must sail tomorrow as planned, and talks with Rörlund about the morality of human losses in business. When Rörlund tells Johan that Dina is his promised wife, Johan storms off, determined to revenge himself on the 'whole pack of you'. When Krap announces that 'it's blowing up for a regular storm', Bernick declares that '*The Indian Girl* is to set sail just the same'.

By Act Four 'it is a stormy afternoon and already dark'. Rummel tells Bernick that the 'town is coming in procession to honour its leading citizen' and advises him to make a speech of thanks, scotching the rumours about his land purchases. Meanwhile, both the decrepit *Indian Girl* and the sound *Palm Tree* can be heard preparing to sail. Lona arrives to say goodbye. Dina is desperate to go to America with Johan and to their amazement Martha gives them her blessing: 'Rebel against it, Dina. Be his wife. Let there be something to defy all this tradition and habit.' Johan and Dina say goodbye 'for ever' and Martha and Lona are left mourning their loss. Bernick tells Lona of his loneliness, but says he 'must go under like all the rest of this social system, rotten and wrecked as it is'. However, he is determined to deprive her of 'the satisfaction of breaking me'. She says Dina and Johan have left on *The Palm Tree* and torn up the evidence of Bernick's past: 'Now there is nothing to bear witness against you.' For Bernick this is too late: he is soon told that Olaf has run away on *The Indian Girl*. The blinds are rolled up and 'the whole street is illuminated': the procession is arriving. But Bernick wants all the decorations pulled down, shocked by the knowledge that he has lost his son. Betty reveals that Olaf has been miraculously saved and that the ship's departure has been delayed until tomorrow. Rörlund makes a speech of salutation, declaring: 'what you have done . . . you have not done with the idea of any tangible reward for yourself', and gives him and all the 'pillars of society' silver and other precious items. Bernick rejects Rörlund's praise, declaring that his 'craving for power and influence has been the driving force behind most of my actions'. He admits to corruption in the purchase of the land and confesses to his own personal guilt from fifteen years ago. Betty tells him that he has shown her 'the happiest prospect for many a year', and Lona tells him that her motivation was that the hero of her youth 'should stand free and clear'. Bernick also makes peace with Olaf, saying he can become whatever he wants, and instructs Aune to overhaul *The Indian Girl* properly. As the sky starts to clear, Bernick declares that 'it is women who are the pillars of society'; but Lona says that 'the spirit of truth and the spirit of freedom' are more worthy of the title.

❧ About the play

Pillars of Society (sometimes translated as *The Pillars of the Community*) is the first of Ibsen's plays to be concerned with problems of social and political morality. It was partly inspired by an English MP, Samuel Plimsoll, who caused an outcry in 1875 by attempting to reform the practice of sending men to sea in rotting ships ('floating coffins'). His campaign struck a chord world-wide, particularly in maritime nations such as Norway.

Pillars of Society had an uncharacteristically long gestation: Ibsen began thinking about it as early as 1869 and it was finally written in Munich in 1877. In a letter to King Oscar I of Sweden, Ibsen wrote that he wanted:

> To lead the vision and the thoughts of the public in a different direction and to show that untruth does not reside in institutions but in the individuals themselves within the community; that it is the inner life of the people, the life of the mind, which has to be purified and liberated; that it is not the external liberties which are to be desired but on the contrary a personal and cultural liberation, and that this can only be acquired and taken possession of by the individual himself, in that his conduct has truth as its basis and point of departure.

In another letter in the same year, he wrote that the play:

Rakes about in all sorts and manners of conditions of things, which is presumably not within the power of literature to reform but upon which literature may nevertheless try to shed a true and proper light.

In the central character, Karsten Bernick, Ibsen has drawn a particularly nineteenth-century figure, a philanthropic millionaire who seems to control everything in the town. His success is based on a set of questionable actions: he married a woman he did not love so as to further his career; as a young man he was caught in a married woman's bedroom and let his fiancée's brother Johan take the blame; now he has secretly bought cheap land knowing that his plans to build a railway on it will make him a fortune. When he lets Johan set sail on a ship that he knows will sink, his actions are seen to be entirely unacceptable. It is only when he discovers that what he has done could result in the loss of his only son that he recognizes the true consequences of his actions.

Bernick's nemesis comes in the shape of Lona Hessel: his former love who went to America, where she has found liberation and strength on its 'wide open prairies' and in its 'bright, white light'. It is thought that Lona is based on Asta Hannsen, a Norwegian feminist of the 1870s who emigrated to America in the face of overwhelming criticism. As such, she is an early draft of Nora in *A Doll's House* and the other independent-minded women who are such a feature of Ibsen's masterpieces. She also prefigures those other female characters in Ibsen – Rebecca West, Hilde Wangel and Ella Rentheim – whose motivation is to release the 'truth of life', however dangerous the consequences, in the men they love.

One of the play's achievements is the way in which it presents a detailed portrait of the stifling conformity, repressed longing and narrow-minded provincialism of small-town life. It is rich with brilliantly drawn cameos: Bernick's wife Betty, their adventurous son Olaf, her long-suffering sister Martha, the adventurer Johan Tönneson, the young Dina Dorf, the insufferable schoolmaster Rörlund, Bernick's corrupt clerk and foreman, the businessmen and their wives, and the rest of the town. Each has his own individuality and affects the action of the play in specific ways.

At first sight, *Pillars of Society* is a classically structured comedy, in which the vain, overreaching man discovers truth through love and society is reformed. However, some commentators have wondered what Bernick really stands for at the end: since his position in society is more secure than ever, what is the reality of his new-found commitment to 'truth'? It has even been suggested that Ibsen's intentions are entirely ironic: that Bernick is manipulating opinion so as to further his own career, and that Ibsen is showing the depth of corruption in such 'pillars of society'.

Pillars of Society is not Ibsen at his greatest. It can feel rather schematic in structure and lacking in human energy. A common criticism is that the play is too wordy, with too many long speeches which are not psychologically or dramatically integrated. Yet, while the play has never had the popularity of *Peer Gynt*, it does suggest more clearly Ibsen's subsequent development. The Danish dramatist Erik Bøgh was lavish in his praise:

> If falsehood is to be stripped bare, [Ibsen] will work at it till its fine feathers cling protectively to the wearer's skin like the shirt of Nessus. If necessary, he will remove the skin too, and should a little flesh be adhering to the skin, that will not deter him . . .

❧ In performance

Pillars of Society was premièred in Copenhagen on 18 November 1877 and in various theatres in Scandinavia over the following two years. It was then performed – in authorized and unauthorized versions – throughout Germany, with the young writer Paul Schlenther saying:

Not until this play did we learn to love him, love him for life. I think I can speak for many of my contemporaries when I say that it was the influence of this piece of modern realism coming at a decisive stage in our lives, that determined our tastes for life.

The twenty-two-year-old Otto Brahm, who was to found the Freie Bühne in Berlin, declared:

It was there that we gained the first inkling of a new world of creative art, first felt ourselves face to face with people of our time, in whom we could believe, and with a criticism which embraced the whole society of our time.

The British première took place in December 1880 (under the title *Quicksands*) at the Gaiety Theatre in London: it was a disaster. But Henry James admired:

the operation of talent without glamour . . . the ugly interior on which his curtain inexorably rises and which, to be honest, I like for the queer associations it has taught us to respect: the hideous carpet and wallpaper (one may answer for them), the conspicuous stove, the lonely central table, the lamps with green shades . . . the pervasive air of small interests and standards, the sign of limited local life.

The play is not often performed professionally, partly because of the size of the cast but also because it is overshadowed by Ibsen's subsequent achievements. The BBC made a television film of it in 1956.

Pillars of Society had an enormous influence on Arthur Miller, whose *All My Sons* (1947), with its badly built aeroplanes being flown by the sons of the manufacturer, has many parallels.

Translated by Michael Meyer, Methuen 1970

A Doll's House
(*Et dukkehjem*)
1879

∽ Characters

Torvald Helmer
Nora, *his wife*
Doctor Rank
Mrs Linde
Krogstad
Helmer's three young children
Anne-Marie, *their nanny*
Maid
Porter

The action takes place in the Helmers' flat

∽ The story

Act One takes place on Christmas Eve. Nora Helmer returns
home from shopping and her husband Torvald – who has just
been made manager of the bank – wants to know how much
money his 'little featherbrain' has spent. Nora's schoolfriend
Mrs Linde arrives, asking Nora to beg Torvald for a job.
Nora tells her that when they were first married, Torvald was
very ill and she secretly borrowed money to finance a holiday
in Italy, which saved his life. She is still paying the money
back, from whatever she can save from her housekeeping
money. Torvald offers Mrs Linde a job, but Krogstad – who
lent Nora the money and is about to be sacked by Torvald –
wants Nora to intervene on his behalf. He knows that she
forged her father's signature and threatens her: 'If I lose
everything a second time, you keep me company.' But when
Nora asks Helmer to be lenient, he is adamant – after all,

Krogstad 'forged someone's name'. Helmer has work to do, and Nora must make everything pretty for Christmas.

Act Two takes place on Christmas Day. Nora is alone, keeping watch on the locked letter-box, waiting for Krogstad's letter to Torvald which will reveal all. She has been invited to a fancy-dress party and Mrs Linde helps her repair a Neapolitan fishing girl costume. Once again she asks Torvald to give Krogstad his job back, promising that his 'little songbird would chirp and sing in every room' if he does. Once again he denies her and despatches the maid with his letter of dismissal. Nora is joined by Doctor Rank, who knows that his inherited disease is incurable. They sit together and, as the light fades, she shows him the silk stockings she will be wearing at the party. When she asks Rank for a favour, he says he will do 'all that a man can do'. But they are interrupted by Krogstad, who has now been sacked. He has a letter for Torvald, telling him everything, which he deposits in the locked letter-box. Nora is increasingly unnerved, and tells Mrs Linde 'What's going to happen . . . is a miracle!' Mrs Linde goes off to find Krogstad and persuade him to get his letter back: 'Once,' she says, when they were together, 'he'd have done anything for my sake.' When Torvald emerges with Rank from his study, he is disappointed that Nora is not yet dressed in her costume, and she desperately dances the tarantella to stop him opening the letter. Mrs Linde quickly returns – Krogstad will be back the next day – but Nora appears oblivious.

Act Three takes place on Boxing Day. Mrs Linde is waiting for Krogstad, while the Helmers are at the fancy-dress party upstairs. It emerges that Mrs Linde broke off with Krogstad because she needed money for her sick mother and brothers and he had no prospects. Furthermore, Mrs Linde has now been offered Krogstad's old job, but what she really wants is Krogstad himself, and the two are reunited. When Krogstad says he will ask Torvald for his letter back, she prevents him. Hearing the Helmers coming home, Krogstad leaves, declaring 'This is the luckiest day of my life!' Nora is wearing the

Neapolitan dress and wants to go back upstairs, but Torvald
will not let her. Mrs Linde encourages Nora, saying that she
must tell him everything, and leaves. Nora has danced the
tarantella, Torvald has drunk 'delicious champagne' and now
he wants her. But Rank interrupts their love-making, to say
goodbye: 'At the next fancy-dress party I shall be – invisible.'
Torvald unlocks the letter-box, and goes off to his study, leaving Nora contemplating suicide. Torvald reappears, having
read Krogstad's letter, and blames her entirely. But the door-
bell rings: Krogstad has sent the contract he drew up with
Nora back, both of them are 'saved' and Torvald forgives her.
Then, to his amazement, she changes out of her fancy dress
and declares that they have to 'come to terms'. She tells him
that she is going to leave him, because she has 'obligations,
just as sacred' to herself, declaring that she is 'going to find out
– which of us is right, society or me'. She gives him back her
ring, takes his, and tells him that the only miracle that could
have saved the marriage would have been if 'we could have
discovered some true relationship'. In the moments it takes
her to reach the front door, Torvald holds out some hope. But
the final stage direction says it all: 'A door slams, off.'

ᴄᴏ About the play

A Doll's House was written in Amalfi (south of Naples) in the
summer of 1879. You can still visit the room in the Hotel
Luna Convento where Ibsen worked. The story of the play
had its roots in a real-life episode. Ibsen's protégée Laura
Kieler was in an unhappy marriage. Her husband contracted
tuberculosis and she borrowed money so that they could go
on holiday to Italy, where he recovered. She confided in
Ibsen's wife and asked Ibsen to champion her novel. When her
husband discovered what had happened, she had a nervous
breakdown and he had her committed to an insane asylum.

    While Ibsen was in Rome, there was a heated debate about
the appointment of a woman librarian at the Circolo
Scandinavo, and he made a famous speech in her defence:

Is there anyone in this assembly who dares to claim that our women are inferior to us in culture, intelligence, knowledge or artistic talent? I don't think many men would dare to suggest that. Then what is it men are afraid of? I hear that it is accepted tradition here that women are such clever intriguers that we keep them out because of this. Well, I have met with a good bit of male intrigue in the course of my life . . . What I am afraid of is men with small ambitions and small thoughts, small scruples and small fears, those men who devote all their ideas and all their energies to obtain certain small advantages for their own small and servile selves.

Ibsen's commitment to women's position in society was not original. His friend Georg Brandes had translated John Stuart Mill's *The Subjection of Women* in 1869 and the 'woman question' was very much alive in Scandinavian intellectual circles. Furthermore, Camilla Collett, a friend of Ibsen's wife Suzannah, was a radical feminist who argued with him about women's rights. Ibsen started to formulate his plans in 1878:

There are two kinds of moral law, two kinds of conscience, one in man and a completely different one in woman. They do not understand each other; but in matters of practical living the woman is judged by man's law, as if she were not a woman but a man.

The wife in the play ends by having no idea what is right and what is wrong: natural feelings on the one hand and belief in authority on the other lead her to utter distraction.

A woman cannot be herself in modern society. It is an exclusively male society, with laws made by men and with prosecutors and judges who assess feminine conduct from a masculine standpoint.

At the centre of *A Doll's House* is Nora Helmer, the wife of the newly appointed bank manager, Torvald Helmer, and the mother of three young children. She pretends to be bird-brained and this appeals to him. But Nora is shrewd and proves quite capable of paying her debt to Krogstad out of her housekeeping money while letting Torvald think she is extravagant. For much of the play her behaviour is conventional: she has done everything for her husband's sake, is content to play games for him, flirt with Rank and dance the tarantella for both of them. Nora eventually arrives at a radical conclusion, but she is hardly a radical feminist.

Torvald is not a bad man, but his thinking is entirely conventional. He is delighted with his new position at the bank and is looking for security and contentment. His attitude to his wife is that of a bourgeois husband of the period. Certainly, he is so wrapped up in his own affairs that he fails to notice what is happening around him, but a reading of the play which sees Torvald as cruel or pathological travesties Ibsen's intentions.

The climax of the play is the transformation that takes place in Nora in the last act. As Ibsen wrote:

> [Nora is] a big, overgrown child, who must go out into the world to discover herself and so may one day be, in due course, fit to raise her children – or maybe not. No one can know. But this much is certain, that with the perspective on marriage that has opened up to her in the course of the night it would be immoral of her to continue living with Helmer: this is impossible for her and this is why she leaves.

Her first instinct is for suicide: she draws a black shawl over her head, muttering about 'water . . . deep . . . black'. When Krogstad's letter arrives and Torvald 'forgives' her, her response is to blame Torvald for not taking 'the whole thing on [his] shoulders'. At the end, when she leaves him, her prospects are bleak: she is leaving everything behind in order to be 'true' to herself. In Ibsen's later plays he explored relentlessly the complex – and sometimes catastrophic – consequences of such an act of self-realization; here, he merely hints at them.

Mrs Linde and Krogstad are an essential part of Ibsen's design. Krogstad's isolation and bitter sense of injustice make him much more than a melodramatic villain. Mrs Linde's practical and independent mind, as well as her radical capacity for love, makes her much more than simply Nora's confidante. In a play which is often seen as an attack on marriage, it is fascinating to see Ibsen's celebration of the romantic reconciliation of an estranged couple.

Doctor Rank is a mysterious figure. To Nora he is more than simply a devoted older man. He knows that he is dying (probably from inherited syphilis), but in his flirtation with her, his delight in Torvald's 'dark Havanas' and his playful melancholy, he not only faces up to his death with courage but also allows her to glimpse the possibility of her own renewal. Indeed, behind the play's naturalist surface lurks a Christmas drama of death and new life: wickedness (Krogstad) is redeemed through love, true love (Mrs Linde) gets its reward, illness (Doctor Rank) faces death with equanimity, tyranny (Torvald) is brought low and the oppressed (Nora) is reborn into a brave new life.

A Doll's House is Ibsen's first chamber play and is an impressive technical achievement, combining concentrated resources with exquisitely controlled stage pictures. An example is the 'tarantella', the Neapolitan dance of death in which catastrophe is imminent even in its jollity (one expert described it as a 'hysterical catharsis which lets women escape from marriage and motherhood into a free lawless world of music and uninhibited movement') and which is traditionally depicted being danced in the shadow of the smoking Mount Vesuvius. Another example is the maid bringing on the lamp in Act Two, interrupting the 'silk stocking' scene between Rank and Nora: propriety intervenes just as the light is fading. The play is faultlessly constructed and carries a tremendous narrative drive, which – if occasionally melodramatic – climaxes in one of the most provocative endings in drama.

What, ultimately, are we to make of Ibsen's intentions? For understandable reasons, the play has been claimed as the first great feminist play (and influenced the 'New Woman' plays that emerged in its wake). Others draw attention to the speech Ibsen made to the Norwegian Women's Rights League nearly twenty years later:

> I am not a member of the Women's Rights League. I have never been deliberately tendentious in anything I have written. I have been more of a poet and less of a social philosopher than people generally seem inclined to believe. I thank you for your good wishes, but I must decline the honour of being said to have worked for the Women's Rights movement. I am not even very sure what Women's Rights actually are.

As ever, Ibsen in *A Doll's House* is obsessed by the question of how to be true to yourself. The remarkable fact is that, in his first great naturalistic play, he should have chosen the particular story of a woman leaving her husband to explore that 'universal' theme.

⇨ In performance

A Doll's House was premièred at the Royal Theatre in Copenhagen on 21 December 1879. Edmund Gosse reported that 'all Scandinavia rang with Nora's "declaration of independence". People left the theatre, night after night, pale with excitement, arguing, quarelling, challenging.' Performances quickly followed in Stockholm, Christiania and Bergen.

In Germany, the actress playing Nora refused to perform the end, saying 'I would never leave my children', and Ibsen was persuaded to write a new ending (a 'barbaric outrage' as he called it), in which Nora does not leave. Some German theatres adopted this, but when the original ending was reinstated, a 'missing fourth act' was 'discovered', in which Torvald visits Nora (who is now staying with the happily married Krogstad and Mrs Linde) and they are reunited. It was not until 3 March 1880 that the Munich Residenztheater performed the play as Ibsen had written it.

Intriguingly, the English-langage première took place in
Milwaukee on 2 June 1882. The first London performance
was of an adaptation called *Breaking a Butterfly* ('*A Doll's
House* with Ibsen taken out', as Harley Granville Barker
called it) on 3 March 1884. There followed a reading of the
play in Bloomsbury on 15 January 1886, with Eleanor Marx
as Nora, her husband Edward as Torvald, William Morris's
daughter as Mrs Linde and Bernard Shaw as Krogstad.
Havelock Ellis, who was in the audience, wrote:

> The great wave of emancipation which is now sweeping
> across the civilized world means nothing more than that
> women should have the right to education, freedom to
> work, and political enfranchisement – nothing in short
> but the bare ordinary rights of an adult human creature in
> a civilized state.

Eleanor Marx and Bernard Shaw subsequently did much to
introduce Ibsen to British audiences.

The first full London performance took place on 7 June
1889 at the Novelty Theatre, with the American actress Janet
Achurch as Nora. Granville Barker described this as 'the
dramatic event of the decade', but one critic said:

> that foolish, fitful, conceited and unlovable Nora is to
> drive off the stage the loving and noble heroines who have
> adorned it, and filled all hearts with admiration, from the
> time of Shakespeare to the time of Pinero.

Other Noras on the English stage have included Gwen
Ffrangçon Davies (1930), Lydia Lopokova (1934), Flora
Robson (1939), Mai Zetterling (1953), Cheryl Campbell
(1982), Kelly Hunter (1994) and Janet McTeer (1996).

Eleonora Duse played Nora in Italian (1893), Meyerhold
directed the play in St Petersburg (1906), Max Reinhardt in
Berlin (1917), and the astonishing Alla Nazimova performed
Nora in New York (1918) to audible gasps of recognition.
Ingmar Bergman directed the play at the Royal Dramatic
Theatre in Stockholm (1989).

Several films of the play have been made, the first in 1911. Patrick Garland directed it for television in 1973 with Claire Bloom, Anthony Hopkins, Ralph Richardson and Denholm Elliott. Joseph Losey made a heavily feminist version in 1973, with Jane Fonda as Nora.

Fassbinder's film *Nora Helmer* (1974) recast Nora as a careerist who does not leave the home but seizes power in it. The Austrian dramatist Elfriede Jelinek wrote a startling sequel called *What Happened After Nora Left Her Husband* (1980).

Translated by Kenneth McLeish, Nick Hern Books, 1994

Ghosts
(*Gengangere*)

1881

∞ Characters

Mrs Helene Alving, *widow of Captain Alving, a former*
  Chamberlain to the King
Osvald Alving, *her son, a painter*
Pastor Manders
Jakob Engstrand, *a carpenter*
Regine, *Engstrand's daughter, Mrs Alving's maid*

The action takes place in the living-room of Mrs Alving's
country estate, near a large fjord in western Norway

∞ The story

At the start of Act One the fjord is 'dimly visible in the pour-
ing rain' through the glass of the conservatory at the back of
the room. Regine tries to stop her father, the carpenter
Engstrand, from entering, warning him that he will awake
'the young master'. Engstrand has saved some money and is
setting up a 'café' for sailors (probably a brothel). He wants
Regine to work there, but she will have none of it. Pastor
Manders arrives to talk to Mrs Alving, and is keen to see her
son, Osvald, who has recently returned from Paris. Manders
tells Regine that she should look after her 'father [who] needs
someone at his side', but she wants to work in a 'thoroughly
respectable house'. Mrs Alving arrives, eager to settle their
business before lunch. Manders is shocked by her radical
books, which, she says, 'seem to explain and confirm a lot of
things I've been puzzling over myself'. Manders is responsible for the business management of a new orphanage named
after Mrs Alving's dead husband, and wants to know whether

it is to be insured, arguing that local people would regard insurance as showing insufficient trust in Divine Providence. Eventually, Mrs Alving agrees, but insists that Regine should not move to town to live with her father. When Osvald appears – smoking his father's pipe and looking exactly like him – he shocks Manders by his bohemian attitudes and tells him that real immorality is seen when Norwegian married men visit Paris alone. When Mrs Alving agrees with Osvald, Manders reminds her that when she left her husband because of his infidelity, he – Manders – persuaded her to return to him. He also accuses her of abandoning her son when he was young. She informs him that her husband 'died just as depraved as he had been all his life', having had an affair with her servant girl. Now she is 'putting up a memorial to this man', and the money saved for it was all her work. As the curtain falls, Mrs Alving hears Osvald and Regine behaving like her husband and their serving maid: 'Ghosts,' she says, 'the two in the conservatory . . . they've returned'.

Act Two takes place after lunch, but already the light is fading. Manders has realized Osvald's attachment to Regine, but has also discovered that Regine is Osvald's half-sister – her father was Captain Alving and her mother was Mrs Alving's maid Johanna, who was persuaded to marry Engstrand for money. It also emerges that when Mrs Alving left her husband she was in love with Manders. She regrets the secrecy of her past and wishes she could tell her son the truth. She is desperate to be free of 'all the ghosts' that haunt her. Engstrand asks Manders to lead the prayers for the orphanage and, when confronted, Engstrand replies that he did not accept any money, was a loving husband to Johanna, brought up Regine and kept a decent home. Manders recognizes a redeemed sinner and goes off to pray with him. Osvald tells his mother about his illness ('It's my spirit that's broken – my mind's gone – I'll never be able to work again!') and declares that this cannot be hereditary, but is punishment for his own behaviour. Mrs Alving is about to tell him the truth about his father when Manders returns. Instead, Osvald announces that Regine is going to Paris as his wife. They are interrupted by Regine announcing that the orphanage is on fire.

Act Three takes place early the following morning. The orphanage has been burned to the ground, and Mrs Alving is worried about Osvald, who is still trying to put out the fire. Manders arrives, followed by Engstrand – full of sympathy for Manders, whom he claims accidentally set fire to the orphanage himself. Mrs Alving decides to give her estate to the parish and Manders buys Engstrand's silence by promising him money for his seaman's home – if he will take the blame. Mrs Alving tells Osvald the truth about his father. She also tells Regine the truth about her parents – which prompts Regine to leave, determined to pursue Pastor Manders. Left alone with his mother, Osvald declares that he has no obligation to love his father, because he has nothing to thank him for. She can resolve his feelings of 'remorse', but not of 'dread'. He tells her that his fatal disease has its seat in his brain, and that he cannot bear the thought of becoming an invalid. He shows her a box of twelve morphine tablets and asks her to give them to him if his condition deteriorates. She tries to get a doctor but he locks her in the room. Eventually, they sit together and she promises him she will do what he asks. As a beautiful day breaks, Osvald sits in the armchair, suddenly paralysed, with his back to the light, repeating tonelessly: 'The sun. The sun.' Mrs Alving is left looking at the pills, incapable of giving them to him.

ᐒ About the play

Ibsen described *Ghosts* as 'a family story as sad and grey as this rainy day'. Paradoxically, he wrote this gloomiest of plays in the extreme heat of Sorrento over the spring and summer of 1881. His subject is the relationship between parents and childen and significantly it is an orphanage that Mrs Alving is opening in her dead husband's name. As in Sophocles' *Oedipus Rex*, the sins of the father are visited on the son, and the ghosts of the dead have a powerful hold on the living.

The action of the play is a slow unveiling of the truth. If the central theme of Ibsen's work is how to be true to yourself, in *Ghosts* he shows the pain of that pursuit.

At the centre of the play is the character of Mrs Alving, the widow of a royal chamberlain. She has reached a point when all the compromises of her life need to be faced. She is reading radical material and is determined to think for herself and confront 'her ghosts'. Many years ago, she walked out on her husband who had made her desperately unhappy; her mistake was that she followed the advice of Pastor Manders and returned to him. Now is the time for truth. As Ibsen wrote: '*Ghosts* had to be written. After Nora [in *A Doll's House*], Mrs Alving of necessity had to come'. However, when she wants to tell her son the truth about his father's corruption, the consequences are more catastrophic than she imagined:

> These women of the modern age, mistreated as daughters, as sisters, as wives, not educated in accordance with their talents, debarred from following their mission, deprived of their inheritance, embittered in mind – these are the ones who supply the mothers for the new generation. What will be the result?

Ibsen's criticism of the Lutheran Pastor Manders is palpable, and his hypocrisy and narrow-mindedness are sharply drawn. Ibsen shows his faults early on: he is a sensual man who had been attracted to Mrs Alving and is not oblivious to Regine's charms. He dismisses Mrs Alving's books and objects to Osvald's life as an artist without knowing anything about either. However, Manders is a gullible fool, a 'big baby' as Mrs Alving calls him, who is too easily hoodwinked by the conman Engstrand. He is caught up in a set of beliefs and dare not see beyond them – at least not in public. His attitudes spring from a deep, spiritual pessimism:

> Yes, that's it exactly – this rebellious spirit, this craving for happiness in life. What right have we human beings to happiness? No, Mrs Alving, we have our duty to do. And

> your duty was to remain with the man you had chosen,
> and to whom you were bound by sacred ties.

Above all, he is terrified of what the world might think of him. Mrs Alving, however, is a more formidable opponent than he imagined.

The return of Osvald Alving ('the Prodigal son') from Paris is the catalyst for the action. He is making his way as an artist, although 'things have gone a little quiet recently'. It soon emerges that he is ill and that his capacity for work is severely limited. His impassioned defence of his bohemian friends is a declaration of a new kind of moral law and his belief in the 'joy of life' radically transforms his mother's understanding of what went wrong in her own marriage. When he appears smoking his father's pipe, flirting with the maid and drinking too much, he looks (and increasingly behaves) like his father's 'ghost'. It soon becomes clear that he has inherited his syphilis (although here Ibsen has made a mistake: it is impossible to inherit syphilis without the mother suffering from it too). Osvald's tragedy is that of the young, promising man destroyed by his inheritance.

Jakob Engstrand is a carpenter. He drinks too much, is full of 'human failings' and sees temptation all around (like the Devil – and Oedipus – he has a limp). Unashamed, he tries to get Regine to work in his 'sailors' hostel' and treats her ruthlessly, despite his protestations of affection. He pretended to be her father in the past and in Act Three assumes the blame for the burned-down orphanage to protect Pastor Manders. His skill is with language and he manipulates Manders's desire to believe in redemption. His life has been circumscribed by his position in the world and he is trying to survive the best he can. The play's conclusion reveals that he and Manders are closer in morality than society would imagine.

Mrs Alving's maid Regine is upwardly mobile and flirtatious: she is learning French, is ashamed of her father and does not want to marry a sailor. She exudes a sexual vitality which the dying Osvald finds compelling, and there is a moment in Act Two when she is asked to drink champagne with Osvald and his mother and all her dreams seem realizable. But when she discovers that Oswald and she share the same father, her life is shattered. She, too, is trapped by her parents ('The way I see it, if Osvald takes after his father, then I'll most likely take after my mother') and leaves saying that if she cannot get a position with Pastor Manders, she will work at her father's hostel. Ruin and prostitution beckon.

Bernard Shaw said that the final scene between Mrs Alving and Osvald was 'so appallingly tragic that the emotions it excites prevent the meaning of the play from being seized and discussed'. At times, their relationship veers close to being incestuous. Osvald's desire for death has often been criticized, but as Ibsen wrote: 'And then they say the book advocates nihilism . . . All it does is to point out that nihilism is fermenting under the surface, at home as everywhere else.' When asked about whether Mrs Alving gives Oswald the morphine after the curtain falls, Ibsen was typically circumspect: 'That I don't know. Everyone must work that out for himself. I should never dream of deciding such a difficult question. Now, what do *you* think?'

The play's meticulous detail – and its position as a key text in the development of 'naturalism' – can obscure its dazzling theatricality. It has an astonishing atmosphere: austere, sensual and evocative. The progression from rain and gloom, through darkness and fire, to the quite extraordinary (if almost unrealizable) stage direction towards the end of Act Three ('The glacier and the mountain peaks in the background gleam in the morning light') is both natural and rich with meaning. As the poet Rilke said: 'there was the tinkle of glass in the next room, a fire outside the window; there was the sun'. Ultimately, *Ghosts* presents us with a human paradox: you can live unhappily in the rain and gloom of lies and concealment, but once you let in the brilliant light of truth, death and disaster may well follow.

⟨⟩ In performance

Ghosts was published in December 1881, but it took some
time for performances to take off, because it had caused such
a scandal. As early as November 1881, Ibsen was predicting
trouble:

> *Ghosts* will probably cause alarm in some circles; but that
> can't be helped. If it didn't there would have been no
> necessity for me in having written it

Astonishingly, the play received its native-language première
at the Aurora Turner Hall in Chicago, on 20 May 1882. Its
Christiania première (attended by the young Edvard Munch)
was presented by August Lindberg's private touring company
at the Møllergaten Theatre in October 1883.

Herman Bang movingly described the atmosphere at the
German première of *Ghosts* in 1887 by the influential
Meiningen players:

> The young people barely heard her [the actress playing
> Mrs Alving]. They read when the curtain was down, and
> they read when the curtain was up. They read furtively
> and amazed, as though fearful, read as the book was
> passed secretly from hand to hand, a little humble,
> yellow, paperbound volume of a hundred pages bearing
> the title *Ghosts*. What a strange evening when all those
> hundreds of young people read as one the play about the
> sins of their fathers, and when, as a drama about mar-
> riage was being acted behind the footlights, that other
> drama of parents and their children forced its way up
> from the auditorium on to the stage. They did not dare
> to read the book at home, and so they read it secretly
> here.

Because of its controversial nature, performances were frequently banned and the play was initially performed in private club theatres, some established for the purpose. Thus
Ghosts had an overwhelming influence on the subsequent

development of 'art theatres' across Europe. It opened the Freie Bühne in Berlin in 1889 and Antoine's Théâtre Libre in Paris in 1890.

The first public English performance took place on 13 March 1891 in J. P. Grein's Independent Theatre production at the Royalty Theatre in London. William Archer collected the press cuttings:

> An open drain; a loathsome sore unbandaged; a dirty act done publicly; a lazar house with all its windows open . . . Candid foulness . . . Offensive cynicism . . . Ibsen's melancholy and malodorous world . . . Absolutely loathsome and fetid . . . Gross almost putrid indecorum . . . Literary carrion . . . Crapulous stuff.

The first fully public performance in England was not licensed by the Lord Chamberlain until 1914.

Stanislavsky directed *Ghosts* at the Moscow Art Theatre in 1905. He was interested above all in 'Osvald's inner drama: the fact that he knows about his illness'. The Scandinavian theatres mostly rejected the play, and it was not staged publicly in Christiania for another eighteen years. Max Reinhardt directed an 'expressionist' production of the play with sets by Edvard Munch which opened the Kammerspiele in Berlin in 1906. In 1934 James Joyce wrote a comic poem inspired by seeing the play in Paris which includes the line: 'I am the ghost of Captain Alving.'

Ghosts was critically panned, wherever it was performed, and not just by the right-wing press:

> What has most depressed me has been not the attacks themselves, but the lack of guts which has been revealed in the ranks of the so-called liberals.

But Ibsen was quite sanguine:

> The violent criticism and inane attacks which people are levelling against *Ghosts* don't worry me in the least. I was expecting this.

Famous English Mrs Alvings include Mrs Patrick Campbell (1928, with the young John Gielgud as Osvald), Sybil Thorndike (1930) and Flora Robson (1959). Irene Worth played Mrs Alving in a production by Jonathan Miller (1974); Katie Mitchell directed the play for the RSC (1994) with Jane Lapotaire as Mrs Alving and Simon Russell Beale as Osvald; and Francesca Annis played Mrs Alving in the West End (2001). Diana Quick and Daniel Evans played mother and son for English Touring Theatre (2002).

Celia Johnson played Mrs Alving on television in 1968, and Judi Dench starred with Kenneth Branagh and Michael Gambon in 1988. Penelope Wilton starred in a Radio 3 production – translated by Doug Lucie – in 2001.

Translated by Stephen Mulrine, Nick Hern Books, 2002

An Enemy of the People
(*En Folkefiende*)

1882

∾ Characters

Doctor Thomas Stockmann, *Medical Officer at the Baths*
Mrs Katherine Stockmann, *his wife*
Petra, *their daughter, a teacher*
Ejlif and Morten, *their sons, thirteen and ten years old*
Peter Stockmann, *the doctor's elder brother, Mayor, Chief of Police, Chairman of the Board of the Baths, etc.*
Morten Kiil, *a master tanner, Mrs Stockmann's foster-father*
Hovstad, *editor of* The People's Messenger
Billing, *a journalist*
Captain Horster
Aslaksen, *a printer*
Men and women of all ages and every class attending the public meeting

The action takes place in a coastal town in Southern Norway

∾ The story

Acts One and Two take place in the living-room of Doctor Stockmann's house. Billing is being given dinner by Mrs Stockmann when the Mayor arrives, wanting to see his brother, her husband Thomas Stockmann. He says he feels no animosity towards the left-wing editor Hovstad, who has also arrived, and that the tolerance and civic pride in the town, as expressed by the 'splendid new baths', means that 'things are looking pretty promising' for everyone. Doctor Stockmann comes in with Horster, calling for 'roast beef' and 'some hot toddy' ('I can't tell you how happy I feel, surrounded by all this growing, vigorous life'). He is pleased to have returned to town after 'those years in the North, cut off from everything'. The Mayor says he is worried about his brother's forthcoming article and says that 'the individual must be ready to subordinate himself to the community . . . to the authorities charged with [its] welfare'. Stockmann pours drinks and hands round cigars. Horster tells them that he is sailing to America in a week's time. Hovstad says he is running the article the next day, but Stockmann wants him to delay. Petra returns from teaching with a letter for Stockmann. Billing announces that he is an atheist and Petra says that if she had any money she would start a school of her own. Stockmann reveals the content of the letter: scientific evidence that the Baths are a 'most serious danger to health', causing typhoid and gastric fever. He says he is going to put the matter right, and relishes the commotion that will be caused. As the curtain falls, he is pleased to have 'been of some service to one's home town and fellow citizens'.

Act Two takes place the next morning. Katherine's foster father, Morten Kiil, appears, delighted at Stockmann's discovery (he wants to exact his revenge for his own downfall which Stockmann had caused) but convinced that no one will believe in the existence of invisible bacteria. Hovstad tells Stockmann that the corruption of the Baths reflects the 'swamp' that is the town and regards it as an opportunity to wrest power away from the rich men who run it. Aslaksen arrives to offer his support – and the support of 'the middle classes' – saying that he wants to 'draft and publish a vote of thanks from the townspeople'. Hovstad offers help, too, and leaves with Stockmann's article. Stockmann is delighted at the support of these key figures: 'How wonderful to stand shoulder to shoulder in the brotherhood of one's fellow citizens.' The Mayor arrives, having read Stockmann's private report. He is shocked by the cost of relaying the pipes and concerned about the economic impact on the town. He says Stockmann's report exaggerates, and hints that gradual improvements might be possible. The Mayor warns Stockmann of the harm he will do himself by behaving recklessly and forbids him, as a member of staff, from expressing his opinions. He also threatens him with dismissal. When Stockmann says that 'the whole town's prosperity is rooted in a lie', the Mayor leaves, saying 'You've had your warning'. Katherine reminds Stockmann of his brother's power and says she is worried about their children. Petra supports her father, however, and Stockmann declares: 'I want to be able to look my boys in the face when they grow up into free men.'

In Act Three the action moves to the Editor's office. Hovstad has read Stockmann's article ('pretty scathing, isn't he?') and Billing says he can see 'the revolution coming'. Stockmann arrives and tells them to print his article: 'it's no longer just the water-supply and the sewers now. No, the whole community needs cleaning up, disinfecting.' Aslaksen is to oversee the printing, but is 'frightened' of 'vested interests': his 'heart is still with the people. But I'll not deny that my head rather inclines me to support the authorities.' Petra arrives with an English story which she refuses to translate, because it 'runs completely contrary to everything you believe in'. Hovstad says it was Billing who wanted it ('a man with all his progressive ideals?'), and Petra praises Hovstad for 'blazing a trail for the advancement of truth'. When Hovstad says that he is only publishing Stockmann's article because of his romantic feelings towards her, she is furious and leaves. The Mayor arrives, telling them of the costs of any alterations and suggesting his brother's argument may be imaginary. He is about to give them a 'short statement of the facts' when Stockmann arrives, impatient for proofs but concerned that there should be no public demonstration. Katherine arrives, furious with him for not caring about the family. Suddenly Stockmann discovers his brother, who had hidden himself earlier, and tells him that 'we are having a revolution in town tomorrow'. He is shocked to hear that Hovstad is not going to print his article and will publish the Mayor's statement instead. He decides to call a public meeting and Katherine supports him. Finally he declares: 'And now, gentlemen, the gloves are off. We'll see whether you and your shabby tricks can stop an honest citizen who wáилɔ in clean up the town.'

In Act Four the action moves to Captain Horster's house, where the public meeting is taking place. Horster ushers in Katherine and her family (while denying that he is being brave) and Stockmann and the Mayor also enter. Aslaksen is unanimously elected Chairman and urges 'moderation'. When the Mayor proposes that Doctor Stockmann should not be permitted to present his account, he is supported by Aslaksen and Hovstad. However, Stockmann wants to speak of something bigger: 'all our spiritual sources are polluted and our whole civic community is built over a cesspool of lies'. He also tells the crowded hall of his commitment to the Baths and the town, despite 'the colossal stupidity of the authorities', declaring that 'the worst enemy of truth and freedom in our society is the compact majority. Yes, the damned, compact, liberal majority . . . the majority is never right . . . that's one of those lies in society that no free and intelligent man can help rebelling against.' His railing against the majority and its hand-me-down 'truths' ('no society can live a healthy life on the old dry bones of that kind of truth') and his declaration that 'free-thinking is almost exactly the same as morality' provokes an uproar, culminating in the denunciation of Stockmann as 'an enemy of the people', a sentiment which is adopted and voted on as the 'resolution' of the meeting. Stockmann asks Horster whether he has 'room aboard for passengers for the New World' and leaves, declaring, like Christ, that 'I forgive you, for you know not what you do'. As the curtain falls, the crowd is heard chanting 'Enemy of the people! Enemy of the people!'

Act Five takes place in Stockmann's study. The windows have been broken and Stockmann is counting the stones. The landlord has given them notice ('he daren't do anything else') but Stockmann says that they are leaving for America ('things are on a bigger scale there'). Petra returns – she has been sacked and her reputation sullied. Horster arrives – he, too, has been given his notice – and is just about to announce

'another idea' when the Mayor enters and the two brothers
are left alone together. The Mayor gives Stockmann his
notice, and informs him that his prospects in the town are
grim unless he publishes an apology. He also says that
Stockmann's attack was his way of ensuring that Morten Kiil
left a considerable sum to Katherine and the children in his
will, declaring 'for now we have a weapon against you'. Kiil
arrives, having bought up shares in the baths very cheaply.
Stockmann has said that the bacteria came from Kiil's tan-
nery, and now Kiil wants him to deny their existence, or say
they have been exterminated. If he does not, Kiil will leave
Katherine nothing. Hovstad and Aslaksen arrive, aware of
Kiil's speculation and that Stockmann will be rich, and offer
him ownership of their paper. Stockmann drives them out
through a broken window, and sends a card with three 'nos'
to his brother, declaring 'But now I'm going to sharpen my
pen; I'll impale them on it; I'll dip it in venom and gall; I'll
chuck the inkpot right into their faces.' Horster offers them
his home and Stockmann speaks with a kind of crazed confidence, taking the boys out of school, planning to look after
and educate the poor. At the end of the play, surrounded by
his family, he declares that he has made a great discovery:
'The thing is, you see, that the strongest man in the world is
the man who stands alone.'

↬ About the play

An Enemy of the People was written quickly by Ibsen's standards and was conceived in reaction to the furore over *Ghosts*:
if the masses rejected Ibsen's revelations of the truth, in his
next play he would show the basis of their cowardice. It was
written in Rome and, like Shakespeare's *Coriolanus*, questions
the wisdom of 'the mob'.

The central role of Doctor Thomas Stockmann is one of
Ibsen's greatest creations. He is passionate and idealistic, sensual and pragmatic, arrogant and foolish. His belief in the
ultimate victory of 'truth' is somewhat naïve and his declara-

tion in Act Four of the individual's duty to it, regardless of the majority, can seem overblown and idealistic:

> The truths the masses recognize today are the same truths as were held by advanced thinkers in our grandfathers' day. We who man the advanced outposts today, we don't recognize them any more.

In some ways, however, this is Ibsen's point: it is foolish to imagine that the 'masses', manipulated by the press and controlled by the powerful, can ever have the necessary independence of mind to care about the truth. It is only a scorned élite who can afford to insist on it, whatever the consequences.

At times, Stockmann's position comes close to anarchy, as Ibsen had written in a letter to Georg Brandes in 1871:

> The state is the curse of the individual . . . the state must go! That revolution is one that I will join. Undermine the concept of statehood, set up voluntary action and spiritual freedom as the sole determining factors making for unity . . . To exchange one form of government for another is merely tinkering with differences in degree, a little more or a little less – altogether useless.

Thus Stockmann is, to an extent, autobiographical; but in a letter in 1882 Ibsen was keen to stress their differences:

> The Doctor is more muddle-headed than I am, and apart from this he has a considerable number of other traits that make people more willing to hear certain things from him which, if I myself had said them, they would perhaps not have taken quite so well.

Ibsen is careful to draw Stockmann's family in some detail: his wife Katherine, torn between the safety of her family and love for her husband; their idealistic and intellectual daughter Petra; and their two young boys Ejlif and Morten. Their friend Captain Horster is one of the most attractive characters in the play: brave but diffident, loyal but independent-minded.

Ibsen also shows Stockmann's opponents. In Peter Stockmann, he has produced one of his most powerful critiques of the hypocrisy of authority. He is not only the Mayor but also Chief of Police and Chairman of the Baths. For all his abstemiousness, he is highly intelligent and can act ruthlessly. It is important to stress, however, that his opposition to his brother is motivated by genuine concern for the economy and stability of the whole town, not simply his own position or income. Other characters include Hovstad, the spineless editor of the so-called liberal newspaper, who loses his radical commitment as soon as he sees the enemy; Billing the revolutionary whose energies are rhetorical and cynical; the hypocritical printer, Aslaksen, the voice of the respectable lower middle class, whose calls for moderation mask deep corruption; and the bitter, wily old tanner Morten Kiil, Katherine's unappealing foster father. Behind these figures are the townspeople, who act like the chorus from a Greek tragedy, sometimes in unison, sometimes individualized, but always representing the overwhelming force of society against which the individual needs to make his stand.

The great Ibsenite choice between individual truth and the hypocrisy of society is dramatized in the central clash between the two brothers. The play explores the dilemma faced by the democrat when he discovers that the masses are misled and misguided, and investigates the possible role of a liberal élite. Indeed, the play seems to dismiss the possibility of an intelligent democratic will altogether, as Ibsen wrote in a letter to Georg Brandes the following year:

> But I maintain that the intellectual avant-garde is *never* able to collect a majority. In ten years, the majority might possibly have reached the point where Doctor Stockmann stood at the meeting. But during these ten years, the Doctor has not been standing still; he continues to be at least ten years further on than the majority; the majority, the masses, the public never catch him up; he can never collect a majority.

The awkward fact is that this questioning of the wisdom of the majority can easily shock modern audiences, brought up to think of democracy as the best possible form of government.

An Enemy of the People has a rolling, rollicking vitality, which, in a good production, makes it tremendously exciting to watch. If at times the play lacks the depth and complexity of Ibsen's greatest dramas, it has a clarity of moral purpose and a direct and powerful dramatic hold, which makes it an ideal first play for the newcomer to Ibsen.

∞ In performance

An Enemy of the People was premièred in Christiania on 13 January 1883, and then performed all over Scandinavia in the same year. It was generally favourably received. Its German première was in Berlin in 1887 and its French première took place in Paris in 1893.

Amongst many letters full of meticulous detail about casting, acting, design and so on, is this to the director of the Christiania Theatre:

> In the so-called romantic drama . . . illusion is not an absolute requirement; during a performance the spectator is perfectly aware that he is only sitting in a theatre and watching a theatrical performance. But circumstances will be different when *An Enemy of the People* is produced. Each member of the audience must feel as if he were invisibly present in Doctor Stockmann's living-room; everything must be realistic here.

The 1905 Moscow Art Theatre production coincided with the first Russian Revolution. Stanislavsky, who was playing Stockmann, described the performance after the Kasanzky Square massacre in Petrograd: 'the atmosphere in the theatre was such that we expected arrests at any moment and a stop to the performances'. There was a particular uproar when Stockmann said: 'You should never put your new trousers on when you go out to fight for truth and freedom.'

The play received its London première on 14 June, 1893, in a production starring and directed by Beerbohm Tree, which William Archer described as 'distinctly below the level of the so-called "scratch" performances to which we have been accustomed' but which was otherwise well received. This toured America throughout 1895 and could still be seen in London in 1909. Tyrone Guthrie staged the play at the Old Vic in 1939 with Roger Livesey as Stockmann, and Joan Littlewood presented a Lancashire version at Stratford East in 1954.

Arthur Miller wrote a remarkable adaptation of the play, declaring in his foreword that 'I have attempted to make *An Enemy of the People* as alive to Americans as it undoubtedly was to Norwegians'. This was premièred in New York on 28 December 1950, with Fredric March as Doctor Stockmann, and received its British première at the Young Vic in London in 1988 with Tom Wilkinson.

The play was staged at the Royal National Theatre in 1997 in a production by Trevor Nunn, with Ian McKellen as Stockmann. The translation was by Christopher Hampton, who wrote: 'It is this even-handedness and refusal to over-simplify that makes *An Enemy of the People* as powerfully relevant in our age of *fin-de-siecle* corruption, ecological vandalism and truculent refusal to accept inconvenient facts.'

Translated by James McFarlane, Oxford, 1960

The Wild Duck
(*Vildanden*)
1884

↻ Characters

Haakon Werle, *businessman and industrialist*
Gregers Werle, *his son*
Old Ekdal
Hjalmar Ekdal, *his son, a photographer*
Gina Ekdal, *Hjalmar's wife*
Hedvig, *their daughter, fourteen*
Mrs Soerby, *housekeeper to Haakon Werle*
Relling, *a doctor*
Molvik, *a one-time student of theology*
Graaberg, *a clerk*
Pettersen, *Haakon Werle's servant*
Jensen, *a hired waiter*
A fat gentleman, a balding gentleman, a short-sighted
    gentlemen and six other guests
Several hired servants

Act One takes place in Haakon Werle's house; the rest of the
play takes place in Hjalmar Ekdal's apartment

↻ The story

The wealthy businessman Haakon Werle is throwing a lavish
party for his son Gregers, who has returned from his father's
logging works in the country. Pettersen and Jensen are
preparing the drawing-room for after dinner. Old Ekdal,
dressed in 'a shabby greatcoat', comes to see Graaberg for
some copying work. Pettersen tells Jensen that years ago
Ekdal was sentenced to hard labour for 'doing the dirty on
old Werle'. Mrs Soerby appears, very much the mistress of
the house, accompanied by a number of guests. Gregers is left

with his old friend Hjalmar Ekdal, who made a clean break after his father's disgrace, married Gina – who used to 'be in service' in the Werles' house – and took up photography. Gregers is shocked when Hjalmar turns his back on his own father, and asks Werle who was guilty of the original misdeed. Werle blames Ekdal and says he can do nothing for his family now, beyond giving Ekdal some badly paid copying work. Gregers wants to know why Werle paid for Hjalmar's photography lessons and suggests a connection between that and his attitude to Gina. Werle offers his son a partnership in the firm, needing his approval for his forthcoming marriage to Mrs Soerby. Gregers knows that his mother was blind to his father's affairs and suggests that his friend Hjalmar's 'home is built on a lie'. He declares that he has finally discovered an 'objective to live for' and leaves the house in disgust.

In Act Two the action shifts to Hjalmar's studio, an attic room with a large skylight, where he lives with his wife and daughter. Hedvig is reading and Gina is doing the accounts: they have little money, but what they have is spent on Hjalmar's luxuries. Ekdal comes in with his copying work and goes into his room. Hjalmar returns from the party; he had promised he would bring Hedvig something delicious, and she is bitterly disappointed when he can only show her the menu. Gina and Hedvig pamper him and he plays his flute: 'What though we have to pinch and scrape in this place, Gina! It's still our home.' Suddenly Gregers arrives. He wants to talk about Hedvig, who Hjalmar says is losing her sight ('Apparently, it's hereditary'). When Ekdal appears, Gregers talks with him about his 'old hunting grounds' and Ekdal shows him an area of the loft he has turned into a version of the wild, with rabbits, pigeons and a 'wild duck' (shot by Gregers's father, but rescued by his hunting dog). To Hjalmar's delight (but Gina's concern), Gregers wants to rent their vacant room. Hjalmar declares that now he can work on his invention and look after his 'poor white-haired old father', but as the curtain falls it is Gina who has to ask him to help carry the sleeping Ekdal off to bed.

Act Three takes place the following morning. Gregers has made a mess of his room by misusing the fire. Hjalmar has invited him to lunch, along with Relling and Molvik. Gina prepares the lunch and Hjalmar does some retouching work. He is interrupted by Ekdal (who goes into the loft), then by his wife (who wants the table for lunch) and finally by Hedvig (who takes over the work, even though it is bad for her eyes). Hedvig tells him about the books she found in the loft, including a history of London with a 'a picture of Death, with an hour glass, and a girl'. She sees her wild duck as mysterious and is astonished at the way Gregers attaches metaphorical meanings to it: a creature that had been down to 'the briny deep', but was rescued by a clever dog. Gina appears and Gregers discovers that she has learned how to take photographs too. A shot is suddenly heard: Hjalmar is 'hunting', and Gina says that 'the two of you will end up having an accident one of these fine days with that gun'. Hjalmar talks about his 'invention' and reveals that he nearly committed suicide when his father was taken to prison. Gregers compares him to the wild duck 'in a poison swamp'. Relling and Molvik arrive, keen for lunch, but Molvik, who got drunk the night before, leaves feeling sick when pork is served. Relling criticizes Gregers for his 'claim of the ideal', but is interrupted by Werle's arrival. Gregers tells his father that he is determined to 'free Hjalmar from all the lies and deceit that are causing his ruination', partly as a way of curing his own 'sick conscience'. Gregers refuses his father's generous financial offer and, to Gina's and Relling's alarm, takes Hjalmar out for a walk.

At the start of Act Four, Hedvig is waiting anxiously for her father. When he returns, he declares that he wants to wring the wild duck's neck, saying 'there are certain demands of the ideal . . . certain claims that a man can't disregard without doing violence to his own soul'. Having sent Hedvig out for her evening walk, he announces that he wants to keep the accounts himself and is determined to cut off any financial support from Werle. He makes Gina confess that Werle 'had his way' with her, before they were married, and declares that 'everything's over and done with now'. Gregers returns, disappointed not to see the 'light of radiant understanding on the faces of husband and wife alike'. Relling turns up and attacks Gregers ('Don't you think the Ekdals' marriage is good enough as it is?'), prophesying that he will 'end up doing [Hedvig] serious harm'. Mrs Soerby arrives, to have 'a little chat [with Gina] and say goodbye'. She says that she has been entirely honest with Werle about her past ('the best policy for us women') and their forthcoming marriage seems meaningful. She also says that Werle is going blind ('retribution for his sins' says Hjalmar). Hedvig has been given a 'deed of gift' from Werle, a great deal of money. When Hjalmar asks Gina if Hedvig 'is mine', her answer is 'I don't know'. He storms off in a terrible state, tearing up the 'deed', with Hedvig sobbing 'he's never coming back to us again'. Left together, Gregers tells Hedvig that she should 'sacrifice the wild duck for his sake'. Gina returns and, as the curtain falls, declares: 'This is what happens when you get these stupid idiots coming round with their fancy demands.'

Act Five takes place 'in the cold grey light of morning'. Hjalmar is moving out and – to Gregers's shock – is in Relling's flat ('lying on a sofa, snoring'). When Relling arrives, he tells Gregers that Hjalmar's 'misfortune is that . . . he's always been considered a shining light' and that his weakness lay in his 'inflamed scruples'. Relling says Hjalmar is sick, but he will keep his 'life-lie going . . . Take the life-lie away from the average man and straight away you take away his happiness.' Left with Hedvig, Gregers reminds her of the 'genuine, joyous, courageous spirit of self-sacrifice'. Hedvig asks Ekdal how to shoot a wild duck. Suddenly Hjalmar returns and declares: 'As I spend these last moments in what was once my home, I wish to remain undisturbed by those who have no business to be here.' Step by step, his plans falter; Gina pampers him, he glues the 'deed' back together, and all the while his protestations become increasingly extravagant. Hjalmar tells Gregers of his love for Hedvig: 'I was so inexpressibly fond of her . . . and I deluded myself into imagining she was equally fond of me, too.' Gregers assures him that Hedvig would sacrifice everything for him when, suddenly, 'a pistol shot is heard in the loft'. Soon they discover the truth: Hedvig has shot herself ('the forest's revenge'). Hjalmar is devastated, and even challenges God ('if thou art there! Why hast Thou done this to me?'). While Molvik starts drunkenly praying, Relling attacks both Gregers's attempt to wrestle meaning from Hedvig's death, and Hjalmar's 'sentimentality and self pity'. As the curtain falls, Relling says: 'Oh, life wouldn't be too bad if only these blessed people who come canvassing their ideal round everybody's door would leave us poor souls in peace', while Gregers declares pompously that his destiny is to be 'thirteenth at table'.

ᙆ About the play

On finishing *The Wild Duck* in 1884, Ibsen wrote to his publisher Frederick Hegel:

> This new play in many ways occupies a place of its own among my dramas; the method is in various respects a departure from my earlier one.

This new 'method' was the introduction of a symbolist element, which takes the play beyond the strictly naturalistic. Of course, the play itself carries a powerful warning against symbolism, against mistaking symbols for real life: the wild duck is just a wild duck, however much meaning is projected on to it. Gina, the voice of realism, gets to the point: 'That blessed wild duck! All the carrying-on there is about that bird!' Elaborate language and metaphor are traps, which often fail to express the unvarnished truth.

The play centres on two families: the Werles and the Ekdals. Werle has made a fortune in logging and been ruthless – particularly toward Old Ekdal – in his pursuit of money. Now he uses his wealth to assuage his guilt: with his continued employment of old Ekdal, financial support for Hjalmar's photography and his 'deed of gift' to young Hedvig. When news comes of his marriage to Berta Soerby, we sense a real possibility: her past is full of pain, which has given her a rare generosity of spirit, and Werle is now capable of redemption. Werle's son Gregers, however, has been cut off from society, and the play shows how his single-mindedness can cause chaos. He is an idealist, who says that if he had the choice he would like to be 'a really absurdly clever dog; the sort who goes in after wild ducks when they dive down and bite on to the weeds and tangle in the mud'. In his relentless pursuit of the 'ideal', Gregers is extraordinarily dangerous.

The other family are the Ekdals. Old Ekdal is a pathetic old man whose glory days are long gone and he is emasculated by the shame that was falsely attached to him. He is reduced to shooting rabbits in a loft, which he pretends are the wild woods of Norway. His son, Hjalmar, is perhaps Ibsen's most self-regarding character – greedy, egotistical, self-pitying and vain. Obsessed with his own comfort, he will never make the invention he keeps talking about. Nevertheless, Ibsen manages to show his vulnerability and elicits our sympathy.

Hjalmar's wife, the working-class Gina, is pragmatic and sober, responsible and in touch with the realities of life. She has a strongly independent view of men ('Always have to have something to deviate themselves with') and, because her past is compromised, has a profound understanding of the complex reality of the world. Her daughter Hedvig is both loving and naïve: 'She doesn't suspect anything. Happy and carefree, just like a little singing bird, there she goes fluttering into a life of eternal night.' She dies a victim of clichéd moralism, and her death lacks any redemptive meaning, beyond demonstrating the futility of Gregers's idealism and the destructive effects of her father's egotism.

These two families are offset by a host of other characters. Relling is a doctor, a hard-edged cynic quite capable of seeing through any amount of idealism. His philosophy is the necessity of telling lies in order to get through life. His friend

Molvik is a one-time student of theology, now a tutor and rapidly turning into an alcoholic. Gina describes them as a 'pair of wasters'. Graaberg is the Werles' clerk, tough and cynical, yet not above slipping Ekdal a bottle of brandy; Pettersen is an all-seeing servant; Jensen has the naïvety of the young hired waiter; the guests in Act One are individually drawn, but all are equally greedy, foolish and self-centred.

In June 1884, in one of his most significant letters, Ibsen wrote:

> I believe that none of us can have any higher aim in life than to realize ourselves in spirit and in truth. That, in my view, is the true meaning of liberalism, and that is why the so-called liberals are in so many ways repugnant to me.

The Wild Duck examines the kind of liberalism which ignores individual circumstances and relies on dangerous notions of the 'ideal'. In his jottings he said:

> Liberation consists in securing for individuals the right to free themselves, each according to his particular need.

In *The Quintessence of Ibsenism*, Bernard Shaw summarized the play brilliantly:

> The busybody finds that people cannot be freed from their failings from without. They must free themselves.

The Wild Duck is a technical marvel. With its artist's studio setting, its meticulous realism and its grandeur of conception, it can feel like a nineteenth-century staging of a Rembrandt. In an interview in 1898, Ibsen said that 'It is to be tragi-comedy . . . or else Hedvig's death is incomprehensible', and it is the play's restless, analytical tone which gives it its unique power. Sometimes regarded as his greatest work, the 'master's masterpiece', it is perhaps more accurate to describe *The Wild Duck* as Ibsen's 'problem play' – like Shakespeare's *Measure For Measure* – which, with its scope and its vision, its moral seriousness and its dramatic power, continues to exact a powerful hold over audiences and readers alike.

ᴄᴏ In performance

Ibsen was very particular about how *The Wild Duck* should be staged:

> The play demands absolute naturalness and truthfulness both in the ensemble work and in the staging. The lighting, too, is important; it is different for each act, and is calculated to establish the peculiar atmosphere of that act.

In a letter to the Swedish director August Lindberg, he demonstrated the detail of his theatrical vision:

> When Hedvig has shot herself, she must be lying on the sofa in such a way that her feet are downstage, so that the right hand with the pistol can hang down. When she is carried out through the kitchen door, I imagined Hjalmar holding her under the arms and Gina her feet.

The Wild Duck was premièred in Bergen on 9 January 1885, and then throughout Scandinavia within weeks. It opened in Berlin in 1888 and at the Theatre Libre in Paris in 1891. It received its English première on 5 May 1894 at the Royalty Theatre, London. The reception was confused. Havelock Ellis detected 'a certain tendency to mannerism, and the dramatist's love of symbolism . . . becomes obtrusive and disturbing', but Bernard Shaw was ecstatic:

> Where shall I find an epithet magnificent enough for *The Wild Duck*! To sit there getting deeper and deeper into your own life all the time; until you forget you are in a theatre; to look on with horror and pity at a profound tragedy, shaking with laughter all the time at an irresistible comedy; to go out, not from a diversion, but from an experience deeper than real life ever brings to most men . . .

The play was revived in London in 1955 with Emlyn Williams as Hjalmar and the young Dorothy Tutin as Hedvig. Modern productions include Ingmar Bergman's at the Dramaten in Stockholm in 1972 with Max von Sydow as Gregers (seen in London in the World Theatre Season), and Peter Zadek's at the Schauspielhaus, Hamburg in 1975. Ralph Richardson played Old Ekdal at the National Theatre in London in 1979, and Peter Hall directed the play in 1990 with Alex Jennings as Hjalmar and David Threlfall as Gregers.

Translated by James McFarlane, Oxford, 1960

Rosmersholm
(*Rosmersholm*)
1886

∽ Characters

Johannes Rosmer, *formerly the parish pastor, owner of
Rosmersholm*
Rebecca West, *living at Rosmersholm, formerly the
companion of Rosmer's dead wife*
Doctor Kroll, *a headmaster, Rosmer's brother-in-law*
Ulrik Brendel
Peder Mortensgård
Mrs Helseth, *Rosmer's housekeeper*

The action takes place in Rosmersholm, an old manor house
near a small coastal village in West Norway

∽ The story

The play opens with the visit of Doctor Kroll to Rosmersholm.
Rosmer tells Kroll how much he – and Rebecca – miss his
dead wife, Beata. Kroll is worried about the growth of radical
politics in the area, and particularly Mortensgård's left-wing
newspaper, *The Searchlight*, which even his wife and children
seem to be reading. Kroll wants Rosmer to lend his influential
support – his 'family name' – to his own paper. Ulrik Brendel,
Rosmer's old tutor ('a distinguished-looking man . . . dressed
as a tramp'), arrives, on his way to town to give a series of lec-
tures 'on equality'. He wants to borrow a clean shirt and some
money. When Rosmer tells Kroll that he stands 'where your
children stand', Kroll is appalled, describing Rosmer's position as 'unforgivable'. Rebecca, who has witnessed this, senses
imminent doom.

Act Two takes place in Rosmer's study. Rebecca confesses
that she wrote a note to Mortensgård, asking him to help

Brendel. Kroll arrives (having not 'slept a wink since yester-
day') and tells Rosmer that Beata committed suicide because
she was jealous of his relationship with Rebecca. Kroll
accuses Rosmer of 'free love', but his real concern is for the
future. Rosmer's answer is direct: 'For generations the
Rosmer family has brought nothing but darkness and oppres-
sion. I think it's my duty to bring light and cheerfulness.' But
Kroll threatens him: 'You're innocent, Johannes . . . You've
no idea what storms are going to break.' Mortensgård arrives,
keen to enlist Rosmer's support ('Nothing helps the moral
standing of the Party more than winning over a convinced
and serious Christian'), but when he discovers that Rosmer
has left the church he is no longer interested. Furthermore,
he owns a letter written by Beata which criticizes his treatment of her, and he uses it to remind Rosmer of the need to
be 'careful'. It quickly transpires that Rebecca has overheard
everything. Rosmer recognizes the truth of Beata's letter and
wonders what his relationship with Rebecca will be now.
When he proposes marriage, she shouts for joy; seconds later,
she dismisses the idea, warning him that if he asks her again
she will 'go where Beata went'. Rosmer is mystified.

The next morning (Act Three), Mrs Helseth tells Rebecca
that Beata killed herself because she could not have children.
Kroll's paper, meanwhile, carries a vitriolic attack on Rosmer,
but Rosmer does not have the energy to counter-attack.
Instead he is struck dumb with guilt: 'I'd no right to such
happiness, at Beata's expense.' Rebecca tells him off for his
'inherited scruples'. Meanwhile, Kroll has arrived and criticizes Rebecca for her 'icy' ambition. He demonstrates that
she is 'illegitimate', points out the contradictions in her 'free-
thinking' and insists that she marry Rosmer. She says that she
came to Rosmersholm full of dreams of freedom; but also
confesses that she manipulated Beata, 'went to work on her',
made her feel that 'because she couldn't have children she
had no right to be here'. Kroll leaves with Rosmer, saying:
'This is the woman you were living with!' As the curtain falls,
Rebecca tells Mrs Helseth to fetch her cases. She is leaving:

'today something scared me . . . I thought I saw the White Horses of Rosmersholm.'

Act Four takes place late that evening. Rebecca is leaving on the midnight boat, and Mrs Helseth tries to comfort her. Rebecca tells Rosmer: 'Rosmersholm has broken me . . . When I came I had free will, spirit. Now strangers' customs have crushed me. I don't think I have the willpower to do anything else again, ever.' She confesses she once felt 'uncontrollable desire' for him and it was this that 'swept Beata into the millrace'. As time went by, she says, that matured into love, but what she calls the 'Rosmer view of life engulfed it' and killed 'all happiness'. Rosmer has given into Kroll's demands. He is in despair and begs her to give him back his faith in her. They are interrupted by Brendel, who is going 'down the dark road'. He is ruined, 'in penury', and Mortensgård, the 'Lord and Master of the Future', controls everything. Brendel warns Rosmer to avoid the 'enchantress', who can only be trusted if she 'goes out to the kitchen, with gladness in her heart, and chops off her soft, white little finger . . . Then slices off her shell-like left ear.' Then, hailing the two of them as 'all-conquering', he wanders off into the dark. Left together, Rosmer and Rebecca once again contemplate their future. He is suicidal, and asks her: 'Have you the courage, the willpower – with gladness in your heart . . . to go where Beata went?' This would allow him to 'have faith in [them] again. In my mission. My power to ennoble human souls.' When she agrees ('You have to go forward! I have to go overboard'), he places his hand on her head and takes her as 'my true and lawful wife'. Together, hand in hand, they go off to the millrace. Mrs Helseth comes in to announce the carriage, but looking out through the window, sees the two drown 'in each other's arms . . . The dead one took them.'

∽ About the play

The first Liberal administration in Norway was elected in 1884, but within a year Ibsen was expressing his disappointment: 'I have found that even the most necessary rights of the individual are not as secure under the new regime as I felt I might hope and expect them to be . . . an element of nobility must find its way into our public life . . . What I am thinking of is a nobility of character, of mind, and of will. That alone will make us free.' *Rosmersholm*, perhaps Ibsen's most explicitly political play, is the result.

The story is based on the romantic elopement of the young Ebba Piper with the great Swedish poet Carl Snoilsky, the husband of one of her relatives. Ibsen knew both of them well and in his notes for the play (originally called *White Horses*) he described them:

> He, a refined, aristocratic character, who has switched to a liberal viewpoint and been ostracized by all his former friends and acquaintances. A widower had been unhappily married to a half-mad melancholic who ended by drowning herself.
>
> She, the governess of his two daughters, emancipated, hot-blooded, somewhat ruthless beneath a refined exterior. Is regarded by their acquaintances as the evil spirit of the house; an object of suspicion and gossip.

These, then, are the real life models for Rosmer and Rebecca West.

The twenty-nine-year-old Rebecca West was hailed by contemporary feminists as a free-thinking, independent-minded woman who pursues her own agenda regardless of the whisperings of society. It is she who has been responsible for Rosmer's liberation: 'we'd march to freedom together . . . side by side. But you couldn't . . . You were pining, sickening, choked in that marriage.' However, in a letter to an actress playing the part, Ibsen was very specific about the nature of her power:

> Rebecca's manner must on no account carry any hint of imperiousness or masculinity. She does not force Rosmer forward. She lures him. A controlled power, a quiet determination, are of the essence of her character.

Thus with the hint of an incestuous relationship with her adopted father, her love of perfumed flowers, her manipulation of Beata, her ability to be deceptive and her power over Rosmer, some have seen in Rebecca West the opposite of a feminist: a *femme fatale*.

The forty-three-year-old Johannes Rosmer is known for his 'decency, high-mindedness [and] integrity'. He has that true 'nobility of character' that Ibsen sought, and his newly found radicalness is highly principled: 'I want to help with equality . . . to make all her citizens princes.' He is anxious not to lose his old friend Kroll, and criticizes him not so much for his politics as for the way that 'he sneered and attacked anyone who disagreed'. However, Rosmer is a man 'who never laughs', from a place 'where children never cry', and he eventually succumbs to Kroll's pressure. He is paralysed with guilt about his wife's death. He has lost both his inheritance and his religious faith and is trying, in vain, to reinvent his future.

Rosmer's relationship with Rebecca is idealistic and unrealistic. They are 'comrades in arms', but he knows that 'our beautiful, innocent friendship was bound to be misinterpreted one day'. The truth is that Rosmer is sexless and Rebecca will never be satisfied. He could not give his first wife Beata any children, and there will be no children by Rebecca. The family of Rosmersholm will eventually die out. Rosmer's idealism is not enough.

Doctor Kroll is the local headmaster and chairman of the Temperance Society. He is full of anxiety about the political situation; it is 'civil war', he says, and people call him a political 'fanatic'. Ibsen seems to take pleasure in showing that the patriarch cannot keep his charges under control: not just the pupils at school, but even his wife and children are a miniature vision of the social rebellion that is happening everywhere. However, Kroll is much more than merely a comic figure: his criticisms of Rosmer and Rebecca as 'an atheist and a freethinker' carry real force, and his attacks are vicious and insinuating in the extreme. Unfortunately, they are also successful.

Kroll's left-wing opponent is Mortensgård, the editor of *The Searchlight*, 'a hack' who Ibsen describes as a 'short weedy man with sparse red hair and beard'. Pastor Rosmer had 'branded' him in church and had him sacked from his teaching job. He had an affair with a married woman with whom he had a child and has suffered considerably. Like a true radical socialist, he is more concerned with ends than means, and is quite capable of blackmail. As Brendel says, 'He's learnt to live without ideals. *That's* the secret: action and victory, the wisdom of the world.'

Part-time actor, part-time orator and scholar, Rosmer's old tutor Brendel is a mysterious figure. His language is peppered with common-place phrases and aphorisms (and is very hard to translate). He is almost a Shakespearean fool: eccentric, alcoholic but ultimately benevolent. He is down on his luck but ferociously independent. On his return in Act Four, he is 'wildly excited': he is 'going down the dark road', and shows Rebecca and Rosmer that death is the only way out.

'Be free, Johannes, be free', Rebecca implores Rosmer in Act Two. But if both are involved in an attempt to liberate themselves, the end of the play suggests that they can only achieve freedom in a spiritual marriage consummated by their death. Life is too difficult. The real world is too compromised. Nobility and truth do not stand a chance. Thus Rebecca, far from being a feminist icon, ends up as a sacrificial victim. What is so moving about the end of the play is the image of two individuals bound together, even in disaster.

The atmosphere of *Rosmersholm* is deeply enigmatic. It is almost a ghost story. Rosmer's drowned wife, the folkloric 'White Horses of Rosmersholm' and the steely portraits of Rosmer's ancestors all exert a powerful grip on the living: 'Inherited ideas, inherited doubts, inherited scruples. The dead rushing back to Rosmersholm like galloping white horses.' Ibsen's stage imagination is as powerful as ever: the opening image is of Rebecca crocheting a white shawl which will double as her bridal veil and burial shroud at the end. Every detail is in place. Even the small part of the housekeeper, Mrs Helseth, has a crucial role to play in Ibsen's design: she is an anxious presence, superstitious and conservative, a living link to Beata and the old world, and her darkest fears eventually come true.

In a letter of 1887 Ibsen summarized the play's unique demands:

> The play deals with the struggle that every serious-minded man must wage with himself to bring his way of life into harmony with his convictions. The different functions of the spirit do not develop uniformly or comparably in any one individual . . . Moral consciousness, however, 'the con-science', is by comparison very conservative. It has its roots deep in tradition in the past generally. From this comes the conflict within the individual.

It is this profound exploration of individual consciousness – and conscience – that accounts for *Rosmersholm's* mysterious power.

ᗡᐤ In performance

Rosmersholm was premièred in Bergen on 17 January 1887, and throughout Scandinavia in the same year, but was received with only moderate acclaim.

In a letter (25 March 1887) to Sofie Reimers, the actress rehearsing Rebecca at the Christiania Theatre, Ibsen wrote one of his clearest and most practical instructions on how he wanted his work to be performed:

> No declamation. No theatrical emphasis. No pomposity at all! Express every mood in a manner that will seem credible and natural. Never think of this or that actress whom you may have seen. Observe the life that is going on around you, and present a real and living human being.

The play received its English première on 23 February 1891 at the Vaudeville Theatre in London. It was exception-ally badly received, with the *Standard* declaring:

Those portions of the play which are comprehensible are utterly preposterous . . . Ibsen is neither dramatist, poet, philosopher, moralist, teacher, reformer – nothing but a compiler of rather disagreeable eccentricities.

The Times dismissed Ibsen as a 'local or provincial dramatist' and *The Stage* described the play as 'studies in insanity best fitted for the lecture room in Bedlam'.

The play's French première was in Paris in 1893, and its German-language one in Vienna in the same year. The *Berliner Tageblatt* said 'it remains a play of contrived untruths even though it is hailed by some thickheads as a work of Orphic profundity'. Gordon Craig directed and designed the play with Eleonora Duse as Rebecca in Florence in 1905. Peter Zadek directed a highly regarded production with Gert Voss as Rosmer at the Akademietheater, Vienna in 2001.

Rosmersholm is not often performed in Britain. Edith Evans played Rebecca in 1926, and Peggy Ashcroft at the Royal Court in 1959. The play was presented at the Haymarket Theatre in 1977 and at the National Theatre in 1987 in a new translation by Frank McGuinness. Paul Miller directed a fine production of the play at Southwark Playhouse in 1997, in Kenneth McLeish's translation quoted above.

Bernard Shaw summarized the difficulties of performing *Rosmersholm* with admirable concision:

The actors must be able to sustain the deep black flood of feeling from the first moment to the last.

The same could be said of Ibsen as a whole.

Translated by Kenneth McLeish, Nick Hern Books, 2002

The Lady from the Sea
(*Fruen fra havet*)
1888

∞ Characters

Doctor Wangel
Ellida Wangel, *his second wife*
Bolette, *his elder daughter from a previous marriage*
Hilde, *her sister*
Arnholm, *a private tutor*
Lyngstrand
Ballested
Stranger
Young people of the town, tourists, summer visitors

The action takes place in summer, in a small fjordside town
in northern Norway

∞ The story

Act One takes place in the garden of Doctor Wangel's house,
on a bright summer's day. Ballested is fixing the flagpole.
Bolette is on the veranda. Ballested shows Lyngstrand his
painting of the 'Mermaid's End'. Lyngstrand wants to
become a sculptor but has to improve his health first.
Ballested leaves – the steamer has arrived and the tourists
may need his services as a guide. Hilde and Bolette are
preparing the house to celebrate their dead 'Mama's' birthday. When their father appears, they pretend it is for the
imminent visit of Bolette's old tutor Arnholm, who, when he
arrives, is delighted with Wangel's 'two grown-up daughters'.
Wangel tells him about his second wife Ellida, who has not
been well ('nothing serious'). Nicknamed 'the mermaid', she
swims every day, but says that the water is 'never cold . . . This
far up the fjord, the sea is sick.' Arnholm apologizes to Ellida

for the 'false step' he took years ago, but Ellida wants to talk to him about her own past. Lyngstrand enters with flowers and tells them why he is ill: his ship was wrecked and he was 'in [the water] for ages before they picked me up'. He is going to make a sculpture of a drowned man and his unfaithful wife. He got the story from an American on the ship. Ellida declares that Lyngstrand's flowers are 'a birthday bouquet' – 'why shouldn't I join in with the rest of you? After all, it's mother's birthday.'

Act Two is set at twilight on the viewpoint above the town. Ballested is showing tourists the way to the top. Hilde and Bolette are pursued breathlessly by Lyngstrand. Hilde mocks him and both girls talk about Arnholm and Ellida. Hilde says '[Ellida] doesn't suit us, we don't suit her', but soon she appears with Arnholm and Wangel. The young people go to the top to see the open sea, leaving Ellida alone with Wangel. He wants to hear the truth about what has gone wrong between them. He knows she 'can't bear this place' and says they should move to the sea – 'for your health, your peace of mind'. Ellida tells him about a previous relationship; Wangel presumes it was Arnholm, and is astonished to discover that it was the 'second mate' on an American ship, who spoke poetically about the sea ('Darkness at sea . . . Sun glinting on the waves') and insisted she marry him. He had been accused of murdering the ship's captain and had to leave her; at their parting, he threw their two rings tied together into the sea. She sometimes thinks she sees him and remembers that her dead child's eyes 'changed colour with the sea'. 'My child', she says, 'had the stranger's eyes . . . Now do you understand why I won't . . . I can't . . . I *daren't* any more with you.'

Act Three takes place in a 'dark, damp, overshadowed' corner of Wangel's garden. Hilde is showing Lyngstrand the fish pond. Bolette says she feels cut off, like a 'goldfish in a bowl'. Her father is incapable of helping her into university, and needs her at home. 'Why should I have to stay here?' she asks. Arnholm is about to respond when Ellida arrives, veering between sadness and joy. Suddenly, the Stranger appears.

Ellida greets him, but she is shocked when he looks into her eyes. She asks him why he has appeared now: 'You know perfectly well, Ellida: to fetch you.' Ellida rejects him and Wangel arrives. The Stranger knew that she was married, but says 'that business with the rings . . . was a marriage, too'. Eventually he leaves, saying: 'Be ready tomorrow evening. That's when I'll fetch you.' Ellida is stunned ('Of my own free will. He said I could go of my own free will'), but Wangel is confident: 'I'll see that he's charged with killing that captain.' Ellida turns to him, begging: 'Oh Edvard, I love you, I trust you, save me from that man'. Lyngstand returns, excited to have seen 'the American' again. As the curtain falls, Ellida declares: 'That man is like the sea'.

For Act Four, the next morning, the action shifts into Wangel's garden room. Lyngstrand is watching Bolette sewing: 'In my opinion, marriage itself may be seen as a kind of miracle, in the sense that the wife gradually evolves and changes in her husband's image.' He also says that he is off to the Mediterranean and wants to imagine her thinking of him there. Wangel talks to Arnholm about Ellida, blaming himself for having confined her: 'I loved her so much, and that made me selfish.' Wangel is perplexed at how Ellida's 'mental problems' are mystically mixed up with the Stranger, and is anxious about his daughters finding husbands. Ellida arrives, worried about the Stranger returning. She says that she and Wangel 'conceal the truth', that he 'bought' her and that she 'shouldn't have accepted, at any price'. Worst of all, she says 'I didn't come to your home of my own free will . . . [now] all I'm asking for, begging for, is freedom . . . I want free choice.' 'Tomorrow, he'll have sailed,' Wangel replies. 'The cloud will be lifted. And then . . . *then* I'll set you free.' Dinner is served and Wangel says that they will drink to 'the lady from the sea'.

Act Five takes place later that evening in Wangel's garden. The young people are punting on the fjord. Ballested is arranging a concert for some English tourists, who have come on the last boat before the fjord freezes. Ellida is waiting for the Stranger and tells Wangel that 'my choice is my own, it's inside me, I can choose him, not you – and if that's what I choose, you can't prevent it'. She welcomes Wangel's offer to look after her, but says she 'longs for the forces that horrify me'. Arnholm tells Bolette that if she marries him, she can 'go out into the world, study all you want'. She is shocked ('Impossible . . . you were my tutor'), but soon accepts, absorbed by the thought of 'Freedom'. Lyngstrand and Hilde are together and he imagines what she will be like when he has returned from Italy. She mocks him, imagining herself dressed in black ('a young bride, cruelly widowed'), and they go down to the pier to listen to the music. The Stranger appears and confronts Ellida. The ship's bell is heard ringing and Ellida feels the sea calling ('the unknown I was born for, the unknown you've barred me from'). Wangel threatens the Stranger, who draws a pistol on himself. Wangel realizes that he is losing Ellida and says: 'So, I break our agreement. It's over. Go wherever you please, in full free will . . . your full responsibility, your choice.' This is the catalyst and she decides to stay: 'I changed . . . don't you understand? From the moment I had free will, I had to change.' She thanks Wangel ('You found the right cure, and you were brave enough to use it') and promises to make the children 'ours'. As the curtain falls, 'the tour-boat passes slowly down the fjord'.

↪ About the play

The story of *The Lady from the Sea* is taken from a Scandinavian myth (retold by Hans Christian Andersen as *The Little Mermaid*) concerning a 'sea-woman' who falls in love with a human, comes ashore, sheds her sea-skin, cannot return to the sea and dies. The greatness of Ibsen's achievement is that he takes this folk story, sets it in a realistic context, weaves into it a sophisticated romantic comedy, and through a series of entirely plausible characters, explores the challenges of marriage, the power of sexuality and the importance of free will.

The play is rich with conflicting literary genres: Scandinavian folk-tales, the Viking sagas, Shakespearean comedy, the well-made play and the romantic pulp fiction of nineteenth-century 'penny dreadfuls'. It shifts from dark to light, from the consequential to the flippant, with extraordinary speed. Water is everywhere: the fish pond, the brackish fjord and the open sea. The stage pictures are more filmic than theatrical: the view of the fjord and the islands from the viewpoint, the young people punting down the fjord, and the last cruise ship heading out to sea before the ice freezes. Technically, it is one of Ibsen's greatest achievements.

In his preliminary notes in 1888, Ibsen touched on the psychological model that lies behind this folk-tale:

The sea's power of attraction. The longing for the sea. People akin to the sea. Bound by the sea. Dependent on the sea. Must return to it. One fish species forms a basic link in the evolutionary series. Do rudiments of it still remain in the human mind? In the mind of certain individuals?

Literally translated, the title of the play means the 'seawife' (in no sense a mermaid) and in the central character of Ellida Wangel Ibsen shows a woman of some maturity, who has reached a critical turning-point in her life, when it seems inevitable that she will succumb to the dark forces which draw her. The Stranger is an abstract figure, something taken straight from American pulp fiction. The important thing is what he means to Ellida: freedom, destruction and the roaring open sea where human beings cannot live. Like the sea, her character is fluid:

Contentment's like autumn sunshine. Shadowed by the dark to come. Hints of sadness shadow human happiness, the way clouds drive across the fjord. One minute calm and bright, then without any warning –

She is one of Ibsen's most rewarding characters: complex and mysterious, attractive and alarming in equal measure.

Ellida's husband Doctor Wangel is a good, kindly man, concerned about the community he serves, his two daughters from his first marriage and his troubled wife. However, he is blocking Bolette's education, has a strong streak of self-pity, enjoys a drink and 'likes to be surrounded by smiling faces'. He eventually comes to recognize his responsibility for Ellida's 'illness', her sexual alienation from him, and the paradox of the play is that he can only win her back when he has renounced his claim on her.

Wangel's elder daughter Bolette is kind and solicitous, taking on responsibility for her father's well-being in the absence of her mother or stepmother. She has been denied a university education by her father and is bitter about it, but will get one through a marriage of convenience to her old tutor. The 'balding' Arnholm is pushing forty and still not married: intelligent, conventional, attracted to Ellida but shown by Ibsen to lack the magnetic force of the Stranger. The deal that Bolette strikes with Arnholm is surely doomed to failure.

Wangel's younger daughter Hilde is a model of youth and health. Energetic, sharp and ruthless, she admits that she is fascinated by Lyngstrand's weakness and treats him with the utmost contempt (Hilde's destructive vitality will later appear as Solness's nemesis in *The Master Builder*). He is a pitiful figure, racked with pain, self-centred and full of received (and reactionary) views about men and women. Despite his volubility and his plans to go to Italy, Lyngstrand is a young man who will soon be dead. Ballested is a comic figure – a jack-of-all-trades: tourist guide, painter, musician and so on – strangely disconnected from the action, but a puckish spirit who is essential to the play's atmosphere. Each one of these characters is set in brilliant contradistinction to the others, and the patterning of Ibsen's scenic structure is reminiscent of a Mozart finale or a Shakespearean comedy.

After the despair of *Rosmersholm*, *The Lady from the Sea* marks a break for Ibsen. It is conversational, chatty, almost 'Chekhovian' in feel – exquisitely counterpointed and dazzlingly constructed. As Edmund Gosse said:

> After so many tragedies, this is a comedy . . . the tone is quite unusually sunny, and without a trace of pessimism.

Some feel that the play's symbolism is not entirely succesful, and criticize the abruptness of its ending, as if Ibsen had decided a comic resolution was necessary and simply tacked one on. This underestimates the intoxicatingly romantic atmosphere of the last act and misreads the earlier scenes between husband and wife: all possibilities are open, and the point is that the choice must be Ellida's own. In *The Lady from the Sea*, Ibsen provides his own answer to *A Doll's House*: under certain conditions of absolute honesty, he seems to be saying, where 'free will' is respected, happiness in marriage is possible. Like Shakespeare in his late romances, Ibsen in *The Lady from the Sea* hints at the possibility of redemption.

∽ In performance

The Lady from the Sea received simultaneous Norwegian and German premières in Christiania and at the Hoftheater in Weimar on 12 February 1889. It was soon produced in Copenhagen, Berlin, Stockholm and Helsinki. The first London performance took place at Terry's Theatre on 11 May 1891, translated (badly) by Eleanor Marx-Aveling (Karl Marx's daughter). Lugné-Poe staged it at the Théâtre Moderne in Paris in 1892.

Janet Achurch played Ellida in 1902, as did Sarah Bernhardt in 1904. Probably the greatest Ellida was Eleanora Duse (first in Turin in 1921 and later in London and New York), about whom James Agate wrote:

> If there be in acting such a thing as pure passion divorced from the body yet expressed on terms of the body, it is here. Now and again in this strange play Duse would seem to pass beyond our ken, and where she has been there is only a fragrance and a sound in our ears like water flowing under the stars.

Vanessa Redgrave played Bollette in 1961 and enjoyed a great success as Ellida in 1976 (New York) and 1979 (London). More recent Ellidas include Josette Simon (West Yorkshire Playhouse, 1996) and Vanessa Redgrave's daughter Natasha Richardson (Almeida, 2003). The play is notoriously difficult to pull off successfully in the theatre, partly because of the mercurial quality of the leading part, but also because of its challenging scenic demands.

Translated by Kenneth McLeish, Nick Hern Books, 2001

Hedda Gabler
(Hedda Gabler)
1890

↪ Characters

Jørgen Tesman, *a cultural historian*
Hedda Tesman, *née Hedda Gabler, his wife*
Miss Julie Tesman, *his aunt*
Mrs Elvsted
Brack, *a circuit judge*
Ejlert Løvborg
Berta, *the maid*

The action takes place in Tesman's villa on the west side of the town

↪ The story

Act One takes place on the morning following the return of Tesman and his wife Hedda from their six-month honeymoon. Berta talks to Aunt Julie about her anxiety about her new mistress, but both are proud of Tesman's brilliant prospects. When Tesman appears, he is delighted that Aunt Julie has come to welcome him, but is concerned about Aunt Rina, who is dying. Julie has mortgaged her annuities to make Tesman's new house possible, and Hedda's family friend, Judge Brack, has been 'very helpful'. The way seems clear for Tesman to become a professor, particularly now his main rival, Ejlert Løvborg, has been disqualified because of drunkenness. When Hedda emerges from her room, she deliberately mistakes Aunt Julie's 'extra-special' hat as something the maid has left behind, and humiliates her husband. Thea Elvsted, a schoolfriend of Hedda's, arrives: she has left her husband and is looking for Løvborg, who used to be her children's tutor, and with whom she has become a 'comrade in arms'. Hedda is jealous: she, too, was close to Løvborg before her marriage. Judge Brack visits and announces there is going to be a competition between Tesman and Løvborg for the professorship. Hedda is excited by this, but disgusted with her husband. The act ends with Hedda saying that she has one thing left to amuse herself with: her father's pistols.

Act Two opens with Hedda alone, loading one of the pistols. When Brack appears in the garden, she shoots at him – deliberately missing. She speaks of her frustration with 'the scholar' (she married Tesman because she 'took pity on him'), and Brack proposes a 'triangular relationship'. Hedda rejects this, saying she has only one talent – 'for boring myself to death'. Soon Løvborg appears, on Tesman's invitation, and disturbs Tesman with the brilliance of his new manuscript. Pretending to look at pictures of Hedda's honeymoon, he quietly reminds her of their previous relationship. She rejects his advances, while revelling in her role as his muse. Brack takes Tesman – and the apparently teetotal Løvborg – off to one of his notorious bachelor parties, leaving Hedda tormenting the anxious Mrs Elvsted.

Act Three takes place early the next morning. The men have not come back and the women are asleep in the drawing-room. When Tesman finally returns, he tells Hedda about the evening and how Løvborg started drinking again. He also reveals that when Løvborg dropped his manuscript, he picked it up. Tesman plans to give it back, but Hedda wants to look through it. Tesman hears that Aunt Rina is 'at death's door' and rushes off to see her. When Brack appears, he tells Hedda that Løvborg has been involved in a fight with a police officer and insinuates that this clears the way for the 'triangular relationship' that he wanted. Løvborg returns and tells Mrs Elvsted that he does not need her any more, adding that he has torn his manuscript into pieces. She is devastated and leaves Hedda alone with Løvborg, who quickly confesses the truth – that he has lost the manuscript – and hints that suicide is the only option. He is just about to leave when Hedda hands him one of her pistols to use. Left alone, Hedda pushes Løvborg's manuscript into the stove, saying: 'Look, Thea. I'm burning your baby, Thea . . . Your baby . . . Yours and his.'

Act Four takes place that evening. Aunt Rina has died, but Aunt Julie takes consolation in the new life that she is convinced Hedda is about to produce, as well as in her own ethic of service. Tesman is worried about Løvborg and is horrified when Hedda tells him that she burned his manuscript, but delighted when Hedda says that she did it for his sake. Mrs Elvsted arrives, convinced that 'something terrible's happened' and Brack confirms that Løvborg has shot himself. Hedda believes that it was her inspiration that made him do it, and Tesman and Mrs Elvsted start reconstructing the book from his notes. Brack soon tells Hedda that her image of Løvborg's 'beautiful deed' is quite false: he shot himself at 'Mamzelle Diana's', in 'the lower parts'. Furthermore, Brack knows that the gun is Hedda's, but the police need never know, so long as he holds his tongue. When it becomes clear to Hedda that she is in Brack's power, she goes into the alcove at the back of the room, draws the curtains and shoots herself, leaving the complacent Brack saying: 'No one does that! No one.'

ᦉ About the play

At the centre of Ibsen's greatest masterpiece is the strangely compelling figure of Hedda Gabler herself, one of the most richly contradictory characters in drama: audacious and cowardly, intelligent and shallow, passionate and dry – a 'pale, apparently cold beauty', as Ibsen's preliminary notes put it. Ibsen insisted that Hedda's father General Gabler was essential to her make-up: 'The title of the play is: *Hedda Gabler*. I intended to indicate thereby that as a personality she is to be regarded rather as her father's daughter than as her husband's wife.' She has a destructive nature, driven as much by cowardice as by a death wish. There are several hints that she is pregnant, but at no point does she confirm this. She dismisses everything her husband can provide (a comfortable home, security and children), but she is too frightened to take up with Løvborg again and is sharply resistant to Brack's suggestions of a *ménage à trois*.

The role of Hedda Gabler has been psychoanalysed probably more fully than any other female role in drama, but no one has managed to capture the strangely mercurial quality of the character. Sexual neglect, profound hysteria, an incapacity for love: Hedda has been cited as a perfect example of all of them. Bernard Shaw said she 'has no ethical ideals at all, only romantic ones. She is a typical nineteenth-century figure, falling into the abyss between the ideals which do not impose on her and the realities she has not yet discovered.' Like Shakespeare's Hamlet, she is pure consciousness. It is perhaps most useful to take Hedda at her own word: 'I have only one talent, for boring myself to death.'

Tesman is too easily dismissed. Ibsen's point, however, is that, unlike his upper-class wife, Tesman has had to struggle. As a result of hard work and natural decency, he has landed on his feet; but he is laden down with responsibility – above all to his family – which he is anxious to fulfil. He tries hard to be even-handed with Løvborg, even though he is intimidated by his intellectual force. He is courteous and friendly to Judge Brack, if naïve in his embrace of his seductive charm. He adores Hedda and is astonished to discover her dark, destructive side. Although Ibsen occasionally allows Tesman to be seen in a comic light (Brack's teasing him for being a 'scholar' always raises a knowing laugh), he is a genuinely sympathetic figure: desperate for peace, eager for happiness and appalled by the catastrophe that eventually envelops him.

Judge Brack is the opposite of Tesman: confident, attractive and fastidious – the 'cock of the walk', as Hedda calls him. He is all too aware of criminality and the darker side of life, but he is also well connected, and skilful in not leaving a trace of his own corruption. He is driven by his own appetites and it is a supreme irony that Hedda – whom he patronizes throughout – is able to surprise him at the end and evade his carefully woven web.

The impact of Løvborg is disproportionate to his actual presence. He is in many ways a romantic figure: a wild 'genius' who lives life to the full and is destined to die young. It is not clear what his new book is about, but it surely reflects the new kinds of social and aesthetic beliefs that were emerging at the time. His talk of 'absolute trust' and his readiness to dismiss Hedda as a 'coward', as well as his manipulation of Thea and his paranoia, all indicate a personality intoxicated with an inflated sense of his own destiny. Ibsen's genius exposes this extravagance for what it is – sordid and indulgent – and it is left to Brack, the man of the world, to make plain the degrading nature of his death to the woman who idolizes him.

Mrs Elvsted is an essential element in Ibsen's design but, like Tesman, is sometimes overlooked and often patronized. Ibsen is clear that she is beautiful with strikingly attractive 'curly hair'. Hedda bullied her at school but is astonished to discover that she has had the courage to leave her husband and support herself. When a feminist critic said that she detested Mrs Elvsted ('these women who sacrifice themselves for men'), Ibsen replied: 'I write to portray people and I am completely indifferent to what fanatical bluestockings like or do not like.' Ibsen brilliantly counterpoints Mrs Elvsted's capacity for love with Hedda's withholding of it as two very different images of nineteenth-century femininity.

Tesman's Aunt Julie has a fleeting presence, but the traditional world of duty and restraint is significant. Her conviction that Hedda must be pregnant is touching but futile. Hedda's deliberate mistaking of her smart new hat may make us laugh, but Julie's dedication to Tesman is real. Following her sister Rina's death, she declares that she is going to give her room to 'some poor sick soul to nurse'. In a play where everyone else is so self-obsessed, her commitment to others is remarkable. Berta is a conventional old woman, who looked after Tesman as a child and is now anxious and flustered about her new job as Hedda's maid. As ever, Ibsen was concerned to give his characters dignity and individuality:

Tesman, his old aunts, and the elderly serving-maid Berta together form a whole and a unity. They have a common way of thinking; common memories and a common attitude to life. For Hedda they appear as an inimical and alien power directed against her fundamental nature.

Hedda Gabler embodies the powerful tension between extremism and moderation, between a Nietzschean celebration of the individual on the one hand, and a balanced, socially orientated, pluralist philosophy on the other. Hedda and Løvborg indulge in an almost Wagnerian 'Liebestod', rich with the aestheticized melodrama of 'vine leaves in his hair', and together fantasize about 'a beautiful death'. This is deliberately contrasted with Tesman, who is deeply involved in his academic study ('domestic crafts in fifteenth-century Brabant'). His attitudes are fair-minded and social, and the ties of family and friendship are important to him. The final image of Tesman and Thea working together in the lamplight on reconstructing Løvborg's manuscript may be comic to Brack, but it is the last straw for Hedda. In a good production, it should provide a powerful, and positive, counterpoint to the self destruction all around it.

From a technical point of view, *Hedda Gabler* is perhaps the most perfect example of Ibsen's naturalistic art, as the English writer Edmund Gosse wrote in 1891:

> In the whole of the new play there is not one speech which would require thirty seconds for its enunciation. I will dare to say that I think in this instance Ibsen has gone perilously far in his desire for rapid and concise expression. The sticomythia of the Greek and French tragedians was lengthy in comparison with this unceasing display of hissing conversational fireworks, fragments of sentences without verbs, clauses that come to nothing, adverbial exclamations and cryptic interrogations.

The play has a tightly controlled structure, with each act shorter than the one before, all leading inevitably to catastrophe. When finally Hedda draws the curtain and shoots herself, it is as if she has gone down into the underworld. Oscar Wilde described this in a letter to a friend:

> I was so pleased to find you were at one with me about the Ibsen play – felt pity and terror, as though the play had been Greek.

Hedda Gabler mystified its first audiences, who were becoming used to seeing Ibsen as a writer of 'issue plays'. In 1890, Ibsen wrote:

> In this play I have not really intended to treat so-called problems. The main thing for me has been to depict human beings, their humours and their destinies, against a background of certain operative social conditions and attitudes.

Nowhere else did Ibsen catch the fluidity and fragility of human passion with more refined dramatic skill or theatrical power than in *Hedda Gabler*.

∽ In performance

Hedda Gabler was written in Munich and premièred at the Residenztheater on 31 January 1891, with a popular actress named Marie Conrad-Ramlo playing the title role. Ibsen was in the audience, but was distressed by her declamatory style. It was not a success, and the audience whistled their dismay. Ibsen was also present at the more successful Berlin première ten days later. The play was produced throughout Scandinavia in 1891, and in Copenhagen met with boos and inappropriate laughter.

The first English performance took place at the Vaudeville Theatre, London on 20 April 1891, with Elizabeth Robins as Hedda, in a translation by William Archer. The response was moral outrage, with Clement Scott of the *Daily Telegraph* saying it 'was like a visit to the morgue . . . What a horrible story! What a hideous play!' The *Standard* announced patriotically that 'the tastes of English playgoers are sound and healthy, and the hollowness and shams of the Ibsen cult need only be known to be rejected'.

The newly formed Moscow Art Theatre put on the play in 1899, and Konstantin Stanislavsky was applauded for his brilliant, dissipated portrayal of Løvborg. The production failed, however, largely due to the inadequacy of Marie Andreeva as Hedda. Eleonora Duse played Hedda in Italian in 1903 to great acclaim and Vsevolod Meyerhold directed the play in St Petersburg with Lydia Yavorska in 1906. Ingmar Bergman has directed three productions of the play: in 1964 at the Royal Dramatic Theatre in Stockholm, in 1970 at the National Theatre in London and in 1979 at the Residenztheater in Munich.

Hedda Gabler is probably Ibsen's most frequently performed play and famous English Heddas include Mrs Patrick Campbell (1922), Jean Forbes-Robertson (1936), Peggy Ashcroft (1954), Joan Greenwood (1964), Maggie Smith (1970), Claire Bloom (1971), Glenda Jackson (1975), Janet Suzman (1977), Juliet Stevenson (1989), Fiona Shaw (1993), Harriet Walter (1997) and Alexandra Gilbreath (1997).

Films were made of the play in 1917, 1919 and 1924 and there have been numerous television versions, including one for the BBC (1962) with Ingrid Bergman as Hedda, Michael Redgrave as Tesman, Trevor Howard as Løvborg and Ralph Richardson as Brack.

Translated by Kenneth McLeish, Nick Hern Books, 1995

The Master Builder
(Bygmester Solness)
1892

∞ Characters

Halvard Solness, *the master builder*
Aline Solness, *his wife*
Doctor Herdal, *the family doctor*
Knut Brovik, *formerly an architect, now working for Solness*
Ragnar Brovik, *his son, a draughtsman*
Kaja Fosli, *Knut Brovik's niece, a book-keeper*
Hilde Wangel
Women, people in the street

The action takes place in Solness's house

∞ The story

Act One opens in Solness's architectural office. It is early
evening. Old Brovik is unwell and his son Ragnar and niece
Kaja think he should go home. When Solness comes in, he
wants to talk to Kaja alone. Brovik urges Solness to give
approval for Ragnar's plans for a new house so that he can set
up on his own and marry Kaja. Solness's response is non-
committal and, when left alone with Kaja, he asks her to persuade Ragnar to continue working for him. Solness's wife,
Aline, and Doctor Herdal appear: she has noticed Solness's
distressed state and wants Herdal to find out what is going
on. Soon Solness confesses the real problem: he is getting old
and is afraid of the 'younger generation knocking on the
door'. Furthermore, he feels he has an ability to make his
wishes and his fears come true. Promptly there is a knock at
the door and Hilde Wangel comes in: with her 'eyes shining',
dressed in hiking clothes, she is the picture of youth. At first
Solness does not recognize her, but she reminds him that

they met exactly ten years previously when she was a child. He had finished building a tower, and she watched him climb to the top and hang a garland on the weathervane. At the celebratory dinner, he took her in his arms and kissed her and promised her a 'kingdom'. Now, she says, she has come to claim it. When Solness remembers the episode, he is both astonished and enchanted. She is given one of the empty children's rooms to sleep in and Solness declares 'You're all I've been waiting for'.

Act Two takes place early the next morning. Solness's attitude to Kaja has become dismissive and he is thinking about Hilde now. He sees her presence as a positive, like the new house that he is building. Aline is desperate: 'Build all you like, Halvard. Build what you like, you'll never build me a home.' The door opens and Hilde walks in, bringing daylight with her. Solness tells Hilde that Aline's family house burned down and that she has still not recovered from the shock. He shows her the site of their new house, with its tower, and says Aline caught pneumonia in the fire and could not feed their twins, who died as a result. Furthermore, he confesses that he made his money by parcelling out the estate and building 'homes for ordinary people'. Ragnar arrives, anxious to collect his plans, which he hopes have been approved. But despite Hilde's protests, Solness has done nothing about it. It soon emerges that Solness blames himself for his children's deaths: he knew the house had a fault and he made the fire happen by wishing it into existence. But Hilde says his 'conscience is scrawny' – it should be strong and independent like a Viking's. Solness tells her that she reminds him of a 'new day dawning' and she persuades him to endorse Ragnar's plans. Solness dismisses Kaja, too, and, to Aline's horror, tells Hilde that he is going to put the garland on the new tower that evening. As the curtain falls, Hilde is left muttering: 'unbearably thrilling'.

Act Three takes place on the veranda of Solness's house. It is evening and Aline is worried about Solness's plan to climb the tower. She confesses to Hilde her estrangement, saying that her real losses in the fire were her childhood dolls: 'They were alive for me, in a way . . . Like little unborn babies.' She has sent for Herdal in the hope that he will persuade Solness to change his mind, and asks Hilde to do the same. When Solness arrives, Hilde announces – to his amazement – that she is leaving. It is as if she has looked into Aline's pain and seen that she has to go. Soon, however, Hilde has moved on – 'If only we could hibernate, get away from it all' – and reminds him that he must build the castle he owes her. When she suggests 'A real castle in the air', he stresses that it will have 'its feet on the ground'. Ragnar arrives with the garland – his father is dying, and he has come to watch Solness climb the tower. Meanwhile, Aline rushes off to attend the ladies who have come to watch the ceremony. Solness returns and explains to Hilde how he had defied God and been punished; now, he says, he will 'build the most beautiful thing in the world . . . Build it with the princess I love'. The visitors gather to watch him as he climbs the tower, but suddenly, with a band playing and handkerchiefs waving, he loses his grip and falls to his death. Hilde, ecstatic, waves her shawl and shouts with furious intensity: '*My* Master Builder! Mine!'

ᔰ About the play

With *The Master Builder* Ibsen entered new and very personal territory, and there are many fascinating parallels between Ibsen's own life at the time and that of his central figure, Halvard Solness. Like Solness, Ibsen was in a state of anxiety about the younger generation 'knocking at the door'; like Solness, he was in a highly respectable marriage driven by duty more than love; like Solness, he had close relationships with very young women (Hildur Andersen, Emile Bardach and Helene Raff) whom he regarded as his muses; and finally, like Solness, he was struggling with the contradictory demands of symbolism and realism in producing art in a world in which God is dead. As Ibsen said: 'Solness is a man somewhat akin to me.'

The Master Builder was the first play Ibsen wrote following his return to Norway. It marked a further shift away from 'naturalism' into a new kind of 'symbolist' drama. The language of the play is rich with folkloric talk about trolls and Vikings. It is notorious for its Freudianism, particularly the phallic symbol of Solness's tower that Hilde wants to see crowned. Hugo von Hofmannsthal called it 'a strange mixture of allegory and real-life description', but George Brandes was keen to point out that:

> Recently the so-called 'symbolists' started a feud against 'naturalism'. That kind of catchword seldom means much, and all such are least applicable to Ibsen. For twenty years or more naturalism and symbolism have been harmonious partners in his work . . . Although both as a man and as a writer he loves reality, he is poet and thinker enough constantly to underlay the reality he portrays with a deeper interpretation.

Ibsen's symbols are rooted in his characters and their actions, and the play works best when given a naturalistic production with psychological acting.

It is difficult to define Solness's class. A 'master builder' is less than a fully qualified achitect, but more than a builder. Solness has needed old Brovik to draw up the detailed plans in the past, just as he will need young Ragnar in the future. He is an entrepreneur – part builder, part surveyor, part architect – who has done well, partly through his own bloody-mindedness but also by marrying into a better class than his own. At the start, he is anxious, depressed, corrupt and untrustworthy – morbidly convinced of his own instinctive destructive powers. He blocks the chances of the hard-working, ambitious young architect Ragnar, abuses the love of the devoted Kaja, disappoints the dying hopes of old Brovik and denies the very existence of the despair of his wife Aline. He has given up on the idea of producing architecture of spiritual worth and now builds 'homes for ordinary people'. He has lost his faith and lost his way. The trolls are eating away at him.

The play describes a marriage in deep trouble. Aline is consumed by the inner drama of her own personal tragedy, while obeying all the strictures of wifely and neighbourly duty. Ibsen's preparatory work includes the following poem:

They sat there, the two of them, in such a cosy house
In autumn and in winter days.
Then the house burned. All lies in ruins.
The two of them rake in the ashes.

For among them a jewel is hidden,
A jewel that can never burn.
But if they look hard it's just possible
It could be found by him or her.

But even if these fire-scarred pair do
Ever find this fireproof precious jewel,
She'll never find his burned faith,
He her burned-out happiness.

The lost jewel is the meaning of their marriage. Aline can confide her anxiety to the good-hearted Doctor Herdal; but Solness is all alone.

The arrival of the young and bewitching Hilde Wangel gives Solness another chance. She is twenty-six, a free spirit, a breath of fresh air in the darkness of Solness's daily life. She understands the nature of his pain, and helps him discover the truth of his own situation. She seems to know everything there is to know about him. She has no baggage and no pre-conceptions. Hilde, it seems, is Solness's salvation. But the strength of Hilde's intuition is also the cause of Solness's downfall. For she is fanatical in her determination to push him towards his own personal truth. Ruthless with Kaja and Ragnar, Hilde only exhibits one moment of tenderness towards Aline in Act Three.

Unlike Hilde, Solness cannot stand alone: he is inextricably linked to the suffering of his wife and the corruption in his work. Furthermore, he suffers from vertigo. Ibsen understood this all too well:

This longing to commit a madness stays with us throughout our lives. Who has not, when standing with someone by an abyss or high up on a tower, had a sudden impulse to push the other over? And how is it that we hurt those we love although we know that remorse will follow?

A man who builds towers he cannot climb is a man who has created a public persona he is unable to inhabit. Soon the pursuit of individual truth turns from an act of liberation into a love affair with destruction. Hilde is only happy in the moment after Solness has fallen and 'smashed his head on the stonepile'. Her triumph is rich in apocalyptic intensity:

He went right to the top. Harps, I heard harps in the sky.

In Ibsen's profound skepticism, every truth is relative, and here the instrument of his central character's liberation is also the agent of his destruction.

The Master Builder poses a set of profound dilemmas which go right to the heart of being human. Should we pursue personal development at all costs, or dedicate ourselves to our family and friends? Should we stand alone in our dreams or work with others to make a better world? Should we build symbolic towers in the sky or construct 'homes for ordinary people'? How can we live? How should we accept the fact that we are going to die? What, ultimately, is the value of truth-telling?

The Master Builder is one of Ibsen's most fiendishly complex plays and there are times when one wonders whether the endless play of image and metaphor are successful. On publication it was met with widespread bafflement. Henry James, having read only the first act, wrote in 1892:

It is all most strange, most curious, most vague, most horrid, most 'middle-classy' in the peculiar ugly Ibsen sense . . . It doesn't as yet begin to shape itself as a play, an action – but only as an obscure and Ibseny tale, or psychological picture, requiring infinite elucidation.

Ibsen himself tried (unsuccessfully) to keep such speculation at bay:

> It's extraordinary what symbols and profundities they ascribe to me. I have received letters which ask if the nine dolls signify the Nine Muses, and the dead twins Scandinavianism and my own happiness. They have even asked if the dolls are connected with something in some Epistle of St Paul which I don't even know, or something in the Book of Revelation. Can't people just read what I write? I only write about people. I don't write symbolically. Just about people's inner life as I know it – psychology, if you like . . .

As so often, Ibsen's own words provide the best guide to one of his most ambiguous plays.

∽ In performance

The first public reading of *The Master Builder* took place at a special matinée at the Haymarket Theatre, London on 7 December 1892. The first full productions occurred simultaneously in Berlin and Trondheim on 19 January 1893. August Lindberg's company gave the play's Swedish première in Gothenburg in March 1893.

The London première took place on 20 February 1893 at the Trafalgar Square Theatre in London in a translation by William Archer and Edmund Gosse. The response was exceptionally negative ('a play written, rehearsed and acted by lunatics', according to the *Daily Telegraph*). Only Henry James praised it generously:

> Ibsen's independence, his perversity, his intensity, his vividness, the hard compulsion of his strangely inscrutable art, are present in full measure, together with that quality which comes almost uppermost when it is a question of seeing him on the stage, his peculiar blessedness to actors.

The play was directed by Lugné-Poe in Paris in 1894 (with Solness played by the director), in a production described by Ibsen as 'the resurrection of my play'.

The part of Solness has attracted a number of distin-guished British actors, including Donald Wolfit (1934–48), Michael Redgrave (1964), Laurence Olivier (1965), Brian Cox (1994), Alan Bates (1995), Timothy West (1999) and Patrick Stewart (2003). Hilde Wangel is a remarkable part for a young actress of strength and magnetic appeal.

The last moment of the play is notoriously difficult to stage and directors usually end up placing an imaginary tower above the audience's head. Ibsen's stage directions are breath-taking, if nigh on impossible to achieve:

> The ladies on the veranda wave their handkerchiefs, and cheers and cries of 'Well done!' echo down the street.
> There is sudden silence, and the crowd shrieks with hor-ror. We can just see planks, scaffolding poles and a body plummeting down among the trees.

Translated by Kenneth McLeish, Nick Hern Books, 1997

Little Eyolf
(*Lille Eyolf*)

1894

↪ Characters

Alfred Allmers, *landed proprietor and man of letters,*
   formerly a tutor
Rita Allmers, *his wife*
Eyolf, *their child, nine*
Asta Allmers, *Alfred's younger half-sister*
Borghejm, *an engineer*
The Rat Wife

The action takes place on Allmers's property near the fjord,
some miles from the town

↪ The story

Act One is set in the 'handsome and expensively appointed
garden room' of Allmers' house, with a view of the fjord visible at the back. Asta has come to visit and is pleased to hear
that Allmers has just returned from a six-week walking holiday in the mountains. Eyolf appears dressed in a soldier's uniform: he has a paralysed leg and uses a crutch. ('He is
undersized and looks sickly, but has fine intelligent eyes.')
Allmers seems 'so happy and peaceful', but says he has been
unable to write his book. The Rat Wife appears and describes
how she and her dog charmed all the rats on to a boat and
drowned them in the fjord. Allmers explains that his life's
work – a 'great, solid book on Human Responsibility' – is no
longer important and that 'Little Eyolf has taken a deeper
and deeper hold' of him: his wife Rita, and his half-sister Asta
will be his partners in the project. They are interrupted by
Borghejm, a cheerful young road engineer. He is about to
take up another job in the mountains, and goes for a walk

with Asta before he leaves. Left together, Rita tells Allmers that she hopes Asta loves Borghejm, because she wants Allmers all to herself. She hated him working so hard, but sees that he is now 'absorbed in something worse': 'I want to be everything for you.' She is not interested in his 'quiet affection', or in her role as Eyolf's mother; it is erotic passion that she misses. The previous night she prepared herself for his arrival, but he rejected her ('You had champagne, but you touched it not'); if he continues to do so, the consequences will be terrible, and she is even tempted to say something 'evil'. Borghejm returns despondent – Asta has rejected him. Rita says it is the 'Evil Eye that has played this trick'. Suddenly, shouts are heard from the fjord: 'a child has been drowned' and Eyolf's crutch is seen floating on the surface.

Act Two takes place in a 'small, narrow glen in the forest on Allmers' estate . . . a heavy, damp day with driving clouds of mist'. Allmers is in despair, staring out over the fjord. He asks Asta about the meaning of Eyolf's death: 'It is pointless, the whole thing.' She sews a black band on his hat and sleeve and he remembers her doing the same when their father and her mother died. They recall their happy years as orphans: she had been like a brother to him and he had nicknamed her 'Eyolf'. Allmers rebukes himself for forgetting his dead son, but is glad to have Asta, who is more of a comfort to him than his wife. Rita arrives, and Borghejm persuades Asta to 'go a little way – along the shore. For the very last time.' Rita says the boys on the jetty saw the drowned Eyolf lying on the bottom ('Deep down in the clear water') with his eyes wide open. Allmers accuses Rita of never loving Eyolf and she admits that Asta 'stood in the way. Right from the beginning.' Rita says Allmers gave up writing his book out of self-doubt, not love for Eyolf. They remember that Eyolf was crippled while they were making love (by falling off a table as a baby: 'I forgot the child – in your arms'). It is a judgement on both of them: 'Here we are now, where we deserve to be.' Allmers has dreamed of Eyolf still alive and asks Rita if she would join him in death. She says she would rather stay with Allmers and he confesses he could not do it either: 'it's here, in the life of the earth, we living creatures belong and are at home'. Rita wonders whether they can ever forget Eyolf, but he says that their love, 'that used to be a consuming fire . . . now must be quenched'. Asta and Borghejm return and Allmers tells Asta that he and Rita 'can't go on living together . . . we are making one another ugly'. He says he wants to go home to Asta, 'to be purified and restored'; a 'brother's and sister's love . . . is the only [relation] not subject to the law of change'. But she has discovered from her mother's letters that he is not in fact her brother. As the curtain falls, he hands her some water-lilies picked from the fjord, a gift from 'Little Eyolf' and himself.

For Act Three the action moves to a more remote part of Allmers's estate, with a view over the fjord far below. It is twilight. Borghejm joins Asta, to run a flag up the flagpole to half-mast, but also to say goodbye to her: both are leaving that evening, in different directions. Asta speaks of her closeness to Allmers, but Borghejm is desperate: 'Miss Asta – this is crazy of you! . . . Somewhere in the next few days, perhaps, all life's happiness may be lying waiting for us.' Asta cannot accept him, however, and they are interrupted by Allmers, who is surprised to hear that Borghejm will be travelling 'alone'. Allmers is tortured by the possibility of being able to leave with Asta, when they are joined by Rita, anxious not to be abandoned. She is terrified ('I feel as if there were wide open eyes looking at me') and begs Asta to stay. Rita even asks Asta to 'take Eyolf's place' for us, but Asta decides she cannot, invites Borghejm to go with her on the steamer and they leave together. Rita and Allmers watch the boat draw up ('with its great glowing eyes') against the very jetty where Eyolf was drowned. Rita says she can hear the 'passing bell': 'Always the same words . . . the crutch – is float – ing. The crutch – is float – ing.' She knows he will follow his 'sister', but encourages him to work again. His answer is 'that it would be better for both us if we parted', adding that he nearly died in the mountains. She recognizes the truth: 'For you think it's only here, with me, that you've nothing to live for.' They hear shouts from the jetty below: Allmers declares the poor who live down there should be forced to leave their houses and the 'whole place levelled to the ground – when I'm gone.' Rita says she intends to welcome the orphan boys into her house and treat them as if they were Eyolf himself. This strikes a chord in Allmers, who knows he has done nothing for the poor ('so perhaps it is natural enough, after all, that they didn't risk their lives to save little Eyolf'). To her amazement, he offers to help. In the last moments, Allmers hoists the flag to the top and says that occasionally they may see a glimpse of Little Eyolf and Asta when they look 'up to the mountain peaks. To the stars. And to the great stillness.'

ᥩ About the play

Ibsen wrote *Little Eyolf* in Christiania in 1894 at the height of his international fame. Perhaps in reaction to the public adulation that he encountered on a daily basis, Ibsen, in his later years, developed an acute interest in young people and children. He had recently been reunited with his sister and found himself in increasing contact with his childhood. Ibsen's own brother had twisted his spine when he was dropped as a baby, and he may have had this in mind when he came to conceive the character of 'Little Eyolf' himself.

The play has the simplicity and terror of a nursery rhyme. The story of the wealthy but lonely crippled boy left to drown by the healthy but resentful orphans has all the archetypal power of Hans Christian Andersen. The Rat Wife ('a little, thin, shrivelled creature, old and grey haired, with deep piercing eyes') is taken from the Pied Piper of Hamelin (although there was also a real rat wife in Skien, where Ibsen was born). In the portrait of Allmers and his half-sister Asta, Ibsen touches on the classic tale of an innocent relationship between brother and sister being exposed – and destroyed – by the complex mysteries of adult sexuality.

However, in *Little Eyolf* Ibsen is only partially concerned with children and the imagination. As so often in late Ibsen, at the heart of the play is a marriage in difficulty. Alfred Allmers is a kindly, sober, academic figure, who has been trying to write a *magnum opus* on 'Human Responsibility'. He has come to the conclusion that the real meaning of 'responsibility' is to devote his life to the education and development of his crippled son. He is wracked with guilt about Eyolf's disability (which he sees as punishment for giving in to sexual passion). Despite his wanderings in the wilderness, he is not a noble figure, but nor is he despicable. For most of the play he is placid and cool – what a later age might call 'passive aggressive'. However, as Ibsen said, 'there are places where a lyrical temperament breaks through'. His profound grief at the death of his son is moving, but it is also indulgent. It is only when Allmers finally accepts that he has failed in his responsibilities not just to others but also to himself that he can begin to love his wife and contribute to the world.

Perhaps more than in any other of his plays, in *Little Eyolf* Ibsen is concerned with sexuality, and in particular Rita's frustration with her husband's apparent impotence. She is quite frank about wanting to make love to him on his return from the mountains. In Act Two, however, she starts to look at him more critically, and recognizes her equal responsibility for all that has happened: 'You too, you too,' she says. Rita's acknowledgement in Act Three of certain truths about their relationship takes him to a new place where, paradoxically, a new connection is possible.

Allmers's sister Asta is a strikingly independent figure, quite capable of looking after herself and, if anything, rather aloof. In contrast to Rita, she is a somewhat asexual young woman: as a young girl her brother called her by a boy's name (Eyolf) and her destiny was to be Allmers's chaste sister: looking after him in his struggles, sewing on black bands in his grief and applauding him in his triumph. As soon as it becomes clear that she is not Allmers's sister and that he wants her as his lover, she knows that she cannot stay with him.

Asta's persistent suitor, the young Borghejm, is one of Ibsen's most attractive characters: cheerful and indomitable, hard-working and full of integrity. We are pleased that Asta never turns her back on him entirely and are delighted when she eventually decides to leave with him. Borghejm is no Allmers – an intellectual incapable of pleasuring his wife – but a manly figure with a powerful appetite and a strong physical presence. As he and Asta leave in Act Three, we wonder whether she is following her true destiny, but are confident that Borghejm will offer her all the love he can.

Some commentators – including the usually shrewd Henry James – have felt that Act Three is a disappointment and argued that in the search for a resolution, the dramatist has opted for a didactic point: if life seems meaningless, look after the poor and you will feel better. What this criticism fails to recognize, however, is the complex relationship between activity and sexuality, energy and happiness. When Allmers expresses his commitment to Rita's project – however unlikely it may be – he abandons his plans to return to the mountains (where he would no doubt die) and declares that he will join her in her work. Then, in an act of rampant sexual symbolism, he raises the flag to the top of the mast. It is not morality that triumphs over grief: instead it is life, and the possibility of new life, that heals the deepest wound.

Little Eyolf is written with an astonishingly concentrated power: relentless, austere and magnificent. If at first sight the plot seems flimsy, the intensity of Ibsen's vision is overwhelming. It is not the most accessible of Ibsen's plays, but has its own extraordinary strengths. The English Ibsenite, William Archer, was effusive in his praise:

> I rank the play beside, if not above, the very greatest of Ibsen's works, and am only doubtful whether its soul-searching be not too terrible for human endurance in the theatre.

❦ In performance

The first public reading of *Little Eyolf* took place at the Haymarket Theatre, London on 3 December 1894. The first proper production took place in Berlin on 12 January 1895, and three days later the play received its Scandinavian première in Christiania, with Ibsen in the audience. The play was soon performed throughout Europe: performances in Milan, Vienna, Munich and Paris all took place in 1895.

The London première took place on 23 November 1895 at the Avenue Theatre with Janet Achurch as Rita, Elizabeth Robins as Asta and Mrs Patrick Campbell ('the most haunting and perfect piece of acting', said Robins) as the Rat Wife. Bernard Shaw was dismissive of the production and most of the initial press response was hostile. The play was performed at the Lyric Theatre, Hammersmith with Robert Eddison as Allmers in 1958, and in the same theatre in 1985 with Diana Rigg and Ronald Pickup. Adrian Noble directed a production of the play at the RSC in 1997 with Joanne Pearce playing Rita and Damian Lewis as Borghejm. A television film of the play was made in 1982 with Antony Hopkins as Allmers, Peggy Ashcroft as the Rat Wife and Diana Rigg as Rita Allmers.

As so often in late Ibsen, the play is scenically ambitious and almost filmic in its demands. As Henry James said about the last act:

> Really uttered, done, in the gathering northern twilight, with the flag down and the lights coming across the fjord, the scene might have a real solemnity of beauty.

Translated by Una Ellis-Fermor, Penguin, 1958

John Gabriel Borkman
(John Gabriel Borkman)
1896

❧ Characters

John Gabriel Borkman, *formerly a bank director*
Gunhild Borkman, *his wife*
Erhart Borkman, *their son, a student*
Miss Ella Rentheim, *Mrs Borkman's twin sister*
Mrs Wilton
Vilhelm Foldal, *clerk in a government office*
Frida Foldal, *his daughter*
Malene, *Mrs Borkman's maid*

The action takes place one winter evening on the Rentheim
family estate outside the capital

❧ The story

The play opens in Gunhild Borkman's living-room, 'fur-
nished rather grandly, but now old-fashioned and faded-
looking'. A fire is blazing and it is snowing outside. Gunhild
is expecting her son Erhart and is amazed when her twin sister
Ella arrives instead. Gunhild is obsessed with her husband's
bankruptcy and the dishonour it caused her and her son, and
says she has nothing to do with him any more, despite the fact
that he lives upstairs. Ella argues that 'he was a great man in
those days', but Gunhild declares that she is 'not giving up.
I'll be recompensed somehow' and says that Erhart 'has a
duty to shine so brilliantly, throughout this whole country,
that people will never again be able to see the shadow his
father cast over me . . . and over my son'. They hear Borkman
walking around upstairs: 'It sometimes comes into my mind
that I have a sick wolf in the house, pacing up and down in his
cage, up there in the salon.' He has no visitors except for the

clerk Foldal and his young daughter Frida, who plays the piano for him. Gunhild says that a young widow called Mrs Wilton has been seeing Erhart. Ella is concerned that he is 'in danger' (she brought him up when his father went bankrupt), but Gunhild says he is immune to everything except his 'mission'. Ella announces that she is moving into the house (which she now owns following Borkman's bankruptcy) and Gunhild presumes that she will have to leave ('So we have to put up with living on your pity and charity'). However, it is Erhart's love that Ella really needs and she wants him to choose between the two of them. When Erhart and Mrs Wilton arrive, Gunhild invites them to stay for the evening. He reluctantly agrees, but Mrs Wilton casts a playful spell over him, urging him to follow her to a party nearby. He cannot resist the 'bright lights down there' and once he has gone, the two sisters find the only thing they can agree on: they would rather Erhart was kept by Mrs Wilton than by the other. When Ella leaves, the piano upstairs plays louder and Gunhild cries 'The wolf is howling again. The sick wolf' and throws herself down on the floor, writhing in agony and whispering: 'Erhart! Erhart – be true to me! Come home and help your mother! I can't bear this life any longer!'

For Act Two, the action moves upstairs. Borkman is listening to Frida playing the last few bars of the *Danse macabre*. He first heard such music down the mines, where 'the metal sings [because] it wants to come up into the light of day and serve mankind'. Soon, she has to go to play at a dance given by Hinkel – the man who betrayed Borkman – and she upsets Borkman by telling him that his son, Erhart, is going to be there too. Foldal arrives and Borkman treats him with his customary gruffness. Foldal is feeling lonely and despised at home (particularly by his children), adding that his only achievement is the tragedy he wrote in his youth. Borkman speaks 'with unshakeable conviction of the 'hour of rehabilitation' that he feels is coming. He says Hinkel betrayed him 'at the very moment of achievement' and laughs bitterly about his son being there tonight, his mind having been poisoned by his mother and his aunt. Foldal momentarily doubts Borkman's hopes of rehabilitation and is summarily dismissed ('now you're like a stranger to me'). There is a knock on the door: Ella has come to see Borkman. They have not seen each other for years and she has changed ('I have no dark curls hanging down my back now'). He is grateful to her for everything she has done for his son, but reminds her that in his hour of need he left her fortune intact. Years earlier, he had married Gunhild for her money and she tells him of his 'terrible crime': 'You have killed the power of love in me.' He had a higher purpose, however – he wanted 'to waken all the spirits slumbering in the gold' – and in losing her love he gained the controlling interest in the bank. When Ella reveals that she is dying, she says it is Erhart whom she loves and whom she wants back from his mother: 'I've got to have my child's heart, whole and undivided – now.' When Borkman consents to Erhart taking on the name of Rentheim, she forgives him everything: 'Thank you! Now everything's completely settled between us. Yes, yes, so be it! You've done all you could to make amends. Now, when I'm gone from this world, Erhart Rentheim will live on after me.' Suddenly, however, Gunhild appears: 'Never, in all eternity, will Erhart be called that name! . . My son's heart will be mine. Mine, and no one else's.' Gunhild leaves, with Ella determined to make Borkman and Gunhild come to an understanding.

Act Three takes place in Gunhild's living-room. Gunhild sends her maid off to fetch Erhart from the party. Both Borkman and Ella have come downstairs. He tells Gunhild that 'the only person I have sinned against is myself': 'the very day I was released, I should've marched straight back out into the real world – out into the iron-hard, dreamless world of reality'. He is determined to do it now. Gunhild has other plans, however: '[Erhart's] life will shine so brightly, it'll be so pure and exalted, that your own vile money-grubbing exis- tence will be wiped off the face of the earth.' When Erhart arrives, each of the three stake their claim to him. He is appreciative, respectful and kind, but rejects all three, passionately declaring: 'I'm young! And I want to live. I want to live my own life!' When Gunhild asks him what he wants to live for, his response is startling: 'For happiness, mother!' and explains he has found it with Mrs Wilton, whom he brings into the room. Gunhild tells her that 'You have destroyed the last remnants of what little I had to live for.' What is more, not only is Mrs Wilton seven years older than Erhart, she is also a divorcée. He knows all this, however, and declares that they are leaving that night for the south, taking Frida with them. The luggage is packed, the sleigh is waiting and, as they leave, Gunhild says that now she is 'childless'; Borkman goes 'out into the storm, alone'. As the curtain falls, Gunhild suddenly cries out: 'Erhart, don't go!'

For Act Four the action moves outside the house: 'the ground is thickly covered with the new-fallen snow'. Ella stops Gunhild from following her son. Soon, Mrs Wilton's sleigh bells are heard passing nearby – celebrating Erhart's 'life and happiness', though to Gunhild they sound like 'funeral bells'. Ella is content that Erhart will be happy. Borkman refuses to come back inside, saying he will never 'set foot inside that house again'. Foldal appears, limping heavily, having been run over by the sleigh. He has received a letter from Frida, telling him of her adventure. He is delighted for her ('Little Frida, travelling in that magnificent closed sleigh. With silver bells') and goes back home to comfort his wife. Borkman decides to head out into the night, and he and Ella (who 'belong together') gradually 'make their way into the low wood on the left'. Then, unusually for Ibsen, the location shifts: 'Far below to the left, a landscape of fjords and mountain peaks, towering one above another, stretches into the distance.' The two remember how they used to sit on a bench on the vantage point, looking out. Ella says 'It was the dreamland of our lives. And now it's all covered in snow.' Borkman, however, sees the steamships 'drawing the world together' and imagines the factories he would have built in that kingdom. Ella points out that he crushed 'a warm, living human heart, that beat and throbbed for you'. Furthermore, she says, 'you will never march in triumph into your cold, dark kingdom'. Suddenly, Borkman's heart is seized by 'a hand of iron' and Ella sets off to get help. She turns back, however, and sits in the snow with Borkman. When Gunhild and the maid appear, Ella tells them that Borkman has died: 'it was an icy iron hand that gripped his heart'. Left together, the two women know that it was 'the cold that killed him . . . And turned us both to shadows'. As the final curtain falls, they stand either side of the bench, stretching out their hands to each other: 'two shadows . . . over the dead man'.

❧ About the play

The painter Edvard Munch described *John Gabriel Borkman* as 'the most powerful winter landscape in Scandinavian art'. Certainly, Ibsen's late, great masterpiece has an icy austerity. With its unity of time ('one winter's evening'), its faded elegance and its concentration of means, the play has a strange, neo-classical power, almost like Corneille or Racine. If at times melodramatic (particularly the episode in Act Three when Erhart rejects all three in turn), the play is so rich with psychological detail and human observation that it is utterly compelling.

At the heart of the play is a portrait of a great capitalist on the rocks. Bernard Shaw described John Gabriel Borkman as a

> Napoleon of finance – He has the root of finance in him in a born love of money in its final reality: a love, that is, of precious metals. He does not dream of beautiful ladies calling to him for knightly rescue from dragons and tyrants, but of metals imprisoned in undiscovered mines, calling to him to release them and send them out into all lands fertilizing, encouraging, creating.

Borkman has a visionary sense of the transformative power of money, an almost mystical appreciation of the mines and the glittering metals hidden in the fields (the angel Gabriel indeed). At the root of his tragedy, however, is the loss of love, not money. Ibsen shows how Borkman's mercenary marriage to Gunhild, and his betrayal of the woman that he loved, is a Faustian pact that must eventually be paid for. When he dies in the snow, it is not a corrupt capitalist who has died, but a nineteenth-century King Lear.

Borkman's estranged wife Gunhild is in many ways an unattractive figure. Tough, bitter and resentful, her greatest ambition is to avenge the humiliation she feels. Borkman describes her as being as 'hard as the iron I once dreamed of digging out of the rocks'. But her determination to control her son is driven by genuine maternal love, as well as bitterness and pride. When played well, Gunhild is like an avenging mother in an Icelandic saga, or one of Wagner's Valkyries: fearful and breathtaking in equal measure.

At first sight, Gunhild's sister Ella seems a very different figure. Full of generosity and eager to resolve lifelong bitternesses and despair, she is a softer woman than her sister, and more obviously attractive in her youth. Now she is dying and wants Erhart to bear her name after her death. When Erhart tells her that he is going, she hopes he can be 'as happy as he can'. Her moral condemnation of the coldness at the heart of Borkman's love of money and power is very powerful. The irony is that in her dogged determination to control Erhart she is not unlike her twin sister, and it is crucial to Ibsen's moral design that the two sisters form a symmetrical shape on either side of Borkman and his son.

This elderly trio is contrasted with the living energy of the young couple: the young and charming Erhart and the older, sexually experienced divorcée Mrs Wilton. Their presence brings a vivid colour to the drama: romantic, attractive and alive. We are pleased when Erhart says he is leaving with Mrs Wilton, even with her unconventional plan to pass him on to Frida later:

Men are so fickle, Mrs Borkman. And women likewise.
When Erhart's finished with me – and I with him – it'll

be good for us both if the poor boy has someone to fall back on.

Borkman's old clerk Foldal and his daughter Frida are unwitting characters in a much bigger tragedy. Foldal is almost a comical figure ('a stooped, weary looking man with mild blue eyes and long, sparse grey hair'), caught up in and brought down by Borkman's tragic fall. Frida is a shy, nervous girl, full of natural talent but intimidated and awkward. Both father and daughter are damaged by Borkman's domineering vision and have been alienated from each other. They are reunited only by the grotesque accident in which the sledge which runs over Foldal's foot carries Frida off to a better life. Like Erhart and Mrs Wilton, Frida must be allowed to live her own life, whatever damage may be done on the way. Her father's redemption lies in the spontaneous pleasure he takes at her new opportunities.

The language of *John Gabriel Borkman* is resolute, carved out of granite and somewhat lacking the poetic ambiguities of some of the earlier plays. One of the play's novelties is the way in which the action runs continuously from act to act, providing a unity of time even while locations shift. Commonly regarded as the greatest achievement of Ibsen's last years, much of the play consists of simple but astonishingly powerful duologues. Henry James was full of praise:

> It is a high wonder and pleasure to welcome such splendid fruit from sap that might by now have shown something of the chill of age. Never has [Ibsen] juggled more gallantly with difficulty and danger than in this really prodigious *John Gabriel*, in which a great span of tragedy is taken between three or four persons – a trio of the grim and grizzled – in the two or three hours of a winter's evening; in which the whole thing throbs with an actability that fairly shakes us as we read; and in which, as the very flower of his artistic triumph, he has given us for the most beautiful and touching of his heroines a sad old maid of sixty.

In old age, Ibsen seems to be saying, you have to face up to the consequences of your youth. It is only the truth that can save you from despair.

⤳ In performance

For complicated copyright reasons, *John Gabriel Borkman* received its first public reading at the Avenue Theatre, London on 14 September 1896. There were simultaneous premières on 10 January 1897 in the Finnish and Swedish theatres in Helsinki and the play was performed throughout Europe in the same year.

John Gabriel Borkman had its London première on 3 May 1897 at the Strand Theatre, presented by the New Century Theatre group. Famous London Borkmans include Bernard Miles at the Mermaid Theatre in 1961 and Donald Wolfit at the Duchess Theatre in 1963. Ralph Richardson, Wendy Hiller and Peggy Ashcroft played the three central characters at the Old Vic in 1975, in a production directed by Peter Hall, which transferred to the Lyttleton in the newly built National Theatre in 1976. Ingmar Bergman directed the play for the Bavarische Staatstheater, Munich in 1985. Richard Eyre directed it at the Royal National Theatre in 1996 with Paul Scofield, Vanessa Redgrave, Eileen Atkins and Michael Bryant (as a particularly touching Foldal) in a new translation by Nicholas Wright. Stephen Unwin directed the play in 2003 for English Touring Theatre with Michael Pennington, Linda Bassett and Gillian Barge.

A television film of the play was made in 1958 with Laurence Oliver.

Translated by Stephen Mulrine, Nick Hern Books, 2003

When We Dead Awaken
(*Når vi døde vågner*)

A Dramatic Epilogue

1899

❧ Characters

Professor Arnold Rubek, *a sculptor*
Maja, *his wife*
The Manager, *at the spa*
Squire Ulfheim
Irena, *a lady traveller*
Lars, *Ulfheim's servant*
A nun
Waiters, guests and children

❧ The story

Act One takes place outside a hotel at a Norwegian spa. A fjord is visible 'stretching right out to sea'. Rubek is a rich and successful sculptor and Maja is his beautiful and much younger wife. They have just finished their breakfast. He confesses that he is unhappy to have returned to Norway and she says she wants to leave immediately. He reminds her that 'tomorrow . . . we'll sail northward all round the coast – right up into the Arctic'. Maja reminds him that he lost pleasure in his work once he had finished his world-famous 'masterpiece . . . *Resurrection Day*', and compares it to the 'portrait-busts' he turns out now. He defends them: beneath their superficial likenesses lurk animal energies. She reminds him that when she agreed to marry him, he promised to take her 'up a high mountain . . . and show [her] all the glory of the world'. He has failed to do so and admits that he is beginning to find the four or five years they have been married 'rather long'. The Manager comes over and

Rubek asks him about one of his patients 'who's in the habit of taking the treatment in the night'; Rubek had 'looked out of the window and saw a white figure down there among the trees', adding that 'behind it came another figure – quite dark – like a shadow'. The Manager points to 'a slender lady, dressed in fine creamy white cashmere . . . followed by a nun dressed in black', who soon disappear into the pavilion. Rubek thinks he knows who she is and Maja suggests she may have been one of his models. Squire Ulfheim appears, 'followed by a servant leading a couple of hunting-dogs'. Maja is instantly attracted and wants to go bear-hunting in the mountains with him. When he leaves to feed his dogs ('great thick marrow bones . . . they swallow them whole'), Maja follows him. Immediately, Irena appears. She asks Rubek about their 'child', saying she wishes she had killed it, 'pounded it to dust'. Rubek asks her why she left, and she declares that she 'went into the darkness – while the child stood transfigured in the light'. To his astonishment – and disbelief – she tells him that she killed her two husbands and her 'many children', and that she is dead herself: 'But now I'm beginning to rise – a little – from the dead.' They remember how she had sworn to 'follow [him] to the world's end, and to the end of life' and be the model for his work 'in frank and utter nakedness'. He wronged her: 'I showed myself, wholly and without reserve, for you to gaze at . . . and never once did you touch me!' His defence is that he was anxious that if he touched her his vision would be 'desecrated'. He had wanted to create his sculpture of a woman waking up from death, and she 'consented so willingly'. She says that once the work was done, he had no more need of her; now she asks him to join her in 'the high mountains'. Maja returns and declares that she is not going on 'that wretched steamer', and that she wants to go with 'that awful bear-slayer' 'up to the mountains'. Rubek is unperturbed. As the curtain falls, Irena tells him that she gave him her 'soul – young and living. And since then I've been empty – soulless. That was why I died, Arnold.'

Act Two takes place at a mountain health-resort: 'The
landscape stretches as a vast treeless plateau towards a lake.' A
brook runs across the foreground. It is a summer's evening,
just before sunset, and Rubek is watching a group of children
playing. Maja appears and tells him that she and Ulfheim are
going bear-hunting in the forest. She says that Ulfheim is
'ugly', but so also is Rubek: 'There's such a tired look in your
eyes – a look of defeat.' She has realized Rubek's lingering
fascination with Irena; he is finding their marriage increasingly difficult and needs someone who is 'near to him'. He
admits that he finds his artistic vocation 'fundamentally
meaningless' and that he has 'suffered a new upheaval – an
awakening to what my life really means'. He also speaks of
having a 'little casket with a secret lock, and in that casket lies
all my vision as an artist, but when she [Irena] disappeared
without a trace, the lock snapped shut'. Now, he says, he cannot open that casket, and 'time is passing – and there's no way
for me to reach the treasure'. To his astonishment, her reply
is quite frank: 'Just attach yourself to whomever you need
most.' Suddenly, Maja sees Irena 'striding along like a marble
statue . . . like the embodiment of resurrection'. Maja leaves
and Irena tells Rubek that after he had finished the sculpture
('our creation – our child') she wanted him never to create
anything again. She was motivated by hatred of the artist who
'so lightly and carelessly took a warm, living body . . . and
wrenched the soul out of it', hatred of the man who could be
so unmoved by her nakedness. To Irena's fury, Rubek confesses that he altered the sculpture, added other figures and
placed himself in it – a man 'racked and tormented by the
knowledge that he will never succeed – never in all eternity
will he be free to live the resurrected life'. She despises him
for being 'a poet' and says she wishes she had children of her
own. Together they play a game in the brook with petals and
leaves (like the swans and water-lilies in Wagner's *Lohengrin*)
as they used to 'outside the little cottage on Lake Taunitz',
and they agree that 'you and I let all that lovely life slip away'.
The sun is going down and Irena remembers that she 'once

saw a wonderfully beautiful sunrise . . . high up on a mountain top'. When Rubek asks her to come and live with him and Maja – 'so that I can begin to live again' – she accuses him of 'Empty dreams – dead, idle dreams. There's no resurrection of a partnership like ours.' Ulfheim appears with Maja, who has written a song about freedom. 'I believe I've woken up now – at last!' she says, and goes off. Suddenly Irena sees the face of the Nun staring out of the bushes. She and Rubek promise each other a 'summer night on the hillside', and Irena tells him that 'we see the irreparable only when . . . we dead wake'. She goes down the hill with the Nun, Rubek sits motionless by the brook and high up the mountains Maja can be heard singing.

In Act Three the action moves higher, to 'a wild jagged mountain-side, with sheer precipices falling away at the back. Snow-covered peaks rise to the right, and lose themselves in high drifting mist.' It is early morning and Maja appears, 'flushed and annoyed', held tightly by the sleeve by Ulfheim, who is 'half angry, half laughing'. She is trying to break free (she wants to go down to the hotel 'before everyone's awake') but the only way out is to 'jump down the chasm'. Both tell their life stories – he was cuckolded and she was tricked 'into a cold clammy cage' – and he offers to 'tack our poor rags together'. They are about to go down ('Come on then, carry me down to the depths!'), when they see Rubek and Irena arriving. Rubek announces that 'from now on, the strange lady and I mean to take the same road', but Ulfheim warns them that the 'storm is almost on us . . . Just look how the clouds are billowing down – soon they'll be all around us like a winding sheet.' Ulfheim advises them to wait in the hut and says he will send a rescue party when the storm is over. Then, 'with Maja in his arms, [he] clambers quickly but carefully down the precipice'. Alone with Rubek, Irena is worried that the 'woman in black' will come and 'put me in the strait-jacket'. She has a knife, however, which she meant to use on him (when 'I heard you say, as ice-cold as death, that I was no more than an episode in your life') until she realized that he was 'dead already . . . long ago'. He replies that there is still time for them to live their lives and says 'then let us two dead things live life for once to the full – before we go down to our graves again'. Together they head off up the mountain, 'right to the topmost peak, climbing in the sunrise', and disappear into the mist. Suddenly the Nun appears, and an avalanche buries Rubek and Irena in a mass of snow. The Nun calls out Irena's name with a scream, intoning 'Pax vobiscum' while Maja's triumphant song of freedom is heard in the depths below:

> I am free, I am free, I am free!
> No longer the prison I'll see!
> I am free as a bird, I am free!

∞ About the play

There were many celebrations in Norway in 1898 for Ibsen's seventieth birthday, and in a speech he talked about writing an autobiographical book:

> which will knit my life and my work into a comprehensi-
> ble whole . . . But you must not therefore suppose that I
> intend to lay down my pen as a dramatist for good. No, I
> intend to take it up again and to cling tightly to it until
> the end . . . I still have a few lunacies in my locker which I
> have not yet found the opportunity to express. Only when
> I've got them off my back will it be time to call a halt.

It took Ibsen three years to produce *When We Dead Awaken*, the longest gestation period in his career. It was not con-ceived as his final work, but as the last of his 'realistic' sequence. When a newspaper reported it as a 'dramatic epi-logue' he was keen to point out that

> All I meant was that the play forms an epilogue to the
> series of plays which began with *A Doll's House* and which
> now ends with *When We Dead Awaken* . . .

If he had not suffered from a stroke in 1900, it seems that he would have returned to the kind of poetic drama he had so decisively abandoned after *Peer Gynt*.

Following his return to Norway in 1891, Ibsen's plays are increasingly inward-looking and autobiographical, and in the sculptor Arnold Rubek he comes closest to an explicit self-portrait in old age: a world-famous Norwegian artist who has just returned to his homeland after a long time abroad. There are many other autobiographical touches, including Ibsen's own fascination with sculpture and his lifelong ambivalence towards his native land. Despite his tremendous fame, Rubek is discontented with his life and is yearning for something better: 'Yes, isn't life in sunshine and beauty altogether more worthwhile than to go on till the end of one's days in some damp clammy hole, tiring oneself to death wrestling with lumps of clay and blocks of stone?' He says that when he finished his masterpiece he 'didn't love [his] own work any longer'. He has sacrificed life for the sake of his art.

Irena is a deeply mysterious figure (and is often accompanied by a strangely silent nun). Maja says the 'people down in the hotel think she's mad', and she is certainly disturbed. She also has a vulnerable aspect: 'I had a life to lead too, and a human destiny to fulfill . . . I should have brought children into the world . . . real children, not the kind that are hidden away in tombs.' Most importantly, she was Rubek's muse and, like all muses, her existence has been defined by the needs and imagination of the male artist. She was used by Rubek and disposed of when she was no longer needed. Incapable of seeing her as anything other, Rubek could not love her as a woman. Her anger and instability derive from the way she has been treated. Most importantly, Irena has a metaphorical role in Ibsen's self-portrait: she is the true spirit of poetry which Ibsen has killed in himself and which at the end of his life he wanted to 'awaken'.

Rubek's wife Maja is described as having a 'lively face and gay, mocking eyes'. She is some years younger than Rubek and from a 'poor background'. She is also sexually frustrated.

She is the antithesis to everything Rubek stands for: anti-intellectual, animal and impulsive. She meets her perfect match in the highly sexual, almost bestial figure of Squire Ulfheim (the 'living image of a satyr'). Their attraction is almost pornographic. It is also instinctual and profoundly liberating for Maja.

When We Dead Awaken is more than anything a play about art and artists. It is a measure of Ibsen's restless spirit that having written – in measured, realistic prose – perhaps the greatest plays since Shakespeare, he should punish himself for having abandoned his muse and contemplate a return to verse drama, the form that he had shown to be inadequate. The result is Ibsen's most obscure and inaccessible play, which attempts, not always successfully, to balance psychological realism with dense poetic symbolism.

The play has had its eminent defenders, however. Bernard Shaw declared that 'it shows no decay of Ibsen's qualities', while the eighteen-year-old James Joyce wrote that it

> expresses its own ideas as briefly and as concisely as they can be expressed in the dramatic form . . . On the whole, *When We Dead Awaken* may rank with the greatest of the author's work – if indeed it be not the greatest.

Sadly, as our own appreciation of the rest of Ibsen's work continues to grow, Ibsen's last 'lunacy' increasingly looks like an artistic failure, collapsing under the weight of its own introspection.

∞ In performance

For complex copyright reasons, public readings were held in London, Christiania and Berlin in December 1899 and January 1900, and the first full production of *When We Dead Awaken* took place at the Hoftheater, Stuttgart, on 26 January 1900. It was performed throughout Europe in 1900 and Vladimir Nemirovich-Danchenko directed it for the Moscow Art Theatre in the same year.

The play did not receive its London première until 26 January 1903 at the Imperial Theatre, and its New York one followed in 1905. It met with bewilderment (Max Beerbohm called it 'old man's work') and was dismissed even by Ibsen's most faithful disciple, William Archer:

> Well here's a cheerful end to the century! And to cheer you up a little more, I send a hurried line to say that at last Hummel *is* an old man, and the new play is a sad fiasco. It is a mere hash up of fifty old ideas and is utterly without dramatic fibre.

The play was not produced again professionally in London until 1938.

When We Dead Awaken was staged at the Almeida Theatre in 1990 and the avant-garde director Robert Wilson produced a 'meditation' on the play for the American Repertory Theatre in 1991. BBC Radio broadcast a production of the play in 1969 with Ralph Richardson as Rubek, Irene Worth as Irena and Barbara Jefford as Maja.

The play is not often staged today, as much because of the practical challenges it poses – mountains peaks, flowing brooks, playing children and so on – as for the obscurity of Ibsen's intentions. Directors and designers find it hard to balance its symbolism with its realism, and actors feel that their characters are pawns in the dramatist's sophisticated game, not 'real people'. The sad fact is that in *When We Dead Awaken* Ibsen's metaphors are so abundant that they lack credibility in the theatre.

Translated by Peter Watts, Penguin, 1964

ANTON CHEKHOV
1860–1904

Chekhov's life

Anton Pavlovich Chekhov was born on 17 January (Russian style – 29 January in the rest of Europe) 1860, in Taganrog, a cosmopolitan port on the Sea of Azov in southern Russia. His paternal grandfather was a peasant who achieved what was, before the serfs were emancipated, an exceptional thing: he saved enough to purchase his family's freedom, so that his children were able to move up into the merchant class. Chekhov's father, an intensely religious and bigoted man, was a grocer; his tendency to beat his sons and to insist on obsessive programmes of religious observance led Anton to say later that his childhood had been so crippled by tyranny and lies that it was no childhood at all.

The future playwright was the third of six children (a seventh died in infancy). As they grew up, his two elder brothers, a talented writer and artist, developed signs of alcoholism and consumption, and in a major setback their father Pavel became bankrupt when Anton was fifteen. Pavel escaped to Moscow, to be followed by the rest of his family, except for Anton, who stayed in the south to complete his schooling and look after what remained of the family's affairs before coming to Moscow to study medicine at the university. Here he became the impoverished family's *de facto* head, supporting them by writing comic sketches and short stories for the Moscow periodicals, thereby gaining a grounding in the comic observation and literary economy which would characterize his mature style.

By the end of the 1880s, Chekhov was established as a major writer of short fiction: in all, he produced, by his own account, about six hundred stories, those of his maturity, such as *Peasants*, *Lady with a Dog* and *My Life*, being masterpieces in the genre. However, his full-length output for the theatre at this stage was limited to an unperformed early play now known as *Platonov*, a qualified success with *Ivanov* in Moscow and St Petersburg and a failure in *The Wood Demon*, a work which he later used as the basis for *Uncle Vanya*. Thus far, his only outright theatrical successes were one-act farces and monologues, a number of which are still performed. In 1896 *The Seagull*, generally seen as the first of his major plays, was premièred in St Petersburg in an unsuitable theatre without adequate rehearsal; it was vigorously booed and rapidly withdrawn. In the following year, *Uncle Vanya* achieved success in the Russian provinces, and in 1898 Chekhov reluctantly permitted a revival of *The Seagull* by the newly formed Moscow Art Theatre; it was a triumph and established him as Russia's most original dramatist. Thereafter, his career was always identified with the new company, which went on to present the remaining three plays on which his reputation rests: *Uncle Vanya*, *Three Sisters* and *The Cherry Orchard*.

Throughout his life, Chekhov also practised as a doctor. His efforts on behalf of the communities in which he lived, both near Moscow and later in Yalta – where he moved after being diagnosed with tuberculosis in 1897 – would have constituted a busy life even without his literary work. In 1890 he travelled in conditions of great hardship across Siberia to the penal colony on Sakhalin Island, off Russia's east coast; here he made a painstaking analysis of climatic, medical and geological circumstances and conducted personal interviews with each of its ten thousand convicts. This eventually led to an exhaustive report, *The Island of Sakhalin*, which mildly influenced government policy. Throughout the 1890s Chekhov worked vigorously to alleviate famine in rural Russia, cultivated the soil, treated local peasants, did much to forestall a cholera epidemic, conducted a district census and opened three schools and a post office.

Though he was intensely attractive to women throughout his life, only one major relationship is beyond doubt: with Olga Knipper, the leading actress of the Moscow Art Theatre, whom he met at rehearsals of *The Seagull*. Their courtship was marked by long separations – Chekhov in Yalta for the sake of his health, Olga working on his plays in Moscow – and is known to us because of their poignant and voluminous correspondence, most of which has survived. The couple married in Moscow in 1901. There were no children.

By the time of his marriage Chekhov was a very sick man. At the opening of *The Cherry Orchard* on his birthday in 1904, colleagues and spectators were shocked at his frailty at a rare public appearance; in May of that year he left Russia for Germany with his wife, and finally died, immediately after drinking a final glass of champagne, on 2 July 1904, in Badenweiler in Germany. His body was brought back to Moscow in a refrigerated car marked 'For Fresh Oysters'; his funeral procession became confused with that of a general, and he was buried in the Novodevichy Cemetery in Moscow, where his grave can still be visited.

Chekhov's theatre

An enthusiastic theatre-goer from his schooldays in southern Russia and then a vigorous critic of contemporary styles as a young journalist in Moscow, Chekhov found himself entering a Russian theatre that, despite the earlier work of Gogol and Ostrovsky, was seriously bogged down in outdated conventions and stock situations that owed less to life than to previous plays. From the early 1880s, a welcome relaxation in state control led to the founding of private companies, a promising development which nevertheless generally led to work of great vulgarity. These trends placed the star actor at the centre of proceedings (there was as yet no conception of the idea of a director) and the author was merely seen as the supplier of product – so unimportant, in fact, that when Chekhov's *Ivanov* opened, his name on the poster was tiny compared to those of the actors and the date of the performance.

Despite his determination to 'get the theatre out of the hands of grocers and into those of literature', it took

Chekhov some time to find his own way: *Ivanov* and *Platonov* depend heavily on the virtuosity of the central performer to the exclusion of most else, and such traditions as the fatal gunshot and the monologue to the audience persist, perhaps due to a reluctance to alienate his audience entirely. However, even these early plays were original enough to be greeted with hostile incomprehension – their novelty interpreted simply as ignorance – and the Petersburg première of *The Seagull* in 1896 was a catastrophe. Audiences and critics continued, even after his reputation was rehabilitated, to have reservations about his plays, and at the time of his death he was perhaps more popular in Russia as a fiction writer than as a dramatist, a situation that has now been largely reversed.

A century later, much of what bewildered early audiences has become a yardstick by which other dramatists are measured. Chekhov's way of suspending moral judgement on his characters once troubled audiences accustomed to didactic simplification and even alerted the censors, who found it unacceptable that in *The Seagull* Arkadina's relatives seemed not to object to her living openly with a man, and could not believe that an enlightened character like Vanya would ever fire a gun at a university professor. Even now, the ambiguities in the central characters which allow for simultaneous sympathy and criticism from the audience, the apparent inconsequentiality of the dialogue (as inconsequential as in life), the manner in which comedy lurks closely behind even the most intensely dramatic situations, can be startling and refreshing. It is fortunate for us that Chekhov had the stubbornness, in a short career, to insist on a style that owed more to life's inconsistencies than to melodrama; one in which, typically, characters suppress their urgent emotions behind commonplace activities – eating, drinking and indulging in banal chatter – which paradoxically reveal far more of their inner life than blatant confession. As Chekhov once said, 'people have dinner, that's all they do, they have dinner; yet during this time their happiness is established or their lives are falling apart'.

His achievement owes an enormous amount to his collaboration with the Moscow Art Theatre, the private company founded in 1898 by the director Vladimir Nemirovich-Danchenko and the actor Konstantin Stanislavsky, which asserted the principles of the director-led ensemble that we now take for granted. These included adequate rehearsal time, the subjugation of the star performer to teamwork, and the abandonment of histrionic display in favour of delicate spatial relationships on the stage and interpersonal hints between the characters. These proved to be tailor-made for Chekhov's style. So when Nemirovich-Danchenko persuaded him to authorize the revival of *The Seagull*, claiming that it 'beat with the very pulse of Russian life', the turning-point was momentous. The triumphant outcome led, in the six years remaining of Chekhov's life, to three more masterpieces which confirmed the Art Theatre's name and Chekhov's place in theatre history. His relationship with the company remained prickly – much of their work he found unnecessarily gloomy, reverential and slow, and he particularly disliked their elaborate creation of 'real' sound effects; but his name and the Art Theatre's are permanently linked, and the emblem of a seagull is still emblazoned on the company's curtain.

Anton Chekhov is often seen as the first absurdist dramatist of the twentieth century: such details as Uncle Vanya's tragicomic assault on the Professor, or the solitary death of Firs in *The Cherry Orchard*, can be seen as the precursors of Samuel Beckett's and Harold Pinter's work, while his grasp of the rhythms of ordinary life and his understanding of human foibles have made him a hero of the realistic school. The range of subsequent approaches to his work – from naturalistic to wildly expressionist, from politically explicit to lyrically sentimental – only proves its durability. It is perhaps surprising that the source of all these different styles is a sequence of four plays representing a relatively narrow social range at a very precise moment in the history of one country – the predicament of the landed gentry in the years immediately before the upheavals of the 1905 and 1917 Russian Revolutions. The palate Chekhov used was small, but his subtlety and insight, his acute sensibility and his wit have transformed what the world expects of its theatre; and beneath all other observable aspects of his talent beats the profound poetry, at once grave and joyous, thrillingly recognizable and deeply moving, of life as it continues to be lived.

Translations and further reading

Appreciation of Chekhov in English was initially expressed, generally in passing rather than in formal biography, by such leading writers as Virginia Woolf and George Bernard Shaw. Distinguished early translators of Chekhov into English included Constance Garnett and Elizaveta Fen, followed later by Ronald Hingley and David Magarshack. The trend currently is for the plays to be translated, sometimes quite freely, by working playwrights: among them, Michael Frayn (who speaks fluent Russian) has done all the major plays and many of the one-act plays; Peter Gill *The Seagull* and *The Cherry Orchard*; Frank McGuinness and Christopher Hampton *Uncle Vanya* and *Three Sisters*; David Hare *Ivanov* and *Platonov*; David Lan *Uncle Vanya* and *The Cherry Orchard*; David Mamet *Uncle Vanya*, *Three Sisters* and *The Cherry Orchard*; and Nicholas Wright *Three Sisters*.

Standard biographies include V. S. Pritchett's *Chekhov – A Spirit Set Free* (1988), Ernest J. Simmons's *Chekhov – A Biography* (1962), Donald Rayfield's *Anton Chekhov: A Life* (1997), Philip Callow's *The Hidden Ground* (1998) and Henri Troyat's *Chekhov* (1984). Criticisms of the plays include Patrick Miles's *Chekhov on the British Stage* (1993), Harvey Pitcher's *The Chekhov Plays; A New Interpretation* (1973), Laurence Senelick's *The Chekhov Theatre: A Century of the Plays in Performance* (1977) and David Allen's *Performing Chekhov* (2000).

Any enthusiasts would also do well to immerse themselves in the various selections of his many letters and short stories.

Platonov
(*Platonov*)

probably 1880/1

❧ Characters

Anna Petrovna, *General Voynitsev's young widow*
Sergei Voynitsev, *General Voynitsev's son by his first
    marriage*
Sonya, *his wife*
Pavel Shcherbuk, *retired soldier and neighbouring
    landowner*
Porfiry Glagolyev, *neighbouring landowner*
Kyril, *his son*
Gerasim Petrin, *a rich merchant*
Maria Grekova, *a student, twenty*
Ivan Triletsky, *a retired colonel*
Nikolai, *his son, a young doctor*
Abraham Vengerovich, *a rich Jew*
Isaak, *his son, a student*
Timofei Bugrov, *a merchant*
Mikhail Platonov, *a village schoolmaster, twenty-seven*
Sasha, *his wife, daughter of Ivan Triletsky*
Osip, *a horse thief, about thirty*
Marko, *a court messenger*
Vasily }
Yakov } *servants of the Voynitsevs*
Katya }
Guests and servants

The action takes place on the Voynitsevs' estate in the south
of Russia

❧ The story

In General Voynitsev's drawing-room on a hot June morning,

Anna Petrovna plays chess with Doctor Nikolai Triletsky. She quizzes him about his relationship with a chemistry student, Maria Grekova; he is non-committal but admits that he misses her in the afternoons. Lunch-time is approaching, much to Nikolai's approval: Anna considers him a glutton, though he claims he is simply saving the food from going off. They are joined by Anna's stepson Sergei, newly married to Sonya; by Porfiry Glagolyev, a sentimental landowner; by an out-of-breath merchant, Bugrov, and by Abraham Vengerovich, a rich Jew everyone regards as mean, though he insists that Jews often lend without security and should be respected. The character of Mikhail Platonov, the local schoolmaster, comes under discussion: to Glagolyev, he is a brilliant but vague modern man who fails to respect women in the old-fashioned way that Glagolyev does. Platonov arrives with his wife Sasha (who is wearing traditional Russian dress), rejoicing at being free from a winter hibernation in which they have done little but huddle together reading. They are followed on by Sasha's father, Ivan Triletsky, a drinking man who approves of women's emancipation mainly because it makes them better at shooting, his favourite sport. More visitors arrive, including Petrin and Maria Grekova, whom Platonov immediately teases, much to the disapproval of Nikolai Triletsky; Vengerovich's intolerant student son Isaak; Shcherbuk, a military colleague of Anna's dead husband; Glagolyev's son Kyril, who is fresh back from Paris and furious with his father for not sending him more money; and Osip the horse thief, whom everyone knows to be a murderer though they lack the courage to bring him to justice. It has emerged that Platonov used to know Sonya: in those days he seemed to her a Byronic figure, while he saw himself as a Christopher Columbus, far from the humdrum village schoolteacher he has become. Later in the act, Platonov will admit that he had an affair with Sonya then and that his interest is now rekindled. As the company go in to lunch, elements of plot emerge, mainly that Anna is fond of Platonov but deeply in debt to Shcherbuk and Petrin, and determined to hold on to her estate; also that Glagolyev hopes to marry her, or at least to buy her estate and charge her rent for continuing to live there.

The first of the two scenes in the second act starts a few evenings later. Drunkenness prevails: most of the men are in pursuit of Anna Petrovna, although there is a general wish for Glagolyev to succeed in his plan since, as her creditors, some of them might then be paid. Nikolai meanwhile cadges a loan from Bugrov with the heartily contemptuous promise that he'll never pay it back: he then distributes the money among everybody who passes by, starting with the servants (because they're 'Yakov and Vasily, not Vasily and Yakov'). A pattern of duologues begins between Platonov and the three women he attracts apart from his wife. While Sergei is concerned at Sonya's depression, this turns out to be due to her awakened attraction to Platonov. She reproaches Platonov for his ambiguous attitude to this, while he accuses her of humbug. Osip the horse thief turns up to meet with Vengerovich, who wants Platonov beaten up. Platonov reappears with Maria, whom he mocks and kisses: Nikolai half-heartedly reproaches him for taking liberties with her. Anna and Platonov, the play's two objects of desire, are the next to be left alone; she propositions him, but he resists because he has too much respect for her in contrast to his other women. Glagolyev arrives to propose a Platonic marriage to Anna but she is uninterested; Kyril immediately does the same, but without the platonism. Maria Grekova, furious with Nikolai for not defending her against Platonov's advances, promises to destroy Platonov's teaching career. To Sonya, Platonov regrets his own decline and hers, in such contrast to what they might have achieved together. Much to his father's dismay, Kyril pretends that he has kissed Anna and struck a bargain with her, so that all he needs is a thousand roubles from him to fulfil it. The scene ends with Glagolyev collapsing in distress while fireworks are let off in the garden.

The second scene of the act shifts to Platonov's cabin in the woods, by a railway line, where Sasha is waiting for her husband's return, passing the time by discussing love with Osip and giving him soup. Osip has fallen for Anna Petrovna, having seen her bathing in a stream; she sent him on a pilgrimage to Moscow to atone for his sins but he only got as far as Kharkov before typically falling in with bad company. Making it clear to Sasha that her husband is pursuing Anna Petrovna, Osip invites her to visit him one day – he needn't give her directions because the birds and lizards all know the way. Platonov arrives home, full of alcoholic self-loathing: Sasha reassures him of her love, but then becomes annoyed by his patronizing tone. A further procession of tottering or amorous figures ensues. Vengerovich's son passes by on his way home, lamenting that Jews haven't romantic faces. Anna arrives in pursuit of Platonov, who continues to resist her on the basis that she is the only woman worthy of respect amidst all the provincial mediocrity; she urges him to smoke her like a cigarette and stub her out. He eventually agrees to go away with her, but they are continually interrupted and forced to hide: first by Nikolai wanting to spend the night in the cabin, then by Shcherbuk and Petrin, then by Sasha, who, apparently unsuspecting, invites the pair inside for glasses of milk. Osip has overheard it all and is disappointed because he thought Anna was a saint, and he wants to kill Platonov. Platonov throws Nikolai out of the house for being drunk and idle, and then turns his contempt on himself for allowing women to become his 'Rubicon'. As he again decides to leave with Anna so that 'a long, tedious, ugly romance' can begin, a servant brings him a proposal from Sonya – she will wait for him in the summerhouse till four o'clock. He stands in an agony of indecision, his family inside the cabin; eventually his curiosity gets the better of him again and he prepares to leave. Sergei, whom Sonya has sent shooting, breaks in to suggest a staging of *Hamlet*: Platonov rushes off towards Sonya. A train approaches as Osip insists to Sasha that Platonov has gone to Anna. In despair, Sasha throws herself on the railway line but Osip saves her as the train comes by.

At the start of Act Three, however, it transpires that

Platonov never ran away with Sonya and is now asleep in his schoolhouse. He is awakened by her, furious to find the 'saviour of her life' drunk and dishevelled. Her anger is matched by Platonov's cynicism – 'Women !' – to him, their relationship is now so sordid that he is horrified that Sonya has told her husband about it. Disgusted as she is, she still makes Platonov promise to meet her at ten that evening to leave for a life of work together: he immediately forgets the time. He resolves to write a letter of explanation to Sasha, and, while he's at it, to Anna, who is also accusing him of neglect. Then Marko arrives with a summons: Maria Grekova has brought an action against Platonov for assault. Secure in the knowledge that he plans to leave before the hearing and delighted by her spirit, he signs the summons and writes her a respectful note. Anna Petrovna arrives. She assumes Platonov has been avoiding her because he has designs on someone, but is more bothered by his drunk and unsanitary condition – her solution to his problems is that he should 'give himself an airing' in Moscow or Petersburg, in her company. On the brink of throwing away his bottles, she decides to drink her way through them with him, and they both descend into extravagant self-hatred. When she has gone, Platonov toys with the idea of postponing his elopement with Sonya in order to run away briefly with Anna first. His next visitor, Osip, assures him that his real destination is the next world; Vengerovich has given him twenty-five roubles to kill him, but first he will tear up the banknote so that Platonov will see he is going to do it for hatred, not money. He also invites Platonov to spit on him, but Platonov won't waste his saliva. Sasha arrives as the two men wrestle on the ground; gallantly Osip decides not to stab Platonov in front of her, hands her his knife and runs off. Sasha is there because their son is sick; Platonov offers no practical help beyond promising that his current affair will be brief; unfortunately he names Sonya, whereas Sasha imagined it was Anna he was involved with. He asks her to stay with him since a man as vile as he is needs a nurse; and after all, whose soup will she put too much salt in if not his?

Sasha leaves in great distress. Now Sergei, the betrayed husband, arrives; having intended to challenge Platonov to a duel, he is in tears instead. Platonov throws him out, and is then approached by Glagolyev, wanting to know if Anna deserves to be married to a man as good as himself. Platonov collapses drunkenly on him; Glagolyev takes this as a negative and he and Kyril resolve to go to Paris.

The final act moves back into the study of the late General Voynitsev. Platonov has disappeared and Sonya's servant Katya advises her to have nothing more to do with the unhealthy business of love. Wishing Sonya well in her imagined new life with Platonov, Sergei ironically observes that it is based on a strong foundation: physical lust and the misery of a third party. Anna arrives to report the lynching of Osip; also, Glagolyev, whom she was counting on to buy the estate on friendly terms, has left for Paris; then, to her horror, she learns from Sergei that Sonya is about to elope with Platonov. Bugrov reports that Glagolyev has in fact bought the estate, but in Bugrov's name; the condition is that Anna can live on it till Christmas, but only if she sells her mines, an idea she rejects. Maria asks for Anna's advice: she no longer wants to sue Platonov for assault but to love him. Platonov arrives and observes that Sergei's life is over, since a man without a woman is like a train without steam, but that even so, he himself is the best candidate for suicide. He denounces those he has injured as uncouth and provincial, and demands to be looked after, parking himself on the sofa. Sonya arrives and to her disappointment he assures her that he does not want a new life since he does not know what to do with the old one. Nikolai Triletsky reports to the company that Sasha has poisoned herself by eating matches – Platonov sees this as a punishment on him, so that he deserves everybody's pity. But in fact Triletsky has managed to save Sasha from death and Platonov asks that he should be saved as well, as he is now seeing toy soldiers with pointed caps and a tiny piano crawling over Anna's breast. Sonya begs Platonov for love; Anna urges her to pull herself together. Platonov now sees that he has not even been a truly passionate Don Juan but a stupid destroyer, committing murder à la Russe. Declaring that 'being Platonov hurts', he takes up a gun but can't bring himself to use it. Maria arrives and he promises to seduce her as well when he is better. As she continues to declare her love, Platonov understands why Oedipus put out his eyes. At this point Sonya rushes on and shoots Platonov from point-blank range. He collapses, then rises for a moment before the company, sees the messenger Marko and demands he be given three roubles, and, on this note of minor heroism, dies. Triletsky condemns the company for not looking after Platonov better and declares that Sasha might as well die now; in fact, they must all bury the dead and do what they can for the living.

↫ About the play

Completely unacknowledged by Chekhov himself, we would not know of the existence of *Platonov* but for two facts. First, his brother Mikhail reports that, as a student at Moscow University, Anton wrote an enormous play without a title which he then offered unsuccessfully to the great actress Maria Yermolova: his brief description identifies this as the play we have. Secondly, such a manuscript was acquired, without a name but in Chekhov's handwriting, by the Soviet Central State Literary Archive in 1920, and published by them in 1923. In the 1933 Soviet State Publishing House collection of Chekhov's works, the play goes under the title *Fatherlessness*, but this is probably an error – there was such an early play, written in 1878 and criticized by Chekhov's brother Alexander, but it has certainly been lost, and its title does not fit the story of *Platonov*.

Impossibly long (two to three times the length of the later plays), full of unmotivated appearances and repetitions, unwieldy, crude and extravagant, featuring attempted suicides, a knifing and the lynching of a horse thief, *Platonov* is more a string of sensations than a narrative. It is as if Chekhov was vigorously exploiting all the melodramatic possibilities of traditional theatre before re-creating it in his own image. With tremendous energy he mixes burlesque and tragedy, throwing into the ring a combustible selection of types, and seems to revel in their farcical eccentricity. But although *Platonov* can be dismissed easily enough as an inexpert prefiguring of the themes of Chekhov's later plays – the threatened estate, the drunken doctor, the failed suicide, the inability of a privileged class to adapt to history – it is also a serious enough attempt to assemble a picture of a dismally corrupt and disappointed society. To this end, the scale of the action veers from the orchestral to the doggedly individual; an opening act in which Chekhov's interest seems to be to bring an entire society onto the stage gives way to a series of chance encounters and duologues punctuated by Platonov's self-castigating monologues – his long disquisitions hardly sustained by the play's weak narrative pulse.

The hero, who never leaves the stage in the third act, dominates the play in a way that Chekhov would never permit to a single figure in his later work, explaining himself to the audience directly in a manner the author would soon abandon as well. He is both a portrait of a familiar type to which Chekhov would return – a 'Russian Hamlet' stagnating in the 1880s – and a farcically self-absorbed seducer who damages all around him: the play was once called *Don Juan in the Russian Manner*. There is little to admire in him, though, interestingly, he is emotionally rather than sexually promiscuous, flailing about in pursuit of the transforming power of love. The women who chase him – providing the play's only real motor – are not humiliated figures, but finely drawn, warm and even powerful – especially Anna Petrovna, who sees that in a better world she would have a more creative outlet than her pursuit of Platonov: she is an educated woman who is not even needed in this society as a horse or a dog is needed. Her scenes with Platonov are the play's most satisfying; while the idealist Sonya and the devoted wife Sasha are dealt with almost as sympathetically, and certainly more sympathetically than are the men.

❧ In performance

After its delayed start (the first performance was probably at the Prussian Theatre, Thuringen in 1928), *Platonov*'s stage history is spasmodic but marked by a number of famous names. Jean Vilar and Maria Casarés starred in the first Paris production at the Théâtre Nationale Populaire in 1956, when it was advertised as a world première, though by then it had been played in Sweden and Czechoslovakia as well as Germany. Giorgio Strehler directed the play for his Piccolo Teatro in Milan in 1958; and in 1960, just as it arrived in New York as *A Country Scandal*, Rex Harrison starred in the first English staging at the Royal Court in London, in a translation by Dimitri Makaroff which finally gave it the name *Platonov*.

It has since been translated under this title by Ronald Hingley and David Magarshack, but, unsurprisingly, the most successful adaptations have been done freely by practising playwrights. Michael Frayn's adaptation with Ian McKellen for the National Theatre in 1984 renamed the play *Wild Honey*. Trevor Griffiths's version, *Piano*, also played at the National Theatre in 1990. David Hare's adaptation played at the Almeida Theatre in London in 2001, and is probably the contemporary version truest to Chekhov's original text. *Platonov* forms a loose basis for Nikita Mikhalkov's remarkable 1976 film *Unfinished Piece for Mechanical Piano*.

Ivanov
(*Ivanov*)

A Play in Four Acts

1887 (revised 1889)

❧ Characters

Nikolai Ivanov, *a local government official*
Anna Petrovna, *his wife, née Sarah Abramson*
Mikhail Borkin, *manager of Ivanov's estate, a distant relative*
Count Matvei Shabyelsky, *Ivanov's uncle*
Yevgeny Lvov, *a young country doctor*
Pavel Lebedev, *chairman of the district council*
Zinaida Savishna, *his wife*
Sasha Lebedev, *their daughter, aged twenty*
Yegorushka, *a dependent of the Lebedevs*
Gavrila, *servant to the Lebedevs*
Marfa Babakina, *a young widow and landowner*
Avdotya Nazarovna, *an old woman with no means of support*
Dmitri Kozykh, *an excise officer*
Pyotr, *Ivanov's servant*
Four guests and other visitors

The action takes place in the countryside of central Russia

❧ The story

The play opens in the garden of Nikolai Ivanov, once a reforming landowner but now fallen on hard times, his financial decline accompanied by spiritual malaise. It is early evening, and Ivanov is reading: Borkin, his estate manager, creeps up on him and points a shotgun in his face. The joke is not altogether light-hearted, since Borkin needs money to pay Ivanov's workers, which Ivanov says he cannot supply until he is himself paid at the end of the month by the local council, for which he now works. Borkin believes Ivanov's difficulties spring from naïvety – if only he would buy up the land on either side of the local river, they could threaten to build a dam and extort money from any neighbours who complained. Meanwhile, Ivanov's uncle Shabyelsky has been playing a duet inside the house with Anna Petrovna, Ivanov's wife. Anna's doctor, Lvov, comes out to warn Ivanov that her tuberculosis requires that they move to the Crimea: she would certainly go if he supported the idea, but to Lvov's disgust he objects on the basis of cost. Ivanov goes for a stroll with Lvov, responding to his disapproval with some shame: Anna has sacrificed her family's support and her Jewish faith to marry him, but now, tired of her, he is reacting to the news that she may die not with sorrow but emptiness. Meanwhile Shabyelsky makes affectionate fun of Anna for her Jewishness, but is harder on himself: he feels no better than a buffoon and scrounger. Both characters display a keen sense of mortality; she is troubled by the sound of a screeching owl, while he longs to go to Paris so that he can die sitting by his wife's grave. Lvov and Ivanov return, Ivanov recommending that the younger man lower his sights in life, largely to avoid the mistakes he himself has made – Lvov should marry someone dull, shun unwinnable battles and forswear all progressive thinking. Lvov, meanwhile, is appalled by Ivanov's determination to woo the daughter of his neighbours, the Lebedevs, whom he plans to visit this evening. Shabyelsky, too, is upset that Ivanov is leaving him in charge of Anna, a job worse than being eaten by crocodiles; if Ivanov would let him accompany him to the Lebedevs, he could save Anna the misery of spending the evening with 'the world's most boring person'. Ivanov agrees to take him along; but Anna must stay at home, despite her pleas to him to stay with her – she longs for them to play music and talk together, sitting in his study in the dark as they used to. Admitting that he is beginning to fall out of love with her, Ivanov asks her to pray for him. Left alone with Lvov, Anna confides that she knows what the matter is with her health. Much as Lvov blames Ivanov for her predicament, Anna insists that she once loved him with all her heart; and she laments, with some dignity, that people will not keep their word in love and only answer truth with lies. Lvov is outraged at such tolerance; tired of him, she decides to follow her husband to the Lebedevs, though she suspects he is there for the female company.

Lebedev's house turns out to be full of expensive furniture, much of it under dustsheets. Lebedev is the chairman of the local council; his wife Zinaida a money-lender. The occasion is a party thrown for their daughter Sasha's birthday; the motley collection of guests includes card players, gossips and a lonely rich widow, Babakina. They hope to find Sasha a husband, but it seems a forlorn hope this evening: to Avdotya, an old woman playing cards, the men are like wet hens. Lebedev finds the whole process unendurable in any case: to him, there's only one good man in the district, Ivanov, but he's married already and seems to have gone off his head. These people have formed an unsympathetic interpretation of Ivanov's marriage: most of them dislike him for having married a Jew, and assume he did so in order to secure her fortune, only to find her cut off by her incensed parents. The rumour is that Ivanov has already thrown Anna in the cellar and forced her to eat quantities of garlic – not only that, but he once infected a herd of his own cows to secure the insurance. Sasha defends him stoutly, claiming he's the victim of unscrupulous men like Borkin, and she urges the gossiping company to talk about something that might make them attractive themselves – at the moment, even the flies are bored to death.

Ivanov and Shabyelsky arrive (to Lebedev's delight, since all his other friends have been driven away by Zinaida's money-lending activities). Ivanov announces Anna's illness, but Shabyelsky pooh-poohs it; to him, tuberculosis was invented by doctors like Lvov wanting to get close to the chests of their female patients. Borkin arrives with fireworks for Sasha, hoping to light up her birthday as she lights up their lives. When Ivanov and Sasha are then left alone, he bewails his depression: he feels exhausted without doing anything, and guilty, but about what? Sasha recommends love, her love, but he does not want that either; she suggests they run away to America, but Ivanov feels he couldn't get as far as the door. It transpires that Ivanov owes the Lebedevs nine thousand roubles; when he asks Zinaida to defer the debt, she is scandalized that he is exploiting her. The guests drift back in from the firework display; starving and rebellious, they feel ready to eat their parsimonious hostess. Borkin pretends to broker a marriage between the lonely Babakina and the impoverished Shabyelsky, on which he will take commission. Sasha again declares her love for Ivanov and he kisses her; Anna arrives just in time to see this.

In Act Three, Borkin, Lebedev and Shabyelsky entertain themselves in Ivanov's study with vodka and cucumbers. They discuss the relative merits of the French and Germans, who are going to war, but really they are interested in how best to prepare mushrooms. Borkin continues to insist that Shabyelsky must marry Babakina, that it would be dishonourable not to, in fact. Lvov arrives, and the thought that Anna may be dying sobers them up. Kozykh, a card fanatic, passes through to tell them of his bad luck at his game; Shabyelsky is so bored that he threatens to shoot him. When Ivanov arrives, it transpires that Lebedev is really here at the insistence of his wife, to collect the interest on Ivanov's debt. Ivanov says he is completely broke, and Lebedev, embarrassed, offers him money of his own to pay off the loan. Once again, Ivanov expresses his loss of hope and idealism; stumped, Lebedev suggests a change of air, but realizes he is inadequate to deal with his friend's misery, and leaves. Ivanov now hates his own voice; even his hands and feet disobey him. It has taken only a year for him to become a man who feels he has betrayed the very land he owns, who runs in cowardice from a sick, pleading wife. Lvov comes on, the untried idealist again confronting the spent force; he accuses Ivanov of longing for Anna's death so that he can take up with Sasha. But Ivanov is familiar with Lvov's version of his story, in which his motives are completely materialistic: Lvov strikes him as over-confident, moralistic and ignorant. Sasha Lebedev arrives to invite Ivanov to visit them again; she turns out to be a better intellectual antagonist than Lvov, mocking the vague basis of Ivanov's guilt: after all, a man can't help falling out of love with his wife, and Ivanov hasn't been caught forging banknotes, for instance. Stung, he retaliates that their romance is like something out of a book – Sasha is the noble young girl who saves Hamlet (a character he despises), and he wonders why women are drawn to such men. But to Sasha, the more effort you have to make in love the better. Borkin arrives and to Ivanov's disgust recommends he marry Sasha; he is overheard by Anna, from whose eyes the scales have finally dropped. After five years without a word of reproach, she now utterly condemns Ivanov; he has no honour, he has lied to her and betrayed her, and now means to seduce Sasha to get out of his debts to Lebedev. Ivanov calls her a Jewish bitch and tells her she is going to die.

When Act Four opens, a year has passed and Anna is dead. Lvov is waiting in the Lebedevs' house for the marriage ceremony between Sasha and Ivanov: as uncharitably honest as ever, he is determined to unmask Ivanov and pitch him into hell. In passing, he demands Kozykh's opinion of Ivanov, and Kozykh declares him to be a bad card player. Lebedev and Sasha come in, and the unfortunate father has a new burden: how to explain to Sasha that her dowry has been reduced to counteract Ivanov's debt to Zinaida. In truth, Lebedev thinks Sasha should abandon the wedding; he is uneasy at the talk of scandal and at the age difference between bride and groom: the whole arrangement feels wrong to him. His doubts infect Sasha – she finds she is impatient with Ivanov, who never smiles at her, trembles physically and continues to ramble on about himself. But she will not cancel the wedding: it is her purpose in life to understand and save him. Shabyelsky, meanwhile, like a parody of Ivanov, is overwhelmed with self-disgust at the marriage he is contemplating with Babakina. Even though it is hardly the moment to remember her,

Shabyelsky is tormented by the memory of his duets with Anna; he begs Lebedev for money so that he can go to his wife's grave in Paris, and rejects Babakina. Ivanov demands a private talk with Sasha. He has seen grey hairs on his head, he says; Sasha has aged five years and probably only loves the idea of him, and so he wants to call off the wedding: he draws the line at destroying her life as he did Anna's. Lebedev begs Ivanov to think more simply – the ceilings are white, sugar is sweet, he and Sasha love each other. Lvov arrives to call Ivanov a scoundrel yet again. For a moment Ivanov feels young again and able to run away with Sasha, but equally suddenly runs to the side of the stage and shoots himself.

ᐒ About the play

If Chekhov had written nothing further for the theatre after *Ivanov*, he would probably still be remembered for this energetic and original study of a mind in crisis. While being comparable to *Platonov* – the play is again preoccupied with the state of mind of the eponymous hero to the exclusion of most else – it clearly marks an advance. Ivanov's tendency to repeat himself is presented as a symptom of his condition – which Chekhov was at pains to insist could be charted as scientifically as that of a clinical depressive, with its predictable peaks of arousal and troughs of apathy. The author's medical objectivity was now influencing his theatrical instincts, to the bewilderment of an audience more comfortable with stereotypes. Better still, the play rests on an unresolved ambiguity: while Ivanov's critics believe his neurosis to be selfishly circumstantial – having lost Anna's dowry, he is now looking for a new wife to get him out of debt – he himself regards his misery as an inexplicable and metaphysical thing, and the audience is uncertain which side to take.

Chekhov himself insisted on Ivanov's fundamental decency; he should be ardent and straightforward in contrast to the petty provincial society around him, with the courage not to excuse himself by means of comparisons with Hamlet.

His estate manager Borkin's lack of scruples is contrasted throughout with Ivanov's dispirited honesty. And the merciless socialist Lvov is a man prepared to throw a bomb under a carriage to prove a moral point: his cruel truth-telling is unfavourably contrasted with the candour of Anna and her husband's moral uncertainty.

There is political insight in the play as well: Ivanov is as common a name in Russian as Smith in English, and Ivanov stands as a kind of Everyman – like Platonov, a disillusioned intellectual in a period of reactionary stagnation after the reforms of Tsar Alexander II. Liberal idealists like Ivanov now felt betrayed and out of step. This was also a decade of deep anti-Semitism, with pogroms all over Russia; however, Chekhov's treatment of Anna Petrovna is markedly sympathetic by the low standards of the time.

Ivanov shows some of the economy and detail of Chekhov's later writing, and the characters are often idiosyncratic, comically subtle and morally ambiguous. For instance, Sasha Lebedev, whom Chekhov described as responding erotically to the whining of men rather than to their style, has an intelligence that matches Ivanov's. Uncle Shabyelsky, cynical, kind, self-despising and oppressed by Borkin's matchmaking, is a three-dimensional figure who anticipates Chebutykin in *Three Sisters*, just as the theme of the impoverished landowner anticipates *The Cherry Orchard*. The big set piece of the second act at the Lebedevs' can be both funny and revealing in the theatre, as can the gathering of Lebedev and his friends at the beginning of the third.

While preparing his new play (in ten days in the autumn of 1887), Chekhov boasted that there would be a punch on the nose at the end of each act; but because of his growing self-assurance, such melodramatic flourishes as the sudden suicide of Ivanov sit uneasily. He continued to tinker with the play for many years, perhaps conscious that it sits uncomfortably between an old form and a new. It is as if, seeing how Russian theatre needed to change, he was able to shift it only so far at this stage.

∾ In performance

Ivanov was premièred immediately, under-rehearsed, at Korsh's Theatre in Moscow on 19 November 1887 to a riotously mixed reception. (In this version of the play, Ivanov died of a heart attack.) At the request of the Alexandrinsky Theatre in Petersburg, the play was revived there in 1889, and Chekhov rewrote it extensively for the occasion; this time, it succeeded – not least perhaps because Ivanov now died as a result of the traditional gunshot. Although the play soon became popular in the Russian provinces, the Moscow Art Theatre never performed it during Chekhov's lifetime; his widow Olga Knipper finally played Anna Petrovna with them a few months after his death in 1904. After the 1917 Revolution the play was virtually forgotten in Russia until the 1960s.

Meanwhile, the great German director Max Reinhardt gave *Ivanov* its German première in 1920. English-speaking versions came more slowly; although the play had been swiftly translated in America, it opened in New York only in 1958. It received its London première in 1925.

It has gained in popularity, and claims have been made for it as Chekhov's fifth masterpiece. John Gielgud was particularly attracted by the play: he directed himself in the central role in 1965 at the Phoenix Theatre in London, with Yvonne Mitchell and Claire Bloom, and on Broadway the following year, before playing the part on British television the year after. Ivanov's compulsive repetitiveness makes demands on any actor, while his psychological complexity rewards them. Distinguished British players of the role have been Derek Jacobi (1972), directed by Toby Robertson; John Wood (1976), directed by David Jones; Alan Bates (1989), directed by Elijah Moshinsky; Ralph Fiennes (1997), directed by Jonathan Kent; and Owen Teale (2002), directed by Katie Mitchell.

The One-Act Plays

Chekhov's 'occasional' pieces – three classic one-act farces, a monologue and several other short dramas of varying quality, of which one was unfinished – generally belong to the late 1880s. He was still making his way in journalism and short-story writing. In the theatre, following the failure of *The Wood Demon* and only limited success with *Ivanov*, he felt more at home with these brief, and financially rewarding, 'vaude-villes', generally written at speed with specific favourite actors in mind: they poured out of him, he said, 'like oil from the wells of Baku'. Distrustful of the practices of the 'serious' theatre at this time, Chekhov certainly found great fluency in the one-act form. His obsessive protagonists, emotions at a pitch of farcical desperation and rebellious bodies afflicted with all manner of disorders, remind us of the essential buoy-ancy, energy and sheer sense of fun of the man who went on to write the great plays. Some of these short works, like *The Proposal*, *The Wedding* and especially *The Bear*, were imme-diately successful and have continued to be popular interna-tionally; others, like *The Evils of Tobacco* and *Swan Song* (which was performed by John Gielgud on British television in 1993 under the direction of Kenneth Branagh) are occa-sionally revived; the rest have remained virtually unper-formed.

On the High Road
(*Na bolshoi doroge*)
1884

Adapted from the story 'In Autumn' (1883)
Probably first performed at the Schaubühne Werkstatt,
Berlin, 1981

The action takes place in a wayside inn during a thunderstorm.
Savva, an old pilgrim, appears to be dying, though he dreams
of getting to Jerusalem first. Nazirovna and Yefimovna are
pious old women; but, as Savva says, there are sinners in the
world as well as servants of the Lord, so a selection of rogues is
lined up as well. These include a factory worker who plays the
accordion; a terrifying tramp, Merik, with an axe he has stolen;
and the innkeeper Tikhon. As the group bicker and argue
about the existence of ghosts and the value of women, Bortsov,
a ruined landowner, begs Tikhon for a drink. Tikhon refuses
him, though he is sufficiently frightened by Merik, who might
even be the Devil, to take his boots off for him. When Bortsov
finally gives Tikhon a gold locket with a picture of a woman in
it, the innkeeper relents. Coincidentally a traveller, Kuzma,
arrives and recognizes Bortsov as the son of his old master, and
he tells the story of Bortsov's life; he has squandered his inheritance for the love of the woman in the locket, who ran away
with her lover on their wedding night, and since then he has
hit the bottle. The story creates sympathy for Bortsov and
misogyny among the men in equal measure; they all buy him
drinks and he collapses, muttering to the girl in the picture. At
this moment a carriage breaks down outside and a lady enters
who turns out to be Bortsov's runaway wife, Mary. She is
horrified to see him and leaves, but not before Merik has
swung his axe at her. At this point, the play abruptly ends.

Chekhov wrote this one-act melodrama before *Ivanov*; it
briefly anticipates Maxim Gorky's far more successful and

full-length *Lower Depths* (1902). Although the motley group in the inn has a certain vitality, the plot is both unlifelike and theatrically predictable, the arrival of Mary and the final use of the axe being the most blatant flourishes. *On the High Road* was duly condemned by the censor of the time – ostensibly for its gloom, but more perhaps because a member of the landowning class is shown as a drunk – and the play remained unpublished until after Chekhov's death. Although virtually unperformed since, there was a Berlin production in 1981, played in a warehouse adjacent to the Wall separating East and West.

The Evils of Tobacco
(*O vrede tabaka*)

1886 (and revised until 1903)

First performed Korsh Theatre, Moscow, 1886

Ivan Nyukhin, author of minor scientific treatises, has been persuaded by his wife to deliver a lecture on the dangers of smoking, even though he is himself addicted to tobacco. At the outset he is distracted by a twitch in his eyelid which, he explains, began the very day his wife gave birth for the fourth time, on the thirteenth of the month – the date, he explains, on which she always does so. She runs a private boarding-school (at number thirteen in the street) and though she makes him teach most of the subjects, she calls him an imbecile and treats him like a servant. Nyukhin feels a complete failure, surrounded by seven daughters and a spouse so bad-tempered that his only chance of getting them married is by entertaining their suitors off the premises, at their aunt's, which also happens to be the only place where he can get a drink. When he drinks, Nyukhin dreams of escaping to the country and standing in a field 'like a tree, or a scarecrow'.

Inspired for a moment in his narrative, he tears off his coat and stamps on it; then, spying his wife waiting in the wings for him, he guiltily puts it back on. In closing, he begs the audience to tell his wife that his lecture has been good, declares briefly that smoking is a bad thing, and exits in tattered dignity.

Chekhov wrote this monologue, as he often did his shorter pieces, with a particular actor in mind, the alcoholic comedian Gradov-Sokolov. He continued to rewrite the play for the rest of his life; the version generally used now dates from 1903. Whereas the earliest text was strictly comic, full of farcical effects expressing Nyukhin's inability to make his speech, more of his inner character emerges in the more mature version: that of a man whose potential has been destroyed by an ill-advised marriage.

Swan Song
(*Lebedinaya Pesnya*)
1887

Based on the story 'Calchas' (1886)
First performed Korsh Theatre, Moscow, 1888

Perhaps anticipating the final dilemma of Firs in *The Cherry Orchard*, the hero of *Swan Song* is Svetlovidov, an old actor who has dozed off after drinking too much after a performance and awakens to find the theatre locked up. Unnerved – he has never been in an abandoned theatre at night – he is at first terrified to see a figure appearing like a ghost, but then recognizes it as Nikita, the prompter, and begs him to keep him company. This is no problem to Nikita, who, having no home, regularly sleeps in the theatre; Svetlovidov has no real home either, and no family. In fact, he blames himself for wasting his life on the illusory world of the theatre and now wishes he had married an early sweetheart who demanded that he change his profession. To illustrate his dilemma, Svetlovidov runs through sections of *Boris Godunov*, *King Lear* (with Nikita as the Fool) and *Hamlet*, momentarily feeling his old power and grace as an actor return. Self-hatred recedes, age and the prospect of death lose their sting for a moment; and with a final rendition of Othello's farewell to arms, he trails calmly enough off into the night.

Chekhov wrote *Swan Song* (in one hour five minutes, he claimed) as a vehicle for Vladimir Davydov, who had just played Ivanov for him in Moscow. *Swan Song* was in fact the more successful project; but Davydov was something of an ad-libber and, though a comic success, was in the end judged to have been too undisciplined a performer to do justice to Chekhov's poignant study of the actor's chronic position – the ability of his talent to give tragicomic dignity to a disappointing life.

The Bear
(*Medved'*)
1888

First performed Korsh Theatre, Moscow, October 1888

Even though he was unfaithful and a bully, Mrs Popov is in deep mourning for her husband, who died seven months ago. Her manservant Luka urges her to forget him and to get out and about; after all, when his own wife died, he only mourned her for a couple of months as that was all she was worth. At this point, Mrs Popov receives a visitor, the dyspeptic Smirnov, a local landowner who was one of her husband's creditors. Eager to pay off debts of his own, he is impatient for settlement from the widow; to make matters worse, he is a man who would rather sit on a powder-keg than talk to a woman. However, it swiftly becomes obvious that his misogyny is a mask: he admits that there have been twenty-one women in his life and he has fought three duels over them. He invites Mrs Popov to make a case for the female sex, and she is furious: when it comes to love, it is men like her husband who are the guilty ones. Smirnov mocks her, pointing out that the fact that she is in mourning does not prevent her from powdering her nose, but soon becomes sufficiently enraged to challenge her to a duel. In reality, however, her anger has attracted him, and he assures her that when the critical moment arrives he will fire his pistol in the air. In any case, Mrs Popov needs his advice on how to fire hers; he gives her a detailed lesson on firearms before declaring his love and proposing to her. Still in a fury, they fall into each other's arms.

The Bear ('a silly little French farce', according to Chekhov) was an immediate success all over Russia: when Chekhov travelled across Siberia in 1890, he found it hard to escape from performances of it. In time, it became so lucrative for him that he was tempted to re-name it 'The Milch-Cow'.

The Proposal
(Predlozhenie)
1888

First performed (for the Tsar) at Krasnoye Selo Theatre, 1888

Ivan Lomov, a landowner, is paying a visit to his neighbour Chubukhov: he wants to ask for the hand of Chubukhov's daughter Natasha in marriage. While Chubukhov goes to find her, we learn that as well as being hopelessly hypochondriacal – his ears buzz, his eyelids twitch and he has inexplicable pains as he tries to sleep – Lomov does not really believe in love. However, at thirty-five he feels he should be marrying someone. Natasha, who at first mistakes Lomov for a passing tradesman, chats pleasantly with him; but when he starts his proposal by making a reference to his and Chubukhov's adjoining land, he makes the mistake of describing a particular meadow as his own. A furious row breaks out between them about its ownership: this is only the latest example of a dispute that dates back to the time of Natasha's great-grandfather and Lomov's aunt's grandmother. The insults escalate – Chubukhov's family are called embezzlers and cripples and Lomov's alcoholics and adulterers. Lomov's rages are accompanied by palpitations of the heart and he leaves, distraught. However, Natasha's father has neglected to tell her that Lomov had called with marriage in mind; hearing this, Natasha has hysterics and demands he be called back. With great reluctance Chubukhov fetches Lomov, and Natasha is conciliatory, even admitting the disputed land may be Lomov's. However, the pair now fall out over the virtues of their dogs, and Lomov's complaints continue to be punctuated by aches and pains and dizziness; at one point, he sees stars and suspects that his shoulder may be falling off. Finally he collapses; terrified that he may have died, Chubukhov and Natasha are so relieved when he recovers that they agree to the wedding, which at least will mean that Chubukhov can be shot of him. As the bride and groom begin arguing about their dogs again, Chubukhov sees that they are well matched and drowns their argument with cries for champagne.

The Proposal, which Chekhov described as 'a rotten little vaudeville', is perhaps the most perfectly constructed and funniest of his farces. Interestingly enough, like the equally successful *Bear*, it is completely original, with no origin in an earlier short story.

A Tragedian in Spite of Himself
(Tragik ponevole)

1889

Adapted from the story 'One of Many' (1887)
First performed Moscow, 1889

Ivan Tolkachov arrives at the home of his friend Alexei
Murashkin weighed down with hat-boxes, a child's bicycle,
clothes, parcels and shopping bags. He begs for the loan of a
gun; he wants to put an end to himself. As Murashkin invites
him to explain, the play virtually becomes a monologue, in
which Tolkachov describes a typical twenty-four hours in his
life. He works alone in his office, as his secretary is on leave
and his staff on holiday; his clients are bad-tempered, and it is
a heatwave. When he leaves at the end of the day, he finds his
troubles have only just begun: he has to run errands for his
wife and neighbours, buying materials, complaining to the
dressmakers on her behalf, exchanging shoes she has bought,
collecting groceries and then being chased by the shopkeep-
ers when he forgets to pay. To remember everything, he has
five lists in his pocket and his handkerchief is strangled with
knots. How is he to fit the bicycle and the beer bottles into
the train and remember not to put the carbolic acid in the
same package as the tea? Sometimes he is turned off his train
for inconveniencing the other passengers. When he arrives
home, his wife drags him to the local theatre, and then to the
club to dance the quadrille, and he falls into bed only to be
tormented by mosquitoes and his wife's impromptu concerts
in the drawing-room. Up at six, he starts it all over again,
feeling like a psychopath who must have blood. He begs
Murashkin, if not for a revolver, then at least for a little fellow-
feeling, but all these tribulations have given his friend an idea:
perhaps Tolkachov could take a sewing-machine and canary
cage back to a friend who happens to be staying not far from

his home. As Tolkachov chases him around the table, as bloodthirsty as his mosquitoes, the curtain falls.

The Wedding
(Svad'ba)
1889

Adapted from the story 'Wedding with a General' (1884)
Probably first performed at the Vakhtangov Studio,
Moscow, 1920–1

The action of this particularly exuberant short play begins during the wedding reception of Dasha Zhigalov; her mother is being attacked by the groom for failing to include two lottery tickets in the dowry as agreed, and for not providing a general for the occasion. As the guests dance across the stage, we learn that Yat, a former suitor of Dasha's with the ability to offend everyone, is pursuing Anna Zmeyukin, a midwife with an exceptional singing voice, and that the bride's father Zhigalov is suspicious of newfangled inventions like electric lights, preferring 'something you can get your teeth into'. However, he is fascinated by the views of Dymba, a Greek confectioner, who claims that everything is better in Greece. As the party drinks to the couple's health, Yat declares that young men get married only for money, and that in this case the dowry is not up to much. Zhigalov begins his speech as father of the bride but seems unable to get his mind off Greece, inquiring whether there are good mushrooms there and demanding that Dymba make a speech too; fortunately this is interrupted by the news that the promised general is after all on his way, but that he is very old. This is Revunov, who, far from being a general, is of fairly low rank in the Navy and does not know the family – he has been secured by Nyunin, an insurance broker, on payment of a small fee.

Revunov is at first flattered by the family's attentions, but is soon critical of the bread and the sour herrings. Finding a sailor, Mozguvoy, among the company, he becomes nostalgic for his life on the high seas; he has to be dragged off the subject, and finally admits that his naval post was only the equivalent of that of a lieutenant-colonel in the army. The family accuses him of taking his twenty-five rouble payment for nothing, and he is insulted and leaves; Nyunin of course has pocketed most of the money. The reception struggles on, with Yat continuing to woo the asphyxiated Mrs Zmeyukin, the band playing and the best man struggling to be heard as the curtain falls.

Tatyana Repin
(*Tatyana Repina*)
1889

Probably unperformed

The wedding of Peter Sabinin and Vera Olenin is in progress. As the three priests, the acolyte and the choir intone their prayers for the Tsar and his family (and indeed for themselves), the congregation, which for unexplained reasons includes a group of actors, gossips about the looks of the couple and recent affairs in the town, while the bridegroom complains about the weight of the crown about to be put on his head. To his horror, he suddenly thinks he sees Tatyana Repin, whom he has deserted and believes dead, in the congregation; at the end of the service, rather than leaving with his bride, he wants to go and hold a requiem at Tatyana's grave. He is dissuaded and the procession leaves, the clergy complaining about the pointlessness of their work; then a woman in black who appears to have taken poison out of sympathy for Tatyana comes out from behind a pillar and writhes on the ground. The brief play ends with the comment that the rest is to be left to the imagination of Alexander Suvorin, Chekhov's publisher.

This cryptic note refers to the fact that Suvorin had written a melodrama (in Chekhov's view, anti-Semitic) based on the real story of an actress who had poisoned herself on stage; it had rehearsed and played in Moscow while Suvorin was overseeing the revival of Chekhov's *Ivanov* in Petersburg. This 'sequel' of Chekhov's, which has her haunting her lover's wedding, is more a private literary joke between the two men than a stageable play; but the counterpoint between liturgical intoning and the gossiping of the congregation is certainly effective.

A Jubilee
(Yubilei)
1891

Adapted from the story 'A Defenceless Creature' (1887)

Khirin, an elderly bank clerk, is writing a speech for Shipuchin, his chairman, to make to his board at the General Meeting on the bank's anniversary. The overexcited Shipuchin arrives and, despite the assistance Khirin is giving him, insinuates that the clerk is a wife-beater. Shipuchin admits that he, too, lives like a pig and a drunkard, but in his job appearances are everything; he is concerned that the old man may lower the tone with the felt boots and tatty jacket that he is wearing to keep out the cold. In general, though, Shipuchin is euphoric: knowing that his shareholders planned to honour him with the presentation of a silver tankard and a short address, he has taken the trouble to buy the tankard and write the address himself. He is interrupted by his scatterbrained wife Tatyana, who distracts him with chit-chat about her admirers, particularly a young suitor who has shot himself in the heart. He is further delayed by a woman called Mrs Merchutkin, who arrives to insist on job reinstatement for her sick husband and the repayment of a small debt he is owed, even though he is a civil servant and has no connection with the bank. When the deputation of shareholders arrives to start the presentation ceremony, they find Shipuchin and Khirin in despair, Tatyana insensible on the sofa and Mrs Merchutkin fainted away in Shipuchin's arms. After an attempt to read the speech Shipuchin has prepared for them, they decide to come back later.

Despite its promising premise, the play lacks real development, as if setting up a comic situation and escalating it to farcical frenzy were enough without a real narrative.

The Night Before the Trial
(Noch' pered sudom)

1891 (unfinished)

Unperformed

Alexei Zaitsev checks into a gloomy and ill-smelling inn on his way to the assizes, where he is to be tried for bigamy, forgery and attempted murder. If found guilty, he plans to turn to a trusty friend, his pistol; looking forward to using it with almost sensual pleasure, he conducts a short dialogue with it. He is interrupted by Zina, a young woman who is staying in the next room and complaining of bedbugs; Zaitsev offers her some insect powder and immediately imagines a 'wayside romance'; he hopes, by passing himself off as a doctor, to get into her room. When she seems to acquiesce, he is dismayed to find that Zina's husband Gusev is with her, and fails to notice that he sounds like a lawyer. Gusev, believing Zaitsev's medical credentials, invites him to examine his wife's chest and cure her cough. Zaitsev finds the wife quite amenable to this, but Gusev, complaining that this sort of frisson arises every time he takes his wife to a doctor, interrupts their progress. As Zaitsev prepares a farcical prescription for Zina, Chekhov's manuscript breaks off.

Apart from the fact that Zaitsev tends to address not the other characters but the audience in a series of clumsy asides, the incomplete play obviously suffers from the fact that the main story of his trial is never developed – regrettably, since there is a promising hint that Zaitsev may be about to meet Zina's husband in court.

The Seagull (*Chaika*)

A Comedy in Four Acts

1895

ᔆᕼ Characters

Irina Arkadina, *an actress*
Konstantin Treplev, *her son*
Pyotr Sorin, *her brother*
Nina Zaryechnaya, *the young daughter of a rich landowner*
Ilya Shamrayev, *Sorin's steward, a retired army lieutenant*
Polina, *his wife*
Masha, *their daughter*
Boris Trigorin, *a writer*
Evgeny Dorn, *a doctor*
Semeon Medvedenko, *a schoolteacher*
Yakob, *a labourer*
A chef
A housemaid

The action takes place on Sorin's estate

ᔆᕼ The story

There is to be a moonlit performance in the garden on Sorin's estate of a new play written by his nephew Konstantin: it will feature Nina, whom Konstantin loves. Among the audience will be Konstantin's mother Arkadina, together with her lover Trigorin, a successful writer. Also assembling for the performance are Sorin's steward Shamrayev with his wife Polina; their daughter Masha, who wears black and takes snuff; the poor local schoolmaster Medvedenko, who is in love with her; and the bachelor Doctor Dorn, whom Polina secretly loves. Konstantin's play seems unlikely to please his mother, an established actress: he tells Sorin in advance that he detests the artifice she lives by and that the theatre urgently needs new forms such as he hopes to provide. His play, which will report life not as it is but as it appears in dreams, will be performed without a backdrop apart from the view of the lake beyond the stage. When Nina arrives – with difficulty, since her father and stepmother disapprove of her association with these 'bohemians' – Konstantin's insecurity is aggravated by her admiration for Trigorin and her preference for conventional theatre. In the event, his play is disrupted by its inattentive audience and especially by Arkadina's noisy complaints: to her disgust, as Nina embarks on the opening monologue (in which she plays the 'universal world soul'), the Devil's red eyes are seen and there is a smell of sulphur. Furious at her interruptions, Konstantin stops the play, dismisses the audience and runs away. Sorin reproaches his sister for hurting her son's feelings, while Medvedenko feels it would have been better if Konstantin had written a play about schoolteachers. When Nina comes out to meet the audience, Arkadina encourages her to go on the stage professionally and introduces her to Trigorin, by whom she is wildly impressed. The company disperses, leaving Dorn alone. He is the only one to have seen some good in Konstantin's play, and, when he returns, urges him to continue writing; although Konstantin is grateful, he is more interested in finding Nina, who has gone home. As Masha arrives to persuade him to join the company inside, Konstantin rushes off in search of Nina; left alone, Masha confesses to Dorn, with whom she feels more comfortable than with her own father, her desperate love for Konstantin.

The second act also takes place in the garden, this time on a sunny morning. Dorn reads Maupassant and hums operatic airs; Arkadina deplores Masha's negativity compared to her own optimism and style; a little way out of sight, Trigorin fishes in the lake. Nina arrives, able to stay for several days as her parents are away. The only anxiety Arkadina feels is for Konstantin, who seems to be avoiding her. Nina has lost interest in him, too; only Masha enthuses about his wonderful sad voice and poet's eyes. The atmosphere is uneventful; Arkadina complains half-seriously about this 'sweet country boredom' and wishes she was in a hotel room learning her lines – which greatly impresses the aspiring Nina. Arkadina decides to go into town; but Shamrayev bluntly tells her he cannot spare her the horses as they are all in the fields, whereupon a row breaks out, with Arkadina threatening to go back to Moscow and Shamrayev to resign. Nina tells the audience how astonished she is to find the great figures of the theatre crying, fishing and losing their tempers like ordinary mortals. Konstantin confronts her with a seagull he has shot; he is heartbroken at her neglect and will soon kill himself in the same way. Nina is puzzled by his gesture, finding the new Konstantin moody and oblique, depressingly unlike the one she knew. Konstantin notices that at the approach of Trigorin, returning from his fishing, her face changes as if the sun had come out. He is right to be fearful: Nina is very taken with Trigorin, who now regrets that he and Arkadina have to leave the next day – he would have liked to stay and study Nina a little further, for literary reasons of course. To Nina, a life such as his is a glorious one, but he decries her admiration: the reality of the writer's work is that it is an exhausting obsession that makes it impossible to register the natural things of life without noting them for future use. Nina believes literary creation must bring extreme happiness; but to him it is associated with inadequacy and purposelessness. As they talk, he makes a preparatory note for a short story in which a young girl grows up by a lake, as happy as a seagull, until a man comes along and idly destroys her. This is a warning Nina is doomed to ignore. As Arkadina calls to Trigorin that they will after all stay another night, Nina declares 'It's a dream'.

The day of Arkadina's and Trigorin's postponed departure arrives. Konstantin has shot and wounded himself and even challenged Trigorin to a duel. Unperturbed, Trigorin sits alone at lunch and Masha joins him: she is now drinking vodka in some quantity. She confides that she is exhausted by her love for Konstantin and has decided to marry the faithful Medvedenko instead – a gesture Trigorin finds 'unnecessary'. Nina follows Masha on: unable to decide whether or not to become an actress, she gives Trigorin as a parting gift a medallion she has had inscribed with a line reference from one of his stories. They are interrupted by Sorin and Arkadina and have to postpone their farewells, but Trigorin hurries off to check the book reference. Brother and sister being about to part, Sorin ventures to advise Arkadina to give Konstantin some financial support – he has no overcoat and feels like the family parasite. Arkadina is extravagantly defensive; what little money she has she must spend on her stage outfits. Lacking the courage to pursue the argument, Sorin has a dizzy turn, and Konstantin arrives to help him away. Konstantin and his mother then confront each other. As she changes the bandage on his head-wound, they remember his childhood and begin to forget their animosities, but Konstantin is suddenly roused by the mention of Trigorin, whose success and effect on Nina he resents. They briefly quarrel, but in fact mother and son face trouble from the same source: Arkadina insists that once she gets Trigorin away, Nina will come back to Konstantin. Trigorin arrives with a copy of his book and Konstantin leaves in a hurry. Trigorin is astonished to find that the line Nina has referred him to reads: 'If you ever need my life, come and take it.' He immediately begs Arkadina to release him so that he can pursue Nina, but Arkadina wins him round with flattery and a show of dependency – he is her king, the last page of her life and Russia's only literary hope. Trigorin feebly promises to stay by her side and the household gathers for the goodbyes, Arkadina leaving the servants with a paltry one-rouble tip to share between them. After they leave, Trigorin returns to the house, ostensibly having forgotten his walking-stick; he finds Nina waiting for him. She has at last decided to go on the stage; excitedly, he gives her his address in Moscow and they embrace.

The fourth act starts two years later. The wind is howling in the chimney as a bed is made up in the sitting-room for Sorin, now an invalid. Masha has married Medvedenko, who is trying to persuade her to come home to their house, where their baby is about to spend his third night without her. However, Masha insists on staying where she is, implicitly to be near Konstantin, whom she still loves; her husband will have to borrow a horse from her father Shamrayev and go alone. With Medvedenko out of earshot, Polina urges Konstantin to pay more attention to Masha; she has learned herself that all a woman needs is 'the occasional kind look'. Wheeled in, Sorin reflects that his life could make a good subject for Konstantin's fiction, under a title such as *L'Homme qui a voulu* – he has failed at everything, even in his choice of a place in which to die. As usual, Doctor Dorn declines to treat him, advising him only that life has to end anyway; he prefers to discuss his recent trip to Italy, where he was delighted to be able to wander the streets freely as part of a crowd: this sense of community reminded him of the 'world soul' Nina spoke of in Konstantin's play. The talk turns to Nina, to whom speculation and some scandal has attached itself. Konstantin confirms that she ran away with Trigorin, who in due course made her pregnant; the baby died and Trigorin abandoned her. Her stage career has been undistinguished (she has never played in Moscow): she has a tendency to overact, Konstantin says, though Dorn believes that that at least shows some sign of talent. She has written to Konstantin quite often, but in distraught terms, signing herself 'the seagull'. However, he has always been obstructed in his attempts to meet her, even though she is staying at this moment in the town nearby: her parents will have nothing to do with her since the scandal. At this point, Arkadina arrives for a brief visit with Trigorin, who comes face to face with Konstantin. Trigorin urbanely commends Konstantin's literary work, saying that he is making quite a stir in Moscow and Petersburg, and presents him with a copy of a magazine containing Konstantin's latest story – though Konstantin will notice later that the relevant pages have not been cut open. The awkward moment passes off, though not before Trigorin tactlessly declares he would like to revisit the old stage in the garden where Nina and Konstantin did their play, as he has a new idea for a short story. Medvedenko meanwhile sets out for home without a horse, and a card table is set up for a game of lotto. With Konstantin gone, Trigorin confides that it is not really true that he is famous in Moscow, while Dorn reiterates his enthusiasm for the young man's work; then Shamrayev offers to show Trigorin the seagull that Konstantin once shot, which he has had stuffed, but Trigorin affects not to remember the incident. Trigorin wins the game and the company adjourns for supper. Alone, Konstantin laments his lack of literary progress compared to that of Trigorin, whereupon to his amazement Nina knocks on the window, very distressed. They barricade the door and talk. Nina has been tempted to come for days, but was afraid Konstantin would be angry with her. For a time, hope revives: when she saw the old stage in the garden, Nina felt a weight lifting from her heart, while Konstantin, whose life has been a misery since he lost her, still kisses the ground she walks on. But Nina's talk is disjointed: she again refers to herself as the seagull, recalling both Konstantin's shooting of the bird and Trigorin's idea for a short story that she has painfully lived out. Horrified by Konstantin's devotion when she feels so riddled with guilt, Nina suddenly prepares to leave: she has an engagement at a local theatre the next day. Konstantin begs her to stay. Suddenly Trigorin's laughter is heard from the next room. Nina explains that Trigorin's indifference to her ambitions made her lose faith, but that she still loves the theatre; she now knows that what matters is not success or failure, but simply the ability to keep going. The conclusive fact is that while missing Konstantin, she still loves Trigorin desperately. She recites some of Konstantin's old play, and leaves. For two minutes Konstantin remains alone, tearing up all his work, and then exits quietly as the company returns: as they prepare for more lotto, a gunshot is heard. Investigating, Dorn calmly tells Trigorin that a bottle has exploded in his medicine bag, but then in a whisper admits the truth: Konstantin has shot himself and Trigorin must somehow get Arkadina away.

➤ About the play

Despite the claims of *Ivanov* in particular, *The Seagull* is generally seen as the first of Chekhov's masterpieces for the theatre, one of the defining works of modern drama. It marks a conclusive break with the melodramatic traditions of Russian theatre (represented by Arkadina) in favour of a style in which characters fulfil their destinies while appearing to do little more than complain about the weather and fish; they reflect on their failures, play cards, suffer and rejoice in the unpredictable rhythms of life.

It happens that *The Seagull* displays an unusual preponderance of themes and characters drawn from Chekhov's own experience. These include the admirer who seductively directs her writer-hero to a line of his own work, a woman acquaintance of Chekhov's who suffered the same fate as does Nina at the hands of Trigorin, and an artist friend who shot himself out of disappointed love. Both writers in the play have teasing echoes of Chekhov himself, as does Doctor Dorn, the first of a series of medical men who echo some of Chekhov's own personality.

His determination had been to write a comedy set by a lake, with 'much talk of literature, not much action and several hundredweight of love', and the central relationships are refracted through the preoccupying themes of the theatre and literature. The play is indeed held together by an essentially comic pattern – a chain of unrequited passion in which virtually all the characters are in love with someone who loves someone else. There are quotations from *Hamlet* (as well as a typical struggle between son and mother) and from Maupassant, including the famous opening lines about Masha's black clothes. The attitudes to the theatre of the established actress Arkadina and the young aspirant Nina are continually contrasted, as are the literary ones of Trigorin, successful but contemptuous of his own work, and Konstantin, whose talent is unconfirmed but whose personal life is blighted by the loss of Nina. In some ways, this young dramatist's efforts echo those of the reforming Chekhov; while much of what Trigorin says also reiterates Chekhov's views, some of the lines attributed to him coming from Chekhov's own work. In fact, Chekhov, like Konstantin, was introducing his audience to a new kind of play – featuring such originalities as a suicidal hero who instead of making a dying speech leaves the stage to do the deed after two minutes of silence – even though he had not yet dispensed entirely with theatrical conventions. The traditional gunshot is there, but its interest lies largely in how Dorn and Trigorin will explain its meaning to Arkadina.

Each character develops in unexpected ways. Arkadina is a complex and self-contradictory figure, both egotistical and generous, loving and self-absorbed; Trigorin is self-critical but destructive with women; difficult as it is to assess the talent of Konstantin, it is easy to agree with his artistic complaints. The play's apparent victim, Nina, meanwhile, finds the strength to survive. Dorn, too selfish to treat his patients, is nevertheless astute enough to recognize Konstantin's talent and is much the most cosmopolitan character. Shamrayev, although a servant, is in control of Sorin and able to refuse everything he is asked to do in the line of his work. Sorin's cowardice, meanwhile, is balanced by the poignancy of his regret that he has achieved none of the things he hoped for – a literary career, talent at public speaking, marriage.

The tragic force of Nina's and Konstantin's final meeting – with its themes of displaced yet ineradicable love and the impossibility of recovering early hopes – has tremendous emotional power in the theatre. Meanwhile, the interplay of the surrounding small community, a group held together as much by circumstance as by family ties, self-regarding yet mutually supportive, is brilliantly done. The apparent inconsequentiality of much of the dialogue and the sense of life passing at its own speed can still be disconcerting. In its own time, Chekhov's play required both a new style of acting and a new kind of attention.

∞ In performance

The première of *The Seagull* at the Alexandrinsky Theatre in Petersburg on 17 October 1896 stands as one of the most remarkable fiascos in theatrical history. The play had been placed with this company for the occasion of a gala evening of several items celebrating one of its regular actresses: the audience was there largely for her rather than for the new play, in which she was not even appearing. Many of Chekhov's original touches – Masha taking snuff, Konstantin's ambiguous play and assault on himself, the tongue-in-cheek symbolism of the dead seagull – were interpreted as dramatic incompetence. Before long, the action was drowned by hissing and booing: Chekhov fled from the theatre, vowing never to attempt a play again, though in fact *Uncle Vanya* followed quite swiftly.

Triumphantly revived two years later by the new Moscow Art Theatre, *The Seagull* went on to be performed frequently in Russia (though far less often than the three later plays) and gradually found its way into the world repertoire – eventually attracting, like all Chekhov's work, the best directors and actors of each generation. Although this process was slow in some European countries – German writers found him difficult to translate, he was too pessimistic for the French and too refined for the Italians – the British theatre, partly due to the advocacy of George Bernard Shaw, reacted more swiftly. A production was mounted in 1909 at the Glasgow Repertory Theatre, but the play really caught the public imagination for the first time when John Gielgud played Konstantin in 1925. In 1936 the famous Russian *émigré* director Theodore Komisarjevsky – his prestige enhanced by the fact he had known Stanislavsky and was related to the actress who originally played Nina – revived it with an exceptional cast including Edith Evans, Peggy Ashcroft and John Gielgud, this time as Trigorin.

Chekhov's progress in the United States was hampered by inadequate translations which nobody wanted to stage; but the arrival of a (rather elderly) Moscow Art Theatre company on tour in 1923 alerted the American public, and the Russian-speaking actress Eva la Gallienne launched a Chekhov repertory season which included a 1929 *Seagull*. The play was taken up by Broadway in 1938, when Alfred Lunt and Lynn Fontanne starred as Trigorin and Arkadina.

Arkadina has been played in America by actresses such as Meryl Streep, Olympia Dukakis and Rosemary Harris, and in Britain by Susan Fleetwood, Joan Plowright and Judi Dench; Konstantin has been Simon Russell Beale, Kevin Spacey, Philip Seymour Hoffman and Peter McEnery; Nina, Vanessa Redgrave, Blythe Danner, Helen Mirren and Victoria Hamilton; Trigorin Robert Stephens, Jonathan Pryce and Christopher Walken. Max Stafford-Clark directed Thomas Kilroy's Irish adaptation at the Royal Court in 1991. Peter Stein brought his production, with Fiona Shaw and Iain Glen, to the Edinburgh Festival in 2003.

Uncle Vanya and *The Wood Demon*

Uncle Vanya is based on a far less successful experiment under-taken by Chekhov several years earlier. This was *The Wood Demon*, which he worked on while revising *Ivanov* and which then achieved an unsuccessful production at Moscow's Abramova Theatre in 1889 – not least because some of the audience imagined that the title promised a pantomime rather than a polemic on forestry. It is not clear when Chekhov decided to use *The Wood Demon* as the basis for *Uncle Vanya*, or indeed did the adaptation – possibly straight away or perhaps after the initial failure of *The Seagull* in 1896 – but a comparison of the texts reveals how far his stagecraft had developed in the meantime. Only half the characters of *The Wood Demon* survive in *Uncle Vanya*, where they are joined by the nanny Marina, a completely new creation; half the dialogue survives as well, but the fourth act is completely rewritten for the better – *The Wood Demon*'s Vanya figure, Yegor Voinitsky, had succeeded in killing himself at the end of the third. Astrov, while based on the 'Wood Demon' Mikhail Khrushchev, is purged of Khrushchev's moralizing tone on both ecological and amorous subjects; Khrushchev's love of Sonya – or indeed anyone else – is removed, and replaced in Astrov by a hint of dissipation, perhaps suggested by the character of young Orlovsky in *The Wood Demon*.

Rather than reiterating the elements shared by the two plays, the account of the earlier *Wood Demon* in this section simply indicates its differences, the features that Chekhov abandoned in developing *Uncle Vanya*.

Uncle Vanya
(*Dyadya Vanya*)

Scenes from Country Life in Four Acts

Probably 1897

❧ Characters

Alexander Serebryakov, *a professor, retired*
Yeliena, *his wife, twenty-seven*
Sonya, *his daughter by his first wife*
Madam Voinitsky, *a widow, mother of Serebryakov's first wife*
Ivan Voinitsky (Vanya), *her son*
Mikhail Astrov, *a doctor*
Ilya Telegin, *an impoverished landowner*
Marina, *an old nanny*
A workman
A watchman

The action takes place on Serebryakov's estate

❧ The story

Marina, the nanny in Professor Serebryakov's house, is in conversation with Astrov, a doctor in attendance on the family. Astrov complains of overwork, the dispiriting people he has to live among, his own declining health and even the length of his moustache; however, his real regret is that a patient has recently died on his operating table. They are joined by Voinitsky (Vanya), who manages the estate, just awake from a siesta but alert enough to complain bitterly about the disruption caused in the house by the recent arrival of Serebryakov and his young wife Yeliena, who now intend to live here permanently. Vanya detests Serebryakov for his meanness and hypochondria, and also believes his academic achievements are fraudulent – 'I pity the paper he writes on'.

However, his view is clearly influenced by his own attraction to Yeliena, as well as by his affection for his dead sister, who was Serebryakov's first wife. Vanya maintains that Yeliena owes it to herself to betray Serebryakov; but this very much upsets the local landowner Telegin (known as Waffles because of his pockmarked face). Reproving Vanya, Telegin remembers how his own wife ran away as soon as they were married, and how he has nevertheless supported her and her children by a new lover ever since: he has lost his happiness but kept his pride, he says, whereas his wife has lost her looks and her lover is dead. They are interrupted by the arrival of Yeliena, of Vanya's niece Sonya (Serebryakov's daughter by the earlier marriage) and of Vanya's mother, an admirer of Serebryakov who spends much of her time reading feminist pamphlets; she is irritated that by comparison Vanya has let himself go intellectually. It is obvious that Astrov has been summoned unnecessarily today – the professor has recovered after a bad night – and in any case he is now called away to the local factory. Before he goes, he invites Yeliena and her husband to visit his estate, and in doing so reveals his private passion – the area's threatened forests and wildlife. His enthusiasm is both spiritual and practical: millions of trees are falling to the axe simply because man is too lazy to bend down and take peat from the ground for his fuel. On his departure, Yeliena and Vanya are briefly left alone while Telegin plays his guitar: Yeliena faults Vanya for his rudeness and negativity, while Vanya criticizes her lassitude. Nevertheless, he loves her and begs to be allowed simply to look at her.

In Act Two it is after midnight in the dining-room, and Serebryakov complains to Yeliena of breathlessness and rheumatism, but even more that in his pathetic state he arouses only resentment – 'Don't worry, I shan't be with you much longer'. He feels that a career as distinguished as his should have earned him the right to more care and consideration, though in fact he receives a good deal. Yeliena is distressed by his carping, but Sonya, far too busy with haymaking to pamper him, is furious that he has once again called Doctor Astrov out for nothing. Serebryakov dismisses Astrov as incompetent in any case, and when Vanya arrives to relieve the women's vigil, Serebryakov sends him away too. The only person able to pacify the old man is Marina, who understands the difficulties of age and promises him lime tea and her prayers: he is suddenly much touched and goes to bed. Yeliena is in despair at the petty animosities prevailing in the house, but Vanya only wants to make love to her – when the storm that is raging subsides, he says, every living thing will revive except him without her affection. Since he is also a little drunk, Yeliena has some difficulty escaping him. Alone, Vanya rhapsodizes about her, regretting that he did not propose ten years ago: then they would be waking together in tonight's storm. Worse, he has spent his best years as a steward, virtually unpaid but making the estate reasonably profitable for Serebryakov, who once seemed to him an intellectual giant but is now a nonentity. Astrov arrives: he, too, has been drinking and is exuberantly self-confident: in this state, he feels he can perform the most difficult surgical operations and make great plans for mankind's future. He ridicules Vanya's 'friendship' with Yeliena, since to him a woman can only be a friend when she has already been an acquaintance and a mistress. Sonya, arriving, is angry with Vanya for drinking – his neglect of his farm work means she has to do everything – and she asks Astrov not to lead him on. Because of the weather, she then invites Astrov to stay in the house overnight and over bread and cheese he admits how much he disapproves of Yeliena's and Serebryakov's idleness. He, on the other hand, works harder than anyone in the district, with no comfort in view: disliking both the intelligentsia and the peasants, he feels affection for nobody, though he sometimes has a pang of desire for Yeliena. Sonya begs him to deepen his belief in himself, and quietly inquires how he would feel about being loved by a friend of hers, say, or a young sister: he is dismissive. In fact, Sonya is speaking for herself, and despite his disappointing response feels happy to have spent time with him, only wishing her looks recommended her to him more. At this point the beautiful Yeliena arrives. Tension has always simmered between stepdaughter and stepmother, and Yeliena wants to make it up. The fact is that she didn't marry Serebryakov for his money, but truly believed her love for him was real, though she now sees it was not. Her candour encourages Sonya to confess how much she loves Astrov. Yeliena is excited for her, and admits that she herself would rather have married a man of that age instead of allowing herself to become the 'unimportant character' she now is. She offers to celebrate their reconciliation by playing the piano for Sonya, but when Sonya goes to get permission from Serebryakov for this disturbance she returns empty-handed: 'He says no'.

Vanya's ridicule of Serebryakov continues at the opening of the third act, while the company prepares for a meeting the professor has called. As for Yeliena, she seems to Vanya to be about to fall to the ground through pure indolence; nevertheless he kisses her hand and promises to gather her roses. Sonya seems to share his conflicting feelings about Yeliena: despite their reunion, she criticizes her for neither working on the estate nor teaching or caring for the sick, but then she embraces her. Left alone with Yeliena, Sonya reiterates her love for Astrov and her regret that it is known to the whole household. Yeliena sees an opportunity to establish the true state of Astrov's feelings towards Sonya: she is about to meet him to look at the maps he has made of the district. Privately, Yeliena is sure Astrov does not care for Sonya, though he might be persuaded to marry her none the less; and her own position is complicated by her susceptibility to him. Astrov arrives with his maps, which demonstrate the decline of the local woodlands over the last fifty years – the disappearance, for instance, of the huge variety of birds that used to fly like solid clouds above them. There have been no new roads and railways that might justify man's spoiling, and no remission in the diseases he has to treat. He notices Yeliena's distracted face and assumes she is bored, though in fact she is preparing to ask him what his feelings are for Sonya. When she does so, he assumes she is covertly enquiring about her own effect on him, whereupon he propositions her frankly; as he moves in and kisses her, Vanya arrives with his bouquet of roses. A moment later, the company gathers for the meeting Serebryakov has called to propose the sale of the estate: he and Yeliena would like to use the proceeds to move nearer to St Petersburg. Vanya is incredulous – what will happen to himself, his mother and Sonya? In any case, he believes the estate belongs to Sonya in law since it was originally bought by his father as a dowry for his sister, Sonya's mother. As for his own inheritance, he gave it up to help his sister and has slaved for ten years without a word of thanks to pay off the mortgage. Confronted by his anger, Serebryakov seems prepared to adjust his idea, but Vanya is implacable; he denounces Serebryakov as a tyrannical fraud who has obstructed Vanya's potential to become a Schopenhauer or a Dostoyevsky, rushes out for a gun, fires it twice at the professor, but misses. The act closes with the company distraught, except for Marina, to whom the men are just cackling geese; she quietly comforts Sonya and recommends raspberry tea.

The fourth act opens the same evening, with Marina again, this time winding wool with Telegin. They both look forward to the departure of Serebryakov and Yeliena, who are going to live modestly in Kharkov, their plan for the estate abandoned. Telegin has taken the precaution of hiding Vanya's pistol in the cellar in case of further trouble; however, Vanya, furious and ashamed, has stolen a phial of morphia from Astrov in order to do away with himself. Succeeding where Astrov fails, Sonya recovers the morphia from him, persuading him to be patient and endure. Yeliena and Astrov bid each other farewell, but not before Astrov has again asked her to meet him in the fields, since she is sure to betray her husband one day and it would be better done with him now than with some stranger in Kharkov or Kursk. In any case, he says, it is time she and her husband left – the whole area has been infected with their idleness and nothing is getting done.

Amused by his effrontery, Yeliena kisses him in parting and claims one of his pencils as a keepsake. She and Serebryakov leave, Yeliena briefly kissing Vanya goodbye and Serebryakov delivering a short lecture to Astrov on the virtues of work; Vanya settles down to the estate's accounts with Sonya. After pausing for a glass of vodka and a moment's conversation – he is unlikely to be needed in the house again but is reluctant to leave it – Astrov also departs. Telegin comes in and gently tinkers on his guitar; Marina sleepily takes her place. Everything is quiet, but Vanya's sorrow and regret get the better of him. Sonya insists that life will go on; the two of them will patiently work for others for the rest of their thankless lives before inheriting a beautiful existence beyond death, under a sky bright with stars, calm and gentle as a kiss. Telegin's guitar continues, Vanya's mother makes notes in her pamphlets, Marina knits, and a watchman taps outside. The play ends with Sonya repeating to her uncle: 'We shall have peace'.

∽ About the play

Uncle Vanya, an undisputed masterpiece, marks Chekhov's near-final break with the theatrical orthodoxies of the past. Where *The Seagull* ended with a suicide, Vanya attempts a murder but farcically fails, and then bungles his plan to kill himself; there is one soliloquy rather than three; there are no self-conscious literary quotations and no discussion of the theatre. Chekhov is developing an entirely original style, in which tragedy and comedy seem not simply to alternate but to operate simultaneously; in which the characters continually gain, then lose, their audience's sympathy because of their failure to live up to their own ideals; and where a pervading sense of misery, frustration and broken hopes is expressed by the author with an energy that the characters cannot always feel for themselves.

New themes and methods are beginning to emerge: a dead person (Vanya's sister) lightly haunts the action, as equivalent lost figures will be sensed offstage in *Three Sisters* and *The Cherry Orchard*. Chekhov's growing technical skill is seen in two remarkable diminuendos: first as the chaos of Act Three resolves into Marina quietly comforting Sonya, and then by the musical effect of the four repetitions of 'They've gone' in Act Four as the household settles back into its routine after Yeliena's and Serebryakov's departure.

The characters' mutual isolation is symbolized by their complicated relationships, formally strong but emotionally sterile. Thus Vanya is Serebryakov's brother-in-law, but the reason for that, his sister, is dead; and Sonya is Yeliena's step-daughter though of the same generation. The familial links have become confusing and encumbering; and the complexity of the argument over the estate's legal status underlines the fact that this small group, stuck in out-of-date agreements and barely moving outside the house, feel their antipathies in an especially claustrophobic way.

Chekhov's sense of human contradiction, evident in Trigorin, Arkadina and Sorin in *The Seagull*, is now much extended. Vanya has let himself go in many ways, but when he first appears, yawning after his siesta, he wears a 'showy' tie, as if he has not quite relinquished some younger image of himself. He then complains constantly and bitterly, but keeps our sympathy because his all-too-human attack on the professor is so pathetically bungled. Meanwhile, Astrov, probably the most complex stage character Chekhov has achieved so far, might seem the mouthpiece for many of the author's own finer feelings, but he is also a heavy drinker, allowing himself to be interrupted in his great speech about forestry in Act One by the arrival of vodka, so that he never finishes his train of thought. He believes, implausibly but convincingly, that he is a better surgeon when under the influence; and for all his ecological passion he is incapable of loving a human being, though he brutally propositions Yeliena. Yeliena herself, condemned by Astrov as a 'virus of lassitude', nevertheless expresses great moral force in her reproaches to Vanya. She is almost blindly loyal to Serebryakov, but unsparingly critical of herself when she analyses how she came to marry him. Serebryakov is a bully and an egotist, but touching in his painful realization that he has worked all his life but now no one wants to hear a word he says. Telegin is ridiculous but moving as well when he speaks of his lifelong devotion to an unfaithful wife. On the other hand, two characters are unambiguously sympathetic. Sonya is so self-aware that she knows that it is only when a woman is as plain as she is that her hair or her eyes are complimented; the play's inspiring last words are left not to a dramatic seagull-turned-actress but to this least self-advertising, most easily overlooked character. Meanwhile, Marina counters all the crises in the disturbed household with patient wisdom and lime tea. She is the only one who knows how to nurse grown-up children: steady as a deep, quiet breath, she provides strategic common sense like a spring of water.

☙ In performance

Uncle Vanya took some time to reach Moscow: first, there was much discussion by the Imperial Theatres Committee, which included a number of university professors, of the desirability of staging a play in which a man such as them was fired at with a gun. Consequently, it initially became known in published form, before being played in the Russian provinces and finally entering history in the Moscow Art Theatre's triumphant production which opened on 26 October 1899. Stanislavsky played Astrov, with Olga Knipper, soon to be Chekhov's wife, as Yeliena. It has remained a permanent fixture in the repertoire, apart from a brief suspension around the 1917 Revolution.

The play travelled rapidly into Eastern Europe after an Art Theatre visit to Poland in 1906. In the United States, though translated in 1912, *Uncle Vanya* barely surfaced until Jed Harris mounted a Broadway production in 1930 with Lillian Gish as Yeliena; Gish returned to the play forty-three years later in the part of Marina under Mike Nichols's direction in a cast that included George C. Scott and Nicol Williamson. In 2000 Derek Jacobi played Vanya in New York, with Roger Rees as Astrov.

In England, a brief outing for the play in 1914 led George Bernard Shaw to want to tear up all his own work, and he became as fierce an advocate of Chekhov as he already was of Ibsen; and Theodore Komisarjevsky's London productions of 1921 and 1926 established the play as an attraction for major actors, particularly in the two male leads. Laurence Olivier played Astrov twice, with Ralph Richardson as Vanya in 1945 and with Michael Redgrave in 1962. Ian Holm, Albert Finney, Colin Blakely and Antony Sher have also played Astrov; Paul Scofield, Nigel Hawthorne and Peter O'Toole Vanya; Joan Plowright, Margaret Leighton, Alison Steadman and Imelda Staunton have been Sonya, and Helen McCrory, Rosemary Harris, Janet McTeer and Julie Christie Yeliena. André Gregory's open rehearsals of the play at the Victory Theatre in New York led to Louis Malle's successful 1994 film version *Vanya on 42nd Street*, with Wallace Shawn and Julianne Moore. Another film version, by Andrei Mikhalkov-Konchalovsky (1971), permanently captures the Vanya of the great Russian actor Innokenti Smoktunovsky.

The Wood Demon
(*Leshiy*)

A Comedy in Four Acts

1889

ᴄᴏ Characters

Alexander Serebryakov, *a retired professor*
Yeliena, *his wife, twenty-seven*
Sonya, *his daughter by his first wife, twenty*
Madam Voinitsky, *mother of the professor's first wife*
Yegor Voinitsky, *her son*
Leonid Zheltukhin, *a rich man, formerly a student of
    technology*
Julia, *his sister, eighteen*
Ivan Orlovsky, *a landowner*
Fyodor Orlovsky, *his son*
Mikhail Khrushchev, *a landowner trained in medicine*
Ilya Dyadin
Vasily, *Zheltukin's servant*
Simeon, *a labourer employed by Dyadin*

The action takes place in and around Zheltukin's estate and
Serebryakov's house

ᴄᴏ The story

The first act is set in the garden of the young and wealthy
Leonid Zheltukhin and his sister Julia, at a lunch party for his
birthday; he is fretful about his chances of attracting Sonya
Voinitsky and depends on Julia to make his case to her.
Together with the landowner Ivan Orlovsky, Yegor Voinitsky
(the predecessor of Vanya) and 'Waffles' (here called Dyadin
and much more garrulous than in the later play), they are
waiting for Serebryakov and Yeliena to arrive with Sonya,

Voinitsky's mother and Mikhail Khrushchev, known as the 'Wood Demon' because of his passion for the forests. As well as complaining bitterly about Serebryakov (whom he criticizes to his face from the outset) and about his mother and Yeliena, Voinitsky is censorious about his niece Sonya's seriousness – she is in this play a very much colder and more limited character, something of a blue stocking, and less loved by her uncle. The dissipated and somewhat alarming Fyodor Orlovsky now arrives, demanding champagne, closely followed by the rest. As Voinitsky and Khrushchev argue about the environment, Voinitsky is notably hostile to Khrushchev's position; when he then declares his passion to Yeliena, Fyodor and Sonya are present as well, playing croquet. Voinitsky is interrupted in these efforts not by Yeliena's determined rejection of him so much as by Serebryakov suddenly demanding her attention in the house.

When Yeliena attends to Serebryakov in the night scene that opens the second act, she is completely worn out and is blunter with him than in *Vanya* – 'Don't be such a bore'. Khrushchev arrives in time briefly to treat Serebryakov, and then, observing Voinitsky's wooing of Yeliena, delivers a moral lecture – Voinitsky shouldn't behave like this when he is related by marriage to her and while Sonya, a young girl, is living under the same roof. Fyodor Orlovsky arrives to drink with Voinitsky, but when Sonya joins them he runs off because he has no tie on (Astrov does the same thing in *Uncle Vanya*). Voinitsky also departs, leaving the stage free for Khrushchev's and Sonya's picnic. Tiresome as the professor is, Khrushchev, unlike Astrov, believes in him; he loves Sonya and would take her away, but Sonya is uneasy for reasons of class – she sees Khrushchev as some kind of reforming socialist, whereas she and her family went to exclusive schools. Khrushchev, stung by this, tells her that her snobbish wariness is making her old before her time – no doubt he will have to treat her gout one day. They part on uncertain terms; during the reconciliation that follows between Sonya and Yeliena, Yeliena, like Khrushchev before, comments on

THE WOOD DEMON 179

Sonya's 'calculating eyes' and urges her to trust people more; particularly, she should follow her heart, which is leading her towards Khrushchev.

In the third act, the meeting which leads to Voinitsky's outburst against the professor is delayed by inconsequential matters, and there is no meeting over the maps between Yeliena and the Wood Demon (a brief version of this appears in Act Four). As this act starts, Yeliena is playing Tchaikovsky on the piano offstage, Sonya is dragging round the house thinking of nothing but Khrushchev, and Voinitsky is simply bored; however, Fyodor (dressed as a Circassian) tells him he does not know the meaning of the word and recounts how in his army days sheer tedium led him and another captain nearly to kill each other with sabres. Next, Fyodor bluntly propositions Yeliena but gets his face slapped, and Julia, who loves Fyodor, arrives with her brother on business. Serebryakov's decision about the estate leads to different consequences: Khrushchev arrives to complain to Serebryakov about the latter's sale of a forest of a thousand precious trees for timber – he is as outraged as Voinitsky, all the more so for being called a madman by the professor. Sonya tries to restrain Khrushchev, but his contempt for her family will not let him stay in the house, despite his love for her, and he storms off. At this moment a shot is heard – Voinitsky has killed himself.

In the absence of Voinitsky, the fourth act takes a completely new direction. The action moves to a third location, a nearby forest, to the home that Dyadin rents from Khrushchev; it is a fortnight later, and Yeliena is staying there as a halfway house in her plan to leave Serebryakov – though Dyadin believes she will ultimately return to her husband. Julia arrives to announce the approach of her brother and Serebryakov, who is staying with them rather than in his house, which feels haunted now that Voinitsky has killed himself. It appears that Dyadin is keeping Yeliena's presence a secret, certainly from Julia and Khrushchev, who now arrives to do some painting, in a poor humour with everyone, including himself. The reason is that he has seen Voinitsky's diary and realized that the assumption he shared with all the local gossips that Voinitsky was sleeping with Yeliena was unfounded. The rest of the company assemble, trying to put the tragedy, for which they feel partly responsible, behind them with a sociable evening, but as Zheltukhin repeatedly says, there is tension in the air. Yeliena reveals herself, and Serebryakov initially rejects her; she is at first unwilling to accept her old role as the submissive wife in any case, but soon capitulates to him. Khrushchev, still deeply dejected about his failure to save Voinitsky and about the spiritual health of the company, has rushed off to attend a fire which is burning down a nearby forest, but immediately returns, and Sonya declares her love to him. Fyodor proposes to Julia and is accepted, and the meandering act resolves itself in a perfunctory happy ending very much in contrast with the tragic earlier events; Khrushchev and Sonya, as well as Fyodor and Julia, are paired off.

∽ About the play

Throughout its composition and performances, critics, friends and theatre committees thought *The Wood Demon* tedious and untheatrical, little more than a short story in another form. Its mixture of bluntly expressed animosities, melodramatic confrontations and fragmentary episodes certainly compares badly with the play that would be built on its ruins. Chekhov himself refused all further productions of the play after the first and would not allow it to be published in his lifetime, the first resolve no doubt due to his plans for revision, and the second to the spectacular way in which *Uncle Vanya* obscured its memory.

Many of the faults of *The Wood Demon* are obvious: the unstageable variety of its settings, an overpopulated yet uneventful first act (almost like a series of tableaux vivants) and the similarly plotless first half of the third act. Also, too many changes of heart depend on old-fashioned devices such as the diary exonerating Voinitsky that Khrushchev discovers. Many characters barely earn their keep in the play (*Uncle Vanya*, by contrast, has the smallest of Chekhov's casts) and the happy ending is so unconvincing that it might be a parody. But some sections are startlingly alive, and end up almost unaltered in *Uncle Vanya* – the night scene in the second act particularly, and much of Serebryakov's meeting in Act Three. Chekhov's characteristic counterpoint of the small things of life with its great crises is already present; and it is also possible to sense his concern for the environment, even though Khrushchev is far more preachy on the subject than Astrov will be – Chekhov was a little influenced by the reforming Tolstoy at the time of the earlier play. In fact, *The Wood Demon*'s sheer unevenness is its most disconcerting feature, as if it were being written alternately by a theatrical novice and a master dramatist in full bloom.

ᐒ In performance

After its initial failure at the Abramova Theatre in Moscow on 27 December 1889, *The Wood Demon* lay unperformed in Russia until it was revived in Moscow in 1960. It did little better then, nor in a further Moscow revival in 1993.

The English-speaking world was a little less respectful of Chekhov's wish to bury the play. In Britain, the Actors' Company presented it in 1973 with Ian McKellen and Edward Petherbridge, and it was shown on BBC TV the following year with Ian Holm and Francesca Annis; a further stage revival surfaced at the Playhouse in London in 1997, in a translation by Nicholas Saunders and Frank Dwyer which had received its world première at the Mark Taper Forum in Los Angeles in 1993.

Three Sisters (*Tri Sestri*)

A Drama in Four Acts

1900

Ꮿ Characters

Andrei Prozorov
Natasha, *his fiancée, later his wife*
Olga }
Masha } *his sisters*
Irina }
Fyodor Kulyghin, *a schoolteacher, Masha's husband*
Lieutenant-Colonel Vershinin, *battery commander*
Baron Tusenbach, *a lieutenant*
Vasily Soliony, *a captain*
Doctor Chebutykin, *army doctor*
Second Lieutenant Fedotik
Second Lieutenant Rode
Ferapont, *an old man, caretaker at the county council offices*
Anfisa, *a nanny, eighty years old*

The action takes place in a large provincial town

Ꮿ The story

The three sisters of the title are the daughters of General Prozorov, who died exactly a year before the opening of the play. This anniversary is a bright spring morning and also the Saint's Day of Irina, the youngest, and they are entertaining officers from a brigade stationed nearby under the command of Lieutenant-Colonel Vershinin. Vershinin is viewed by his colleagues with respectful amusement: Lieutenant Tusenbach warns the sisters that as well as displaying a philosophical turn of mind when he arrives, he may bore them with tales of his two little daughters and his wife, who frequently attempts suicide. However, Tusenbach himself tends to philosophize: in his view, Russia is about to be transformed, its idleness swept away and all its citizens usefully employed. His enthusiasm is shared by Irina, who at twenty dreams romantically of a return to Moscow, where the family used to live, and of a life of useful work, though at present she lies in bed for most of the morning. For this she is teased indulgently by Chebutykin, an old army doctor who lodges in the house, and who, it transpires, was in love with her mother. He claims not to have opened a book since he left university, preferring to pass the time making notes of what he reads in the newspapers, or on this occasion presenting Irina with a samovar as a Saint's Day present, a tradition usually reserved for a married woman.

The arrival of Vershinin causes great excitement, especially as it transpires that he served in the brigade commanded by General Prozorov before he left Moscow: Vershinin knew the sisters as little girls and even lived on the same street for a while. Inspired by meeting them again, he begins to speak philosophically, just as Tusenbach promised, speculating on what view future generations will take of the present. The sisters are impressed: they and their brother Andrei still think of Moscow as home and long to return, though this will be difficult for Masha, the middle sister, who is married to a local schoolteacher. She, however, is especially affected by Vershinin: she decides to stay for lunch rather than going home as she intended. Andrei, who has been playing the violin in the next room, is reluctantly brought in to meet Vershinin: he has fallen in love with a local girl, Natasha, whom his sisters regard as common, and is being mercilessly teased by them. When Andrei denigrates the education his father has forced on him, Vershinin eloquently reproaches him – it is only cultured and intelligent people like him and his sisters who can change society for the better. Introducing the subject of his wife and daughters at last, he is immediately interrupted by the arrival of Masha's husband Kulyghin, who presents Irina with an even less attractive present than a samovar – a book recounting the history of the local school, which in any case he gave to her last Easter. Kulyghin is in high spirits, though inclined to pepper his talk with Latin tags; however, Masha is plainly tired of her role as a provincial schoolmaster's wife. As the company begins to move off for lunch, Tusenbach declares his love to Irina, to her discomfort. At the last moment Natasha arrives, nervous of her reception by the family; Olga, the eldest of the sisters, tells her that she is wearing an inappropriate belt. At lunch, Natasha is teased by the company about Andrei and runs from the table: Andrei follows her and asks her to marry him.

By the beginning of the second act, Andrei and Natasha are man and wife and have a small son, Bobik; it is night-time and Natasha is worried about the baby's health, the untidiness in the house and the imminent arrival of a Shrovetide carnival party. Andrei pays little attention, and when the old servant Ferapont arrives with papers for him to sign (he is now secretary of the local council), he admits that he regrets having sacrificed his academic training for a lowly job and unhappy marriage. Ferapont, however, is deaf – although this does not prevent him responding to Andrei's enthusiasm about Moscow's restaurants by telling random anecdotes about the city, even though it hasn't been 'God's will' that he should see it himself. Masha and Vershinin arrive, Masha complaining about her life as it is; she misses the old days and declares that the most civilized people in the area are the military. Vershinin frets about his children being in the hands of his wife – although it is now twelve hours since he left them with her and he hasn't troubled to go back. He is increasingly drawn to Masha as the only woman who can understand his predicament; soon he is professing love to her, and she is responsive. Irina and Tusenbach arrive; he, too, is full of love, but Irina is out of sorts – she has been unaccountably rude to a bereaved woman who wanted to send a telegram from the post office where she now works. Irina plays patience; Doctor Chebutykin reads his paper while Tusenbach and Vershinin settle in for an evening of philosophical talk. Vershinin believes that though the present generation can expect no happiness, it will come in the distant future; Tusenbach thinks that life does not change any more than do the cranes who fly south in the autumn. Natasha regales the company with talk of her Bobik, but they are barely interested; the taciturn and misanthropic Captain Soliony declares that he would be inclined to cook the child in a frying pan and eat him. Suddenly Vershinin is called away; his wife has attempted suicide again. Tusenbach makes a serious effort at conversation with Soliony, who admits that he feels awkward in company, though he is fine when alone. A silly argument breaks out between Soliony and Chebutykin about Caucasian recipes; to save the evening, Tusenbach plays the piano and the company starts to dance, only to be stopped by Natasha, worried about her sleeping baby. They decide to go into town for entertainment (Andrei and Chebutykin in order to gamble); when they are gone, Soliony declares his love to Irina, which frightens her as he threatens to kill any rivals. Natasha suggests to Irina that she should move in with Olga so that Bobik can have Irina's room; when she is then invited out for a coach ride with Protopopov, chairman of the local council, she decides to do so 'just for a quarter of an hour'. Vershinin returns to find the company dispersed; he pursues them into the town, and Irina is left alone with her dreams: 'Moscow, to Moscow!'

In Act Three a fire has broken out nearby; it is past midnight, and the house is open to anyone whose home has been burned. Olga's bedroom is now shared by Irina, as Natasha suggested, but it is currently a thoroughfare. The old nanny Anfisa is terrified that she will be thrown out of the house; Olga reassures her, but then Natasha arrives and shouts at her for sitting down to rest. She cannot grasp why Olga keeps the old servant in employment: Olga and Masha are too exhausted to do anything but mildly demur. Kulyghin arrives, looking for Masha, and parks himself, followed by Chebutykin, whose response to the disaster has been to get roaring drunk.

Talking to himself, he is disgusted by his ignorance, and haunted by his negligence in recently letting a patient die. Meanwhile, Irina, Tusenbach and Vershinin discuss putting on a concert in aid of the victims of the fire; at the suggestion that Masha could play the piano, Kulyghin becomes fretful that this might not be a seemly thing for his wife to do. Chebutykin, still drunk, shocks the company first by breaking a china clock that belonged to the sisters' mother and then by blurting out that Natasha is having an affair with Protopopov. Vershinin, affected by the sight of his children in their night-shirts during the fire, reflects on the wretchedness of the present compared to the future. Second Lieutenant Fedotik arrives, laughing uproariously that everything he owns is lost; Soliony is offended that the Baron is allowed in the room with Irina but he is not; Vershinin and Masha provocatively hum snatches of opera to each other; Tusenbach pleads with Irina to come away and embark on a working life with him. Suddenly Masha bursts out that Andrei has mortgaged the house to pay his gambling debts; but Irina is more distressed at the scandal surrounding Natasha and Protopopov. Masha tells her sisters how she loves Vershinin, but they do not want to hear about it, least of all now. Andrei, who had retired to his room to play the violin, arrives to explain how it is that he mortgaged the house without their permission; trying to brave it out, he breaks down at the loss of his sisters' confidence. In fact, exhausted by the continuous traffic through their room, they have withdrawn behind their screens – except for Masha, who hears Vershinin calling to her in code and goes to him. Kulyghin bursts in, still looking for Masha and increasingly insecure. As things settle, Irina quietly accepts Olga's advice to marry Tusenbach, on condition they all try one last time to go to Moscow.

Now (Act Four) the brigade is leaving for Poland, all except for Chebutykin, who is following a day later. Forgetting any differences, the company stand on the porch, toast each other with champagne and take photographs. It comes to light that Soliony and Tusenbach have quarrelled and there is

to be a duel, about which Irina is extremely anxious; she and
Tusenbach are to be married the next day, before going to
work in the local brickworks. Kulyghin has shaved off his
moustache, perhaps to fall in line with his headmaster's current style, perhaps in an attempt to attract his wife. As he
talks, he never mentions her relationship with Vershinin,
though he knows she is even now waiting to say goodbye to
him. As Andrei passes, wheeling baby Sofya in his pram,
Chebutykin advises him to pack his bag and never come back.
On his way to the duel, Tusenbach, feeling that he is seeing
the fir trees and birches for the first time, movingly repeats
his love for Irina, though he knows she does not return it;
Irina assures him of her loyalty even though her heart is like
a piano whose key has been thrown away. He begs her to 'say
something' to him, but she can't; finally, he asks her simply to
arrange some coffee for him on his return. When he is gone,
Andrei suddenly finds his voice: what has happened to his
aspirations in life, now that he lives in a town in which there
is not a scholar, not an artist, and where the inhabitants do no
more than drink, gossip, sleep and die? He finally manages to
visualize a beautiful future in which his children are liberated
from this endless round of roast goose and cabbage; but
Natasha interrupts him – he is disturbing the baby. Olga
arrives with the nanny Anfisa, one person who has benefited
from events; she now lives in the local school where Olga
teaches, with a room and bed of her own. Vershinin and Olga
fill the time with uneasy conversation till Masha arrives,
whereupon she and Vershinin embrace. A moment later,
Vershinin is gone, his place taken by Kulyghin, trying to
entertain his heartbroken wife with a beard and moustache he
has confiscated from one of his pupils. He assures her that
their life will go on as before. Natasha, too, outlines the
future: Andrei will be moved into Irina's old room to make
more space for the children, and she will cut down the maples
and fir trees. Before making her final exit, she criticizes Irina's
choice of belt, as Olga once faulted hers. Chebutykin, who
has officiated at the duel, arrives and whispers to Olga that

Tusenbach has been killed. As the band plays for the brigade's departure, Olga brings the bereaved Irina and heartbroken Masha together; one day, their pain will be understood and even enrich the lives of others; one day, they themselves will know why they live and suffer. The band plays on, while Chebutykin, pretending indifference to everything, continues to mutter a characteristic little rhyme: 'Ta-ra-ra-boom-de-ay, I'm sitting by the road today'.

ᏟᎭ About the play

Three Sisters is the only one of his major plays which Chekhov described as 'a Drama', rather than 'a Comedy' (*The Seagull*, *The Cherry Orchard*) or 'Scenes from Country Life' (*Uncle Vanya*). Despite its characteristic humour, the prevailing tone of this great play is indeed tragic.

Much of this has to do with a nagging sense of displacement. The military are *en route* through the town towards another posting, and the sisters live here but long to be elsewhere. Chekhov visualized the location as something like Perm in the Urals, seven hundred miles from Moscow and barely within reach by railway at that time – so it might as well be Siberia. Only the two truly local characters, Kulyghin and Natasha, are fully adapted to their habitat – she with a ruthless determination to look after her own interests and what she sees as those of her children, he treating his wife's affair with a determined toleration which is both moving and fanatical. The rest, uneasy in time as well as place, either hanker after the past or long for an imagined future; but both of these are burdens, the future emphasizing the poverty of the present, and the past, in the form of General Prozorov, paralysing his children.

Chekhov once said that the true meaning and drama of a person's life lies inside, not in outward events, which he generally saw as random accidents; and in reality the sufferings of the Prozorov family are not geographical but a consequence of their own obsessions. The frustration of their hopes of returning to Moscow seems tragic to them, but in reality they are the victims of their affections – Masha's love for the itinerant Vershinin; Irina's acceptance of the kindly Tusenbach, doomed to be destroyed by his devotion; Andrei's failure to foresee the consequences of marrying Natasha, to whom he has been drawn as an escape from his family's expectations. All these misfortunes eventually result in some self-knowledge, giving the play the depth of tragedy – Andrei finally finds his voice, and Olga, emotionally imprisoned for much of the action, finds the strength to sustain her sisters in its deeply moving final moments. For other characters there is less hope. Chebutykin has isolated himself through intellectual idleness and a general refusal to engage; alcohol opens his eyes to himself, but still he ends as he began, almost criminally indifferent to everyone except Irina, whom, significantly, he treats as a daughter. Kulyghin has nothing to look forward to and has perhaps learned little by the end, for all his efforts to hold on to Masha. Vershinin will presumably do the same thing again elsewhere; Tusenbach is dead. These last two characters provide the broader frame in which Chekhov sets all the intimate events. They long for a future Russia in which people will understand why they live, but their own actions belie their idealism: Tusenbach's love for Irina leads him to a pointless death in a duel, while Vershinin breaks Masha's heart and leaves.

Chekhov's great sense of ambiguity means that the audience's sympathy continually flows towards and away from his protagonists. Even the 'villain' Soliony is not without dignity. The inadequacy of the three sisters to deal with life is initially poignant, but we gradually see that their hopeless nostalgia masks a degree of snobbishness – as in their unkind reception of Natasha at the lunch party, and the feebleness of their protests later at her cruelty to Anfisa. But while we criticize them, Chekhov ensures that we maintain our affection and respect for what they think they want. Significantly, their yearning is discredited by a particularly unreliable witness – the destructive Vershinin, who declares that once they get to

Moscow they will not notice anything special about it. He may be right, but it is difficult to like him for pointing it out. Natasha's revenge on the sisters' exclusiveness is in any case thorough and lifelong: she takes over their house and emasculates their brother. If the Prozorovs represent a superannuated past, Natasha looks forward to a new world, a more Soviet one perhaps – more efficient, less sentimental, but much reduced in spirit.

Chekhov matches his insights with technical mastery, including the subtlest counterpoint. At the play's opening, Irina and Olga announce their longing for Moscow, but at the same moment our eye is caught by Tusenbach and Chebutykin drifting in, talking about something else:

Chebutykin: Not at all, not at all.
Tusenbach: Certainly, that's rubbish

and later the girls' yearning is implicitly contrasted with old Ferapont's stoical acceptance of why he never got to Moscow:

It wasn't God's will.

The play is also dotted with moments of great terseness: Chekhov senses the theatrical power of a single word in the right place. At the start, Masha's dawning interest in Vershinin is expressed by no more than the removal of her hat and a simple interjection, as funny and serious as in life:

I'll stay to lunch

and near the end, Andrei, torn between the loneliness of bachelorhood and the solitude of his marriage, expresses his turbulence with the utmost simplicity:

A wife is a wife.

Chekhov is also in full control of the diminuendo effect he attempted at the ends of *The Seagull* and *Uncle Vanya*. After the fire in Act Three, individual importunacies keep breaking in without destroying a gradual return to life's normal rhythms. Confessing her love for Vershinin, Masha starts a forward pulse just as everyone is ready for bed: with the same inappropriate energy, Andrei arrives to justify himself, blustering and then breaking down in front of three blank screens. The drunken doctor bangs on the floor. All these crises flare up and relapse while time ticks on, undisturbed. Finally, Irina reveals that the army is leaving and calmly decides to marry Tusenbach: she is the only one carefully taking her own pulse, as if she knew that it is only when one does so that big decisions can be quietly and clear-sightedly made.

∽ In performance

Three Sisters was premièred at the Moscow Art Theatre on 31 January 1901 and, though greeted cautiously by the critics, succeeded with the public, many of whom soon referred not to going to a performance of the play but to paying a call on the Prozorovs. For the first time, Chekhov was writing for actors he knew, and with whom, through his relationship with Olga Knipper, he was deeply involved, and this may be a reason for the play's surefootedness. Certainly the opening production extended the Moscow Art Theatre's reputation to Petersburg and made Chekhov a great deal of money.

There was a relatively quick response outside Russia; as early as 1907, a production in Prague was based closely on the style of the Art Theatre, although the play was not subsequently performed there for twenty-five years. The German première was in 1926 in Berlin; the most famous Berlin production, however, is probably Peter Stein's at the Schaubühne in 1981, meticulously detailed in the Stanislavskian manner.

Three Sisters reached Broadway with Katharine Cornell and Judith Anderson in 1942. Lee Strasberg's controversial 1963 Actors Studio production (Kim Stanley, George C Scott) was booed in London, though popular in New York. In England, the play appeared briefly at the Royal Court in 1920, but it was Theodore Komisarjevsky's 1926 production at the tiny Barnes Theatre that made its name – despite some brutal changes made to the play by the director in an unnecessary attempt to make it easier for English audiences. Thus, the Russian names were much simplified and all references to Tusenbach's plainness were cut to allow an unwilling John Gielgud to play up to his romantic image. Gielgud went on to play Vershinin in Michel Saint-Denis's legendary 1938 production, with Michael Redgrave (Tusenbach) and Gwen Ffrangcon Davies (Olga).

In 1967 Laurence Olivier brought the great Czech designer Josef Svoboda to the National Theatre to work on a production in which he was playing Chebutykin. Janet Suzman played Masha in Jonathan Miller's 1967 version; Trevor Nunn directed an RSC cast in 1979; Mike Alfreds memorably presented the play in 1986 with his own company, Shared Experience. In 1988, at the Donmar Theatre in London, Mustapha Matura reset the action in the Caribbean as *Trinidad Sisters*. Cyril Cusack and three of his daughters played in Adrian Noble's production in Dublin and London in 1990: in the same year, the Georgian director Robert Sturua had three of the Redgrave family as the sisters in the West End. In 2003, Michael Blakemore directed Kristin Scott Thomas, Douglas Hodge and Eric Sykes as Masha, Andrei and Ferapont at London's Playhouse Theatre.

The Cherry Orchard
(*Vishneviy Sad*)

A Comedy in Four Acts

1903–4

∽ Characters

Lyubov Ranevskaya, *a landowner*
Anya, *her daughter, seventeen*
Varya, *her adopted daughter, twenty-four*
Leonid Gaev, *Ranevskaya's brother*
Yermolai Lopahin, *a businessman*
Petya Trofimov, *a student*
Boris Simeonov-Pishchik, *a landowner*
Charlotta Ivanovna, *a governess*
Simeon Yepihodov, *the estate clerk*
Dunyasha, *a maid*
Firs, *a footman, aged eighty-seven*
Yasha, *a young footman*
A Passer-by
The Stationmaster

The action takes place on Ranevskaya's estate

∽ The story

It is May; the blossoming cherry trees are just visible at day-break as Lopahin and Dunyasha prepare for Ranevskaya's return home after five years abroad. To his annoyance, Lopahin has fallen asleep and failed to meet her at the railway station as he had hoped – he has been fond of her since he was a boy, and specially remembers an occasion when, beaten by his serf father, he was looked after by her. At that time he was her 'little peasant'; now he is rich, but unsure of himself: in his white waistcoat and yellow shoes, he feels like a pig in a sitting-room. Led by the ancient manservant Firs, muttering to himself, Ranevskaya's party appears – her daughter Anya, the governess Charlotta and manservant Yasha, together with her brother Gaev and her adopted daughter Varya, who have been to the station to welcome her. Ranevskaya is delighted to be back in what was once her nursery; we learn from Anya that she has been living far beyond her means in Paris, surrounded by bohemians. Now she is coming home to the prospect of having to sell off the estate to pay the family's debts. Lopahin, who has to leave very shortly, explains to Gaev and Ranevskaya his plan to save the estate: they must build summer cottages on their land for holidaymakers to rent. Profitable as this scheme looks, both brother and sister are offended at the thought of destroying their much-loved cherry orchard. Lopahin leaves, frustrated by his inability to make them focus on the problem. His timing has certainly been bad: excited by her return, Ranevskaya believes she can see her dead mother among the cherry trees outside the window. At this moment, Petya Trofimov arrives to welcome her: he used to tutor her son Grisha, whose death by drowning five years ago, coming soon after that of her husband, resulted in her flight to Paris. Taken by surprise, she is distressed at the memories Trofimov evokes. Gaev assures Anya that he is truly trying to find a solution to their difficulties, perhaps by marrying her to a rich man or borrowing money from an aunt in Yaroslavl. He is interrupted and bossed off to bed by Firs, who always treats him like a disorderly child – unsurprisingly, since Gaev habitually sucks boiled sweets and entertains himself with imaginary shots at billiards, his favourite game. As Anya falls asleep and is carried to bed by Varya, Trofimov watches, whispering 'My springtime'.

The second act takes place in open fields beyond the estate, by a wayside shrine. The local clerk Yepihodov (sometimes known as 'Twenty-two Misfortunes') plays the guitar to Dunyasha, to whom he has proposed but who loves Yasha – who is intent on seducing her and perhaps already has. With them is Charlotta, who explains a little of herself: she is the daughter of fairground performers but does not know who they were, and she has grown up as a lonely eccentric. The group is joined by Lopahin, Ranevskaya and Gaev – Lopahin continuing to urge on them his plan for the estate, but even less able to hold their attention than before, while Gaev recuperates from a long lunch in town and his sister laments her expenses. Also, she has had a letter from her lover – a feckless man she took up with after her husband's death – urging her to come back to him in Paris. Her and Gaev's solutions to the problem of the estate continue to be erratic : Ranevskaya wants Varya to marry Lopahin for his money, while Gaev is proud of having been offered a job at the bank, though on nothing like the terms he needs to break the deadlock. The 'eternal student' Trofimov crosses ideological swords with Lopahin: though both men are industrious and progressively minded in their own ways, they are politically incompatible; Lopahin dreams of an entrepreneurial future while Trofimov eloquently longs for revolution. Trofimov believes Russia can only be transformed by hard work such as his hearers cannot understand; they are the lazy intelligentsia who fail to treat their servants or children properly, while the workers live in squalor, thirty or forty to a room. As the company absorbs his passionate speech, a mysterious distant sound is heard, 'as of a breaking string'; disconcerted, they assume it is a cable snapping in a mine or some strange bird. The unexplained event is immediately followed by the arrival of an itinerant peasant, slightly drunk, singing and begging; Varya is terrified by him, but Ranevskaya gives him more money than he expected. The company go back to the house, leaving Trofimov alone with Anya. She is clearly attracted to him, or at least to his ideas, but he believes that they are 'above love' and should see each other as partners and comrades. All Russia is their orchard, he insists, and so she should be unconcerned about the fate of this one, from whose trees he sees the faces of the oppressed gazing out in reproach. They run down to the river together while Varya calls out for Anya to come inside.

In Act Three a party is in progress, though this is the evening when the fate of the cherry orchard will be sealed by auction in the town; Gaev hopes to buy it in the name of the aunt from Yaroslavl, although she has put up too little money for the purchase. Dancers spill into the sitting-room, among them the local stationmaster and postmaster – to the disgust of Firs, who remembers the days when generals and admirals used to visit. The stationmaster recites a poem; Charlotta entertains the guests with card tricks and ventriloquism, and even prestidigitates Anya and Varya from behind a rug. A disagreement breaks out between Trofimov and Ranevskaya: Trofimov believes she should forget the past and move on, but to her he is too young to understand what giving up the cherry orchard means – her life would make no sense without its links with her past. Meanwhile, her lover is still begging her to return to him and she feels herself weakening. Trofimov disapproves of this, and Ranevskaya taunts him for his lack of experience – at his age, he should have a mistress. In distress at the idea, he rushes from the room and falls downstairs. As the two make up their disagreement and dance, news arrives that the orchard has been sold, though nobody knows to whom. The party continues: Dunyasha's head is being turned by the flirtatious postmaster, so that the jealous Yepihodov is 'reduced to a state of mind'; Varya loses patience with him and threatens him with Firs's walking-stick, with which she accidentally hits Lopahin as he arrives back from the auction. Gaev is just behind him, in tears, but he cheers up at the sound of billiards in the next room. Lopahin admits that it is he who has bought the estate. Varya hurls her housekeeper's keys to the floor, but he is dancing with delight that he, the barefoot peasant boy, now owns the great orchard where his father and grandfather were serfs. He can barely wait to chop down the trees and make a new life for his children, though he also feels for Ranevskaya – 'Dear love, if only you'd listened to me'. Ranevskaya is devastated and Anya comforts her as the act closes, promising that they will go away together, plant a new orchard and one day smile again.

Finally, it is October and the house is being packed up; the family is leaving for the last time. They decline Lopahin's offer of champagne, but Yasha accepts it; he is eager to be gone to Paris with Ranevskaya and to be rid of Dunyasha's passionate affection. Lopahin himself is leaving for Kharkov for the winter, now that the business of the house is completed. Trofimov – when he can find his galoshes – is on his way to Moscow, and he bids a surprisingly fond farewell to Lopahin; he remarks that he has sensitive hands and the soul of an artist. Lopahin offers him a loan, but Trofimov refuses the obligation. The sound of the cherry trees being chopped down is heard, and Lopahin rushes off to stop the work, tactlessly started before the family has left. There is some doubt as to whether Firs, who is unwell, has been taken to hospital as planned. Ranevskaya and Gaev bid an emotional farewell, though they also acknowledge that now the thing is settled they feel rather better; Gaev is starting his job at the bank, and Anya too will stay behind and study. Lopahin assures Charlotta that he will find a job for her. Simeonov-Pishchik, a local landowner, arrives in jubilation – he has spent the whole play cadging money from Ranevskaya, but now gold has been discovered on his land and he wants to pay back his debts; hearing that the family is to be dispersed, he departs in distress. Ranevskaya persuades Lopahin to propose to Varya once and for all; left alone with her, he loses his nerve and flees after a few embarrassing moments, leaving Varya wretched. Ranevskaya and Gaev bid a last farewell to the house: they feel as if they had never really examined it before. They are both overcome: 'my sister . . . my dear sister . . . farewell, my happiness . . . farewell, my youth'. As they leave, the house is locked up; there is silence. Then Firs wanders on, ill and forgotten; he was never taken to hospital and is now incarcerated inside. He frets briefly that Gaev may have left in too light an overcoat for the weather, and lies down, it would seem for the last time. The sound of the mysterious breaking string is heard again; then there is nothing except the thudding of axes into the cherry trees.

∽ About the play

Chekhov's final play, set at the very start of the twentieth century and once described by its author as 'a four-act vaudeville', is taken by some to be the first expressionist drama of the modern theatre. Certainly, there are elements of *The Cherry Orchard* that seem to carry more of a symbolic than an actual meaning. The two-and-a-half thousand acre orchard, for instance, is far too big to harvest, bigger perhaps than any Russian orchard of the time, so it can easily be seen as representing a huge Russian potential no longer fulfilled; the breaking string that interrupts the action remains unexplained; and there is a surreal element to the third-act party, when the crucial news of the sale is accompanied by the antics of the party-goers, in what the director Vsevelod Meyerhold later described as 'the nightmare's vortex, the dance of the puppet show'. Such were the elements that attracted the attention of the new symbolists. The play's extraordinary end is more challenging still; an audience never fails to gasp when, after a great silence, Firs wanders on alone, as forgotten by them as he has been by the cast. These final moments – the last Chekhov was to put on a stage – foreshadow both Harold Pinter and Samuel Beckett in their simultaneous bleakness and comic incongruity. Most of all, though, Chekhov is delivering a last word on the cruelty of people who half-care; Ranevskaya loves her country, her nursery and her table all in the same breath, but forgets about a loyal old man, whom Gaev has only ever considered in relation to his choice of boots in the morning.

Politically, the play is extremely alert. For the first time, Chekhov explicitly acknowledges the upheavals that would shortly engulf Russia – in the following year's uprising in Petersburg, and then in 1917. The arrival of a passer-by to frighten the company, declaiming his ominous poem, is an obvious hint; and Trofimov's character is partly absurd because the provocative views he expresses would otherwise offend the censors, so that the author is covering his tracks by using a strategic element of burlesque. The development of both capitalism (in Lopahin) and revolution (in Trofimov) as keys to Russia's future is closely examined; the two characters are curiously aligned and even friendly. Typically, within this debate Chekhov confuses our sympathies. Lopahin, who could be seen as a destroyer, receives an affectionate description from the author: he should not be a crude peasant or typical merchant, but a gentle person, dignified and intelligent, capable of arousing love in a religous girl like Varya and the grudging affection of Trofimov. As for Ranevskaya and Gaev, it is possible, as with the three Prozorov sisters, to sympathize with their dilemma while being as frustrated as Lopahin by their snobbish refusal to face contemporary reality. Meanwhile one of the most welcome changes of Chekhov's lifetime, the emancipation of the serfs in 1861, is criticized from among the liberated by Firs, who is so reactionary that he pines for the old days when masters were masters and servants knew their place.

For all its experimental instincts, however, in many ways *The Cherry Orchard* is more of the inspired same. Chekhov returns once more to that country estate, its liberal, displaced inhabitants now being overtaken by daunting new men and women – the merchants, beggars, revolutionaries and far-sighted survivors of the new dispensation. To predict the future, Chekhov also digs for the last time into his own past: the orchard he had once planted on his Melikhovo estate, which he had just sold, was being chopped down by its purchaser; he remembers from his youth a particular family of friends in the same difficulties (and with some of the same feeble solutions) as those of Ranevskaya and her brother. Some of the play's best jokes, such as Varya clouting Lopahin with Firs's walking-stick on his crucial Act Three entrance, as her subconscious would require, and then the arrival of real billiards (Yepihodov breaking a cue) to distract Gaev from giving the news, are old-fashioned comic Chekhov; as are the selfish eccentricities of many of the characters, who are now marked both by self-interest and a tendency to fall asleep at inopportune moments. Thus Lopahin starts the action by kicking himself for taking a nap just when he meant to meet Ranevskaya at the station; when Varya talks quietly to Anya about her difficulties keeping things going at home, Anya nods off; Simeonov-Pishchik has a few winks in the middle of touching Ranevskaya for a loan, and even sleeps in mid-sentence during the Act Three party. Chekhov's characters have always had great energy for pursuing their own ends while ignoring those of others; even that seems to be flagging now, as if they are going through wearisome motions. In many ways, *The Cherry Orchard*, if not exactly the frivolous play Chekhov describes, works very simply: there are no aimless philosophical evenings, there is little sense of empty time meandering on, and even at the most discursive moments in Act Two there are pressing negotiations behind the talk. In many ways, Chekhov was ending his life with a highly suggestive but plain story, haunted by intimations of change and told with the acquired simplicity of genius.

∞ In performance

Composed with great difficulty by an author in rapidly failing health, *The Cherry Orchard*'s first performance was given by the Moscow Art Theatre on Chekhov's final birthday on 17 January 1904, as part (to his horror) of a jubilee celebration. However, the play's impact was overshadowed by the outbreak of the Russo-Japanese War a week afterwards (immediately followed by the sinking of the Russian fleet), by Chekhov's death later in the year and by the first Russian revolution of 1905. In any case, the production was disapproved of by Chekhov and seems to have been a sombre and elegiac affair, not at all the 'light-hearted comedy' he somewhat perversely described.

In western Europe, the play was much admired by George Bernard Shaw, whose *Heartbreak House* (1919) consciously echoed it. The original first succeeded in 1925 at the Lyric Theatre, Hammersmith: John Gielgud counted Trofimov as his first good performance, and the play became a popular hit, preparing the ground for Theodore Komisarjevsky's production the next year (with Charles Laughton as Yepihodov), and for Tyrone Guthrie's success with the play in 1933 (this time with Laughton as Lopahin, as well as Elsa Lanchester and Flora Robson). The first successful French productions came after the Second World War; to mark the anniversary of Chekhov's death, Jean Louis Barrault directed the play in Paris in 1954, himself playing Trofimov in his forties. Influenced by the Moscow Art Theatre's visit of 1958, Michel Saint-Denis directed Gielgud as Gaev and Peggy Ashcroft as Ranevskaya in London in 1962; in 1978, Peter Gill put the play on at the Riverside Studios with Julie Covington as Varya, Judy Parfitt as Ranevskaya and Eleanor Bron as Charlotta, as did Peter Hall at the National Theatre with Albert Finney as Lopahin and Dorothy Tutin as Ranevskaya. In Giorgio Strehler's dazzling 1974 production at the Piccolo Teatro in Milan, Gaev and Ranevskaya played with toys in Act One, and the snapping string was audible to the characters but not to the audience. Peter Brook's remarkable version in Paris in 1981 was cast with English, French and Scandinavian actors. Mike Alfreds, seen by many as the doyen of English directors of Chekhov, has directed the play three times: in 1982 at the Oxford Playhouse, with Sheila Hancock, in 1985 at the National Theatre, and then with his Method and Madness Company in 1998. For the Royal Shakespeare Company, Penelope Wilton and Alec McCowen played Ranevskaya and Gaev under Adrian Noble's direction in 1995, while in the same year Peter Stein directed the play at the Salzburg Festival with Jutta Lampe as Ranevskaya. Sam Mendes directed Judi Dench at the Aldwych Theatre in 1990.

The political undercurrents of *The Cherry Orchard* have led to adaptations: in 1977, Trevor Griffiths rendered Trofimov as a positive Marxist hero and the bourgeois characters were heavily criticized; a 1950 production at the Martin Beck in New York had Helen Hayes presiding over a southern plantation, with all the servants as slaves; the 1973 Public Theatre version (with James Earl Jones as Lopahin) was played entirely with black actors as a protest against their exclusion from the classical repertory. Janet Suzman's 2000 *The Free State* is *The Cherry Orchard* transplanted and fully adapted to post-apartheid South Africa.

AUGUST STRINDBERG
1849–1912

Strindberg's life

August Johan Strindberg was born in Stockholm on 22 January 1849. His father, Carl Oscar Strindberg, was a shipping agent of aristocratic descent, whose business success was modest. His mother was a serving maid from a working-class family. Strindberg had a poor and miserable childhood, and his mother died when he was thirteen. When his father remarried, he bitterly disliked his stepmother.

After five years of intermittent attendance at the University of Uppsala, Strindberg was variously employed in Stockholm as schoolteacher, tutor, newspaperman and librarian. He returned to his studies in Uppsala and in 1872 completed a senior candidacy. In 1874 he became an assistant librarian at the Royal Library, where he worked until his resignation in 1882. He tried to be an actor, and wrote three plays, all of which were rejected. His early works – novels and essays as well as plays – were written in revolt against the prevailing romanticism of Swedish literature. His first major play, the historical epic *Master Olof*, was written in 1872, but Strindberg did not achieve any critical success until the publication of his satirical novel *The Red Room* in 1879.

In 1877 Strindberg married the aristocratic actress Siri von Essen, who was seven months pregnant. The child died within a week, but she soon gave birth to two other daughters, Karin (1880) and Greta (1881). Strindberg wrote *The Swedish People* in 1882, which attacked many of the nation's values and earned him many enemies. In 1883 he moved to France, where his son Hans was born in 1884. The publication of his two volumes of *Getting Married* (1884, 1885) outraged the Swedish establishment and he was prosecuted for blasphemy, but acquitted. Under financial and marital pressure, he started to show symptoms of emotional crisis.

In 1887 Strindberg moved to Germany, where he wrote *The Father*, and in 1888 to Denmark, where he wrote *Creditors*, *Miss Julie* and *The Stronger*. In 1889 he founded the Scandinavian Experimental Theatre in Copenhagen, which premièred *Miss Julie* with Siri von Essen in the title role. He returned to Sweden in 1889 and wrote his novel *By The Open Sea* in 1890. He divorced Siri in 1891, and wrote seven plays – including *Playing With Fire* – in 1892.

Strindberg moved to Berlin in 1892, where he met the Austrian journalist Frida Uhl, whom he married in 1893. They separated following the birth of their daughter Kerstin (1894). In the late 1890s he suffered his 'inferno crisis' – a period of severe mental anguish and paranoia, exacerbated by absinthe poisoning – in which he abandoned literature for almost six years, and dedicated himself to alchemy and pseudo-scientific studies. His two autobiographical works, *The Occult Diary* and *Inferno*, appeared in 1896 and 1897.

By 1898 Strindberg had regained some balance and returned to Sweden, where he wrote the innovative *To Damascus Parts One and Two*. This was followed in 1899 by three historical dramas: *The Saga of the Folkurgs*, *Gustav Vasa* and *Erik the Fourteenth*. In 1901 he married his third wife, the young Norwegian actress Harriet Bosse, with whom he had a daughter, Anne-Marie, in 1902. They were divorced in 1904, but continued their relationship for several years. Between 1898 and his death, in addition to a vast output of short stories, essays and scholarly works, he wrote no less than thirty-six plays, including *Easter* (1900), *The Dance Of Death* (1900), *To Damascus Part Three* (1901), *Swanwhite* (1901), *Queen Christina* (1901) and *A Dream Play* (1901). In 1907 he founded the Intimate Theatre in Stockholm, for whom he wrote his four chamber plays: *Storm*, *After The Fire*, *The Ghost Sonata* and *The Pelican* (all 1907). His last play was *The Great Highway* (1909).

In 1907 Strindberg settled into a house outside Stockholm that he called the Blue Tower, and fell in love with the nineteen-year-old Fanny Falkner. He was awarded an 'Anti-Nobel prize' by the socialist politician Hjalmar Branting and died of stomach cancer on 14 May 1912.

Strindberg's theatre

Strindberg is perhaps the most unappealing of all great writers. This would not matter if his views did not affect his work so profoundly. To appreciate the plays, it is perhaps best to come to an honest appraisal of the man.

Wherever you look in Strindberg, you are confronted by contradiction and extremes. As a young man, he was an atheist and a socialist. But this changed in 1888 after he read Nietzsche, whom he described as 'the modern spirit who dares to preach the right of the strong and the wise, against the foolish [and] the small'. In the last years of his life Strindberg returned to socialism, but was increasingly drawn to Catholicism, anti-Darwinism, virulent anti-Semitism and a deep fascination with the occult – much influenced by his reading of the eighteenth-century mystic Swedenborg. Although many of Strindberg's plays show an empathy for the working man, he was fascinated by the aristocracy and the élite. He managed to combine social radicalism with liberalism, anarchism with conservatism. His deep nihilism was partnered by his romanticism; his hatred of Swedish provincialism by his patriotism. One of Strindberg's most unattractive characteristics was his extreme paranoia, which was matched only by his astonishing arrogance.

Strindberg's attitude to women was extremely complicated and it is Strindberg's misogyny which is most shocking to the modern sensibility. At its worst, in 1888, he wrote:

> Woman, being small and foolish and therefore evil . . .
> should be suppressed, like barbarians and thieves. She is
> useful only as ovary and womb, best of all as cunt.

Strindberg loathed the emerging feminism of the time, above all for its emasculating effects, and in 1895 published a long article entitled 'On Women's Inferiority to Man'. But behind all the violent rage and bravado, Strindberg was a writer obsessed by the complexities of sexuality and the challenges of marriage:

> Actually my misogyny is entirely theoretical, and I can't live a day without supposing that I warm my soul at the flame of their [women's] unconscious, vegetable way of life . . . Can you understand my misogyny? Which is only the reverse image of a terrible desire for the other sex.

His view of women was so obsessional and extreme that one could almost say he loved women as much as he hated them.

Strindberg's work was shaped by a spirit of restless experimentalism. He had highly ambivalent feelings about the notion of fiction itself, and spent an inordinate (some say wasted) amount of energy on various non-fiction undertakings: autobiography, history, travel writing, foreign languages, alchemy, pseudo-science and so on. Although he read widely, his interest in fiction was limited: Edgar Allen Poe's stories and the novels of Balzac and Dickens were the high points. Most of his reading was scientific and political, or mystical and spiritual. He was an accomplished amateur painter and admired the work of Edvard Munch, Arnold Böcklin, Paul Gauguin and Alphonse Mucha. He enjoyed playing the guitar and was a friend of Frederick Delius; he loved the music of Beethoven, but loathed Mozart and Wagner.

For one of the world's great dramatists, and despite marrying two actresses, Strindberg had a profound distrust of the theatre. He was scornful of his rival playwrights Bjørnsterne Bjørnson and Henri Becque, but reserved his greatest loathing for Ibsen. It was only when Edvard Brandes introduced him to André Antoine's theories of an 'intimate theatre' that he returned to playwriting after sixteen years and wrote *The Father*. In 1888 he set up the short-lived Scandinavian Experimental Theatre with very little attention to practicality, and even less love of the form. He was intrigued by the writings of Gordon Craig and came to admire the great director

Max Reinhardt. He founded the Intimate Theatre in November 1907 with the young actor Augustus Falck – perhaps the first theatre to be dedicated to the performance of one writer's work, but its productions were of a very variable standard: money was scarce and the actors were young and inexperienced. He was not interested in directing himself, but wrote up his ideas in his *Open Letters to the Intimate Theatre* (1908).

The plays themselves are of a very variable standard: a handful of masterpieces, a dozen best regarded as curiosities, and a large number of failures, dashed off too quickly, which are hardly ever revived. A clue to this unevenness can be found in a letter in 1902:

> A work of art should be a little careless, imperfect like any natural growth, where not a crystal is perfect, not a plant lacks its defective leaf. As with Shakespeare.

What most of his plays have in common is an extraordinary energy: a style which takes your breath away with its vigour as it appals you by its content. The young Norwegian novelist Knut Hamsun (whose own views are just as unattractive) admired Strindberg enormously:

> I have found in no literature such a velocity as Strindberg's. It is no tempest, it is a hurricane. He does not speak; he does not say his opinions, he *explodes* them . . . what is called his 'contradictions' seems to me psychologically consistent. He uses no deliberate planning, and not the method of positive criticism; he guesses his way, throws about ingenious forebodings, bold paradoxes . . . He is a far-seeing observer of a rare sort.

It is this restless, mercurial quality that gives his best plays their edgy modernity and transforms their author's malignancy into magnificent drama.

Strindberg was convinced of the impossibility of happiness and the inescapable pain of existence and his best work is characterized by this despair. In *The Occult Diary* he wrote:

Life is so hideously ugly, we mortals so abysmally evil, that were an author to portray everything we have seen or heard, no one could endure to read it. There are things I remember having seen or heard done by good, respectable, well-loved people, which I have blotted out, never been able to bring myself to mention and refuse to remember. Breeding and education seem only to be masks for the beast in us, and virtue a dissimulation. The best we can hope for is to conceal our meanness. Life is so cynical that only a swine can be happy in it. And anyone who can see our ugly life as beautiful is a swine. Life must be a punishment!

Although in his last years Strindberg tempered some of this pessimism with growing spiritual beliefs, drawn from several different traditions, his true greatness lies in his astonishing commitment to expressing the truth of this despair, however unpleasant and revealing it may be. In a letter in 1907, Strindberg wrote:

My whole life seems to me to have been planned like a play, so that I might both suffer and depict suffering.

It should perhaps be left to the playwright John Osborne – 'Strindberg's Man in England', as he called himself – to have the last word:

Often he [Strindberg] takes up these unremitting postures of confrontation because it was a way of getting most accurately at the heart of something in all its stark awfulness. His men strike a note of unwelcome battle which puts the fear of benighted godlessness into the ranks of the faint-hearted and pussy-footed. He gives off a shocking smell of a pervasive and longed-for notion of innocence that has been irredeemably replaced by knowledge, leading to turbulence, opposition, deception and, finally, a fight to the death. A profoundly religious romantic, he wades up to his ears in opposites of almost neurasthenic proportions and makes assaults on anything and anybody who seeks to threaten his capacity for conquering the world. Such men, such poets, are not to be easily forgotten.

Translations and further reading

Strindberg's international reputation has been dependent on his translators. It is a shame, therefore, that there is not a complete edition of his plays in English.

The most readily available translations appear in Michael Meyer's three volumes, published by Methuen (1964). Peter Watt translated three plays for Penguin (1958) and Michael Robinson has produced an excellent collection of five plays for Oxford World Classics (1998). One of the most interesting recent developments is the playwright Gregory Motton's four volumes of translations for Oberon Books. There are also various one-off translations such as John Osborne's *The Father* (1988), Kenneth McLeish's *Miss Julie* (1995) and Frank McGuiness's *Miss Julie* (2000) and *The Stronger* (1993).

Strindberg's numerous essays, novels and other writings have appeared in English somewhat sporadically, with translations of *Inferno* and *By The Open Sea* both published by Penguin, and Michael Robinson has translated Strindberg's letters and essays. The most authoritative biography in English is Michael Meyer's *Strindberg* (1985). Robert Brustein's *The Theatre Of Revolt* (1991) and Evert Sprinchorn's *Strindberg As Dramatist* (1982) are stimulating, as is Raymond Williams's *Drama from Ibsen to Brecht* (1952, revised 1968).

One of the most acute commentators on Strindberg is the great Swedish film and theatre director Ingmar Bergman, whose *Magic Lantern* (1988) is full of fascinating insights, as is the monograph *Ingmar Bergman, Four Decades In The Theatre* (1982).

The Father
(*Fadren*)

A Tragedy

1887

∽ Characters

The Captain
Laura, *his wife*
Bertha, *their daughter*
Doctor Östermark
The Pastor
The Nurse
Nöjd
The Orderly

The action takes place in the Captain's house in the country

∽ The story

Act One takes place before dinner, in a room in the Captain's house. The Captain asks his brother-in-law, the Pastor, to have a word with Nöjd, a cavalryman in the Captain's regiment: he has been 'sniffing up' the kitchen-maid, who is now pregnant. Nöjd freely admits to a relationship, but refuses to acknowledge paternity. Both the Captain and the Pastor admit that they are sympathetic to Nöjd's predicament: 'Who'd ever know for sure whether the lad's guilty or not? But her – she must be guilty – if there is such a thing.' The Captain complains that 'This house is filled with women, all intent on raising my daughter' and announces his decision to move Bertha into town. The Pastor leaves, expressing concern about the Captain's nervous disposition. Laura, the Captain's wife, discovers him counting the housekeeping money and is told that, due to their financial difficulties, he will control the accounts from now on. Furthermore, he tells her that Bertha is leaving. When Laura asks whether she has any say in the matter, he replies: 'None whatever. [A wife] surrenders all her rights and possessions to her husband. In return he must agree to support her and her children.' She asks him about his meeting with Nöjd, and the Captain repeats his belief that you can never prove paternity. She then asks how, if that is the case, he can claim so many rights over 'his' child. Laura welcomes the new Doctor and tries to convince him that her husband is 'deranged'. The Captain returns and impresses the Doctor with his understanding of science, and says that Bertha should make up her own mind. His old religious-minded Nurse is trying to calm him down when they hear a scream. Bertha runs in; she has been holding a séance with her grandmother, who is furious at her lack of conviction. Bertha says she would love to live in town, but would miss her father. Laura arrives and threatens him with the possibility that Bertha is not in fact his daughter. The Captain leaves the house and tells them he will not be back before midnight.

Act Two takes place several hours later. The Doctor tells Laura to be careful: her accusation of the Captain's insanity could result in him being certified and he senses that she is exaggerating his problems and interfering in his affairs. Laura and the Doctor withdraw, leaving the Nurse reading her hymnal. Bertha comes in and tells the Nurse that she heard someone singing in the 'little empty room . . . where the cradle lies'. The Captain returns home and asks the Nurse if she knew for sure who her child's father was. The Doctor comes in and the Captain tells him how 'untrustworthy' women can be. The Doctor expresses his concern about the 'unhealthy' nature of these thoughts. Laura is caught listening at the door and admits to intercepting the Captain's letters and thus hindering his scientific work. He tells her that she is better off if he remains sane: if he kills himself, she will not get his pension. He begs her to resolve his uncertainty over being Bertha's father: 'Free me from my doubts, and I will give up arms.' Laura swears that Bertha is his child, but he refuses to believe her and insists – in tears – that she confess to her adultery. They remember their early relationship ('The mother was our friend. But the woman is your enemy') and acknowledge that they have struggled for dominance ever since: a battle which Laura says she will win. She announces that she is having him certified, on the evidence of his own letter to the Doctor admitting to his insanity, and will bring Bertha up on his pension. He throws a burning lamp at her as she escapes through the door.

Act Three takes place the next day. The Captain can be heard pacing in the room upstairs. Laura asks the Nurse if the door to the stairs is safely locked and takes the Captain's keys. Nöjd brings a letter from the Captain's superior officer and confirms that he has removed all the cartridges from the Captain's guns. The Pastor arrives and Laura tells him what has happened and shows him the pathetic contents of the Captain's table. He says her husband must have loved her very much. He is half-admiring, half-horrified at what he suspects Laura has done, but she denies everything. The Doctor arrives, still unconvinced that the Captain is mad, despite his violence towards Laura. He admits, however, that it is best to commit him to prevent him from harming anyone. He unpacks a strait-jacket and asks the Nurse to put the Captain into it. The Captain bursts through the locked door, carrying books which cite famous examples of female infidelity, and suggests that the Doctor's and Pastor's wives might have been similarly unfaithful. The Captain admits that he is insane, but as he believes Bertha is not his child, says he 'no longer exists'. Bertha arrives, concerned about his violence against her mother, and when he asks her 'why it matters' says 'you're not my father when you talk like that'. She repeatedly calls him 'Papa' and convinces him that she is his child. He tells her she must choose between him and her mother: 'You must have one soul alone. Otherwise you shall never find peace and nor shall I.' But she just wants to be herself. Raving about being 'Saturn, who ate his own children because it had been foretold that otherwise they would eat him', the Captain fetches a revolver from the cupboard, only to find the cartridges have gone. The Nurse is left alone with him and coaxes him into the strait-jacket by pretending that it is a night-shirt. Discovering himself bound, the Captain rails further against women. Laura arrives and wraps him in her shawl. Its softness and its smell reminds the Captain of their youth, and he asks to be covered instead in his military uniform. He rests his head against the Nurse's breast and has a stroke. As they stand around the dying man, Bertha enters, crying for her mother, who claims her to be 'My child! My own child!'

↷ About the play

Strindberg wrote *The Father* in early 1887 in Bavaria, following the scandal and court case surrounding volume one of *Getting Married*. He saw *The Father* as part one of a trilogy of plays about marriage:

> I am now writing for the theatre, because otherwise the bluestockings will take it over; and the theatre is a weapon . . . it's easier than novel-writing once you get the knack . . . Gondinet says that one needs to be a bit stupid to be able to write plays. I think that's true of all creative writing. Once I started to think, my art went to pot. . . . My wife no longer reads what I write, partly because she doesn't understand it, and it doesn't concern her what I write, since she has her department as wife and mother . . . so I write as ruthlessly as I please.

He was acutely aware of Ibsen's success with his 'feminist' dramas *Pillars of Society* and *A Doll's House* (some of *Getting Married* is a direct riposte to the latter), about which he felt undisguised hostility:

> One does not choose what one writes about . . . Just now I am preoccupied with this question of women's rights, and

shall not drop it until I have investigated and experi-
mented in this field . . . I won't let myself be silenced on
so big and important a matter as this, which has been
befogged and made a farce of by such *sometime* men as
Ibsen and Bjørnson.

By 1887 his relationship with his first wife Siri von Essen was
rapidly deteriorating, and it is perhaps best to regard *The
Father* as a psychological laboratory in which Strindberg
could analyse his own feelings about women, marriage and
Siri in particular.

At the play's centre is the complex and fascinating figure of
the Captain, who is increasingly convinced that he is not the
father of his own daughter and is regarded as insane for
thinking so. Strindberg wrote that he 'symbolizes for me a
masculinity which people have tried to pound or wheedle out
of us and transfer to the third sex!' Although the Captain is a
military figure, he is also a 'distinguished man of science' who
collects books. He can be charming, witty and intelligent. But
like Strindberg himself, he is prone to extremes of paranoia,
nervousness and impatience. He is often angry, stubborn and
overbearing. Paradoxically, again like Strindberg, he has a
rich feminine side which gives him a real capacity for feeling.
Echoing Shylock, he says 'If you humilate us, are we not
shamed? If you sever our hearts, do we not wither? If you poison us, do we not die? Can a man not shed tears or a soldier
grieve? Is it unmanly?' Strindberg's great achievement is to
create a figure with such honesty and blazing energy that
despite the play's ferocious misogyny, we are given an intimate glimpse of male inadequacy in the face of femininity
and motherhood.

The Captain shares his house with the three most important women in his life: his wife Laura, their daughter Bertha,
and his Nurse, Margaret. At the start, Laura shows all the
symptoms of the nineteenth-century New Woman: full of
energy, intelligence and spirit. But she also has a powerful
feminine intuition ('we women are a little cleverer in the way

we manage these things') and Strindberg mercilessly exposes her deviousness, her ferocious instinct for survival and her determination to keep her daughter at all costs.

Bertha is a picture of youth, full of love for her father, free-spirited and energetic – and he loves her deeply: 'My child was my afterlife,' he says, 'She made me immortal. She was my ultimate reality. Take that from me and I am nothing.' It is all the more shocking that he gets to the point where – like Abraham – he is prepared to kill her.

The Captain's Nurse is a surrogate mother figure: sooth-ing, loving and tender on the one hand, terrifying, manipula-tive and humiliating on the other. She is the mother the Captain so desperately needs, but she is also his nemesis, who, like Clytemnestra, manipulates him into the soothing and catastrophic embrace of the strait-jacket.

The Father has sometimes been hailed as a masterpiece of naturalistic theatre. Strindberg preferred to speak of 'the greater Naturalism which seeks out those points where the great battles take place', while Zola, in a letter to Strindberg, criticized the play for its abstraction:

> I like characters to exist in the round, one should be able to elbow them, they should breathe our air. And your cap-tain who has not even a name, your other characters who are virtually abstract creations, do not give me the full sensation of life that I demand.

The play revolves round the uncertainty that a father can feel as to whether his children are actually his. Strindberg was increasingly interested in suggestion and psychological control, and this, combined with the Captain's – and Strindberg's – misogyny is the motor that drives the play. Whatever its shortcomings, *The Father* is Strindberg's first major work for the stage, a genuine tragedy which anato-mizes with extraordinary theatrical energy the war between the sexes. Its subsequent success has belied Strindberg's bitter prophesy:

And in ten years, when we shall have these women-devils
over us with their right to vote and everything, down-
trodden men will dig up my trilogy, but will not dare to
stage it . . .

☙ In performance

On 12 November 1887, Strindberg wrote a letter to the
young Danish writer, Axel Lundegård (who was translating
the play):

> It seems as if I'm walking in my sleep; as if my life and
> writing have got all jumbled up. I don't know if *The Father*
> is a work of literature or if my life has been; but I feel as
> if, probably quite soon, at a given moment, it will sud-
> denly break upon me, and I shall collapse either into mad-
> ness and remorse, or suicide. Through much writing, my
> life has become a shadow life; I no longer feel as if I am
> walking the earth but floating weightless in an atmos-
> phere not of air but darkness.

Despite this tone of despair, the play's world première took
place two days later at the Casino Theatre in Copenhagen
and was a success. Ibsen read the play and wrote that 'If it is
acted as it needs to be, with merciless realism, the effect will
be shattering'. Nietzsche's response was even less ambivalent:
'I read your tragedy twice with deep emotion; it has
astounded me beyond measure to find a work in which my
own conceptions of love – with war as its means and the
deathly hatred of the sexes as its fundamental law – is so mag-
nificently expressed.'

The first Swedish production was on 12 January 1888 at
the New Theatre in Stockholm. The critic Georg Norensvan
described the atmosphere:

> The longer the passionate play proceeded, the more one
> noticed in the audience an unrest, a surge of emotion
> which, from the disturbing scene when the old nurse

tricks the sick man into donning a strait-jacket, took the form of a continuous murmur which mounted after almost every line. It was, no doubt about it, indigation at the content of the play, at its furious assault upon the whole female sex, at expessions such as one has not hitherto been called upon to hear in a theatre, which whipped up our normally calm audience to fever pitch.

The play was performed in 1890 at Otto Brahm's Freie Bühne in Berlin, the first of Strindberg's plays to be performed outside Scandinavia. Lugné-Poe staged it successfully, but with a changed ending, at his Théâtre de l'Oeuvre in Paris in 1894. The première was attended by both Rodin and Gauguin. In 1908, August Falck – son of the August Falck who played the original Captain – staged the play to much acclaim at the Intimate Theatre in Stockholm. This production was filmed.

The London premières of the play in 1911 were staged first in Yiddish at the Pavilion Theatre in Whitechapel, and then in English at the Rehearsal Theatre. It was first performed in New York in 1912 and by 1914 had been seen all over the world. Subsequent English Captains include Robert Loraine (1927), Malcolm Morley (1929), Michael Redgrave (1949), Wilfred Lawson (1953), Trevor Howard (1964) and Alun Armstrong (1988). Al Pacino and Julianne Moore played husband and wife in New York in 1996.

John Osborne produced an outstanding translation for the National Theatre (1988). He described first reading the play:

The sensation was like being pitched headlong from page to page astride an unstoppable beast of pounding dramatic energy.

Translated by John Osborne, Faber, 1988

Miss Julie
(*Fröken Julie*)

A Naturalistic Tragedy
1888

ᴄᴐ Characters

Miss Julie
Jean, *a servant*
Kristin, *a cook*
Peasants

The action takes place in the kitchen of a nobleman's house

ᴄᴐ The story

It is Midsummer's Eve. The kitchen is dominated by a large
stove and above the door is a servant's bell and a speaking
tube. As Kristin cooks his supper, Jean tells her that Miss
Julie's 'wild again tonight'. The servants are holding a dance
in the barn, and Miss Julie, the daughter of the house, has
been dancing with all of them, including Jean. She has
recently broken off her engagement, having humiliated her
fiancé by making him jump over her whip, 'like a puppy dog'.
When she arrives, Miss Julie orders Jean to come and dance
with her again. He thinks it might cause comment for her to
dance with the same 'beau' twice, but when Miss Julie takes
offence, he crumples. As she leads him out, she says to
Kristin: 'I'm not going to steal him.' Kristin is left alone, and,
with a dance playing in the distance, cleans up the kitchen
and arranges her hair. Jean returns, shocked at the way Miss
Julie was dancing and reassuring Kristin: 'You're a good
understanding girl, Kristin. You'll be a good wife.' Miss Julie
comes back, angry, and orders Jean to change out of his livery.
He returns in morning coat and bowler, speaking French.

She orders him to share a beer with her, and insists that he drink her health and kiss her foot. But he tells her that 'they can't go on like this' – a servant and his mistress alone together – as people will begin to talk. While Kristin slips off to bed, unnoticed, Julie tells him of a dream she has had: she is on the top of a tall pillar and longs to be down on the ground, burrowing into the earth. He says he has dreamed of trying to climb a tall tree to reach some golden eggs, but the branches are slippery and the climb is too hard. He warns her that she is 'playing with fire'. When he catches dust in his eye, she provocatively tries to remove it. When he tries to kiss her, she slaps him. When she asks him if he has ever been in love, he says he was – with her: 'You stood for everything I could never have, the gulf between what I wanted and what I was.' They hear the servants singing a song about 'a pretty girl who walked in the woods one day, she walked in the woods one day and lost her way', and run off into his room to hide.

The servants enter, dance and sing, and leave. Miss Julie and Jean come in again, dishevelled, and Jean says 'we can't stay here now'; they should leave together and establish a hotel on Lake Como. She says she has no money of her own and he says that this makes their plan impossible. She begs him to take her away, but he becomes disdainful and brutish. She realizes that she was only the 'first branch' on Jean's climb up the social tree and becomes increasingly desperate ('you talk as if you were higher than me already') as she tries to regain control over him. He tells her that no woman of his class would have behaved the way she has: 'what servant d'you think would throw herself at a man the way that you did tonight?' She grows submissive ('Hit me. Kick me') and he becomes more conciliatory. She tells him about her mother who hated men and, having brought her up 'like a child of nature', taught her to hate them too: 'I promised her I would never be a slave to any man.' She suggests that they should run away, be happy for a few days and then commit suicide together. But he does not want this and suggests that they both stay where they are. She frightens him by suggesting that 'it could happen again' and says she must leave – alone. She goes upstairs to get ready.

Kristin enters, dressed for church, and realizes what has happened. She is disgusted but not jealous, and decides she does not want to stay in a house with 'people who lower themselves'. She tells Jean he must start looking for another position – 'seeing as we're going to get married'. The sun begins to rise and Miss Julie enters, ready to travel, with a greenfinch in a cage. She has found some money and asks him to leave with her. When he agrees, she asks him to kill her bird as it cannot go with them. As he brings the axe down, she screams 'Kill me too!' and starts to rave, telling Jean that she would 'like to see all [his] sex swimming in a sea of blood'. Kristin enters and Miss Julie runs to her, asking her protection from Jean. He goes next door to shave while Miss Julie tries to persuade Kristin to come with them. As he sharpens his razor, she describes a fantastic vision of what the hotel will be like, but falters towards the end. Kristin leaves for church, warning them that she will tell the grooms not to let the horses out, effectively stopping the pair from leaving. Miss Julie asks Jean what he would do if he were a woman in her position: would he kill himself? He says that he would, but as he is a man he would not. The bell rings. Miss Julie jumps to her feet and Jean responds into the speaking tube: 'At once, milord.' She asks him to tell her what to do, saying she will obey him 'like a dog'. He says that since his master is back in the house, he cannot. She asks him again and he gives her the razor, whispering an order in her ear. She hesitates, frightened of the bell and the 'hand that sets it in motion'. The bell rings. Jean cringes and orders Miss Julie to go. She walks 'firmly' out through the door – to her death.

∽ About the play

Strindberg wrote *Miss Julie* in Denmark over the summer of 1888. His relationship with his wife, the aristocratic actress Siri von Essen, was at its worst, and Strindberg exhibited powerful feelings of inferiority – and rage – towards her aristocratic background. The play is also drawn from what appeared to be a real-life affair between the Danish Countess Frankerau and her bailiff Hansen. The greatness of the play lies in the way that it perfectly expresses Strindberg's two great obsessions: the sex war and the class war.

In 1887 Strindberg read Nietzsche and corresponded with him, and the play's Preface gives a powerful sense of his influence:

> Will the day ever come, I wonder, when we are so advanced, so enlightened, that we take no interest in the brutal, cynical, heartless pageant that is human life? If so we shall have shed those minor, unreliable thought-mechanisms we call feelings, which become dangerous and unnecessary as our reasoning faculty develops.

This sense of the inevitable brutality of the world is almost Marxist in its crude class determinism; it also looks forward to the ugliest kind of Social Darwinism. In the Preface, Strindberg says that he saw his characters as people of today: 'They live in a world in transition, in turmoil. I've made them shifting, changing, vacillating, a blend of old and new.' It is this which gives the play its three-dimensional reality.

Miss Julie is one of Strindberg's most extraordinary creations: a sexually liberated, provocative and experimental woman, open-minded and daring, who is also an entirely characteristic product of her aristocratic background. Strindberg's Preface summarizes the reasons for her tragic end:

> Her 'bad' mother; her father's mistaken ideas on how to bring up a daughter; her own character; her lover's influence on a weak and vacillating mind – not to mention the Midsummer festival, her father's absence, her period, her devotion to her pets, the headiness of the dance, dusk, the aphrodisiac perfume of the flowers, the coincidence that brings her and Jean to the same room at the same time, the man's urgent sexuality.

Jean is equally well drawn. In the Preface, Strindberg described him as:

> a founder, the initiator of a dynasty. A farmhand's son, he has trained himself to become a gentleman – and it was easy, given his well-developed appreciation of what he hears, tastes and sees, and his sense of beauty. He's on his way up, and is strong enough not to care who he stands on as he climbs. He's already a stranger to his fellows: he despises them as part of the life he's rejected, and he's afraid of them, runs from them, because they know his secrets . . .

Strindberg is careful to show that Jean drinks wine, not beer, speaks French and is getting an education: 'I read books, go to the theatre. And I listen when my betters are talking. I listen and I learn.' He is attractive and manipulative, charming and cruel. For all his finesse, his social ambition is utterly ruthless, like a true Nietzschean Superman: 'As soon as I get hold of the lowest branch, just watch me climb!'

The third character is Jean's fiancée Kristin, described by Strindberg as:

> A peasant woman, as unselfconsciously hypocritical as an animal, full of servility and sloth honed at the kitchen range, crammed with the religious moralizing which cloaks both original thought and conscience.

However, Kristin has more idiosyncracy and strength than Strindberg's description suggests.

Strindberg called *Miss Julie* 'the first Naturalistic Tragedy in Swedish Drama', and it was written under the influence of the French naturalist director André Antoine. In the Preface – one of the key texts in the history of naturalism – he describes various technical innovations: swift, natural dialogue, in which the talk is sent 'spinning in a thousand directions'; no act divisions or interval break; 'three specific kinds of theatrical spectacle: monologue, dumbshow and ballet'; a set which draws on the 'asymmetry and economy of Impressionist paintings'; the absence of footlights; actors being positioned in a way that they are three dimensional and not always looking at the audience, and so on. The play is, above all, written for:

> A small stage and a small house, [where] perhaps a new kind of drama would arise, and theatre would once again become an entertainment-form for educated people.

But these formal innovations are only a small part of the overall achievement of the play. The depth and resonant sparseness of its language gives it a biblical, mythical quality that takes it out of the domestic and the realistic and transforms it into a masterpiece of poetic drama:

> It was ridiculous. That's why I didn't want to tell, before. But now I'd better. You know what the world looks like from the bottom – no, of course you don't. Hawks, falcons – they soar above us, most of the time; who sees their backs? I lived in a cottage; seven brothers and sisters; a pig; waste land all around, not even a tree. But out of the window I could see the wall of his Lordship's estate. Apple trees, on the other side. The garden of Eden . . . angel-guardians, sword of fire . . . Mind you, they didn't stop us, me and the other boys. The Tree of Life.

Strindberg was aware of the quality and significance of the play, and in a letter to Brandes wrote that: 'I feel that in them [*Miss Julie* and *Creditors*] I have written my stage masterpieces.' In a letter to his publisher Albert Bonnier in 1888, he wrote: 'This play will be remembered in history', and for once his prophecy has come true: if *Miss Julie* was the only play he had written, Strindberg would have earned an important place in world drama.

☙ In performance

Miss Julie was written for Siri von Essen to play the title role and was scheduled to receive its première on 2 March 1889 under the auspices of Strindberg's newly formed – but short-lived – Scandinavian Experimental Theatre at the Dagmar Theatre in Copenhagen, as part of a double bill with *Creditors*. Despite some deletions which had been urged on him by his publisher, the play was banned by the Danish censor, and received its première on 14 March in a single private performance at Copenhagen University Student Union.

Miss Julie had to wait three years until it was performed in Germany, on 3 April 1892 at the Berlin Freie Bühne, but again for one performance only, and it was not performed at André Antoine's Théâtre Libre until 1893. Antoine was delighted:

> Everything gripped the audience – the subject, the milieu, this concentration into a single ninety-minute act of a plot that would suffice for a full-length play. Of course there were laughter and protests, but one found oneself in the presence of something quite new.

In 1899 Chekhov read the play: '[Strindberg] is a remarkable writer. He has a quite unusual power'. Maxim Gorky wrote: 'He is bold, this Swede. Never have I seen the aristocracism of serfs so lucidly presented . . . the idea of the play struck me forcibly, and the author's power awoke in me feelings of envy and surprise.'

Productions followed in Stuttgart (1902), Hamburg (1903) and Berlin (1904), and finally in Stockolm in 1906. Alla Nazimova played Miss Julie in New York and St Petersburg (1905) and Strindberg revived the play at his Intimate Theatre in 1907 where it ran for 134 performances, including a performance specially put on for Bernard Shaw in Stockholm in 1908.

The British première took place at Grein's Little Theatre in 1912, but the play was banned by Lord Cromer in October 1925:

> There is a sordid and disgusting atmosphere, which makes the immorality of the play glaring and crude. There is the very questionable theme of the relationship

between masters and servants, which the play tends to undermine.

The ban was eventually lifted and *Miss Julie* became the most often performed of Strindberg's plays. Subsequent Miss Julies and Jeans have included Maggie Smith and Albert Finney for the National Theatre (1965), Helen Mirren and Donal McCann for the RSC (1971), Cheryl Campbell and Stephen Rea (1983) and Aisling O'Sullivan and Christopher Eccleston (2000). The play has been translated into English dozens of times and some of the most interesting versions include Kenneth McLeish (1995), Gregory Motton (2000) and Frank McGuinness (2000). The playwright Patrick Marber produced his own television and radio response to the play, *After Miss Julie* (1995), which was revised and rewritten for the stage (Donmar Warehouse, 2003).

Ingmar Bergman's remarkable 1986 production of the play at the Royal Dramatic Theatre Stockholm (which was paired with Bergman's production of Ibsen's *A Doll's House*) was seen at the 1987 Edinburgh International Festival.

Translated by Kenneth McLeish, Nick Hern Books, 1995

The Dance of Death
Parts One and Two
(*Dödsdansen*)

1900

First performed 1905 (Part One), 1906 (Part Two)

ᦉ Characters

Edgar, *Captain at the Artillery Fortress*
Alice, *his wife, an ex-actress*
Kurt, *Quarantine Master*
Jenny
The Old Woman
Sentry
Judith, *Edgar's daughter*
Allan, *Kurt's son*
The Lieutenant

The action takes place in a round tower in a granite fortress

ᦉ The story

Edgar is the Artillery Captain of a garrison overlooking a harbour somewhere in Sweden. He is a late-middle-aged misanthrope who sits in his tower – a fortress which used to be a prison – drinking whisky, smoking cigars and trying to control the lives and feelings of all who come into contact with him. His companion in this misery is his wife, Alice, an ex-actress from a rich family, tight with her money, abusive of the servants and full of hatred for her husband. They have two surviving children: an adult son and their daughter Judith. They play cards, bicker and moan about their acquaintances. Their marriage is at boiling-point on the eve of their silver wedding anniversary.

Edgar's cousin Kurt arrives to take up the post of Quarantine Master. Years earlier, Kurt had left his wife and lost contact with his children. The wind rises and Alice invites Kurt to stay for dinner. Edgar insists that Kurt saddled him with Alice. When he says that 'there are corpses under the floorboards; there's so much hatred here it's hard to breathe', Edgar 'crumples up and stares vacantly ahead as if he was dead'. Alice returns from preparing dinner and tells Kurt that her husband is an 'utter stranger' to her. When the bugle sounds outside, Edgar jumps to his feet and leaves. Alice tells Kurt about her misery: 'I've spent a lifetime in this tower as a prisoner, watched over by a man I've always hated, and now hate so boundlessly that the day he died I'd laugh aloud for joy.' When pressed, she says that their mutual hatred is groundless, 'without centre, without purpose, but also without end'. She tells him that two of their children are dead, and that the other two live in town: 'in order not to destroy the children, we had to send them away'. She also reveals that there is no food in the house. Alice's hopes for his death are almost fulfilled when Edgar gets her to play 'The Entry of the Boyars' on the piano and he dances to it and collapses. Kurt rings the local doctor, who refuses to visit. Alice tells Edgar that their servants have left because they have not been paid. Meanwhile, Kurt has spoken to another doctor and tells Edgar that he must change his lifestyle: no more cigars and whisky, just milk. As the night draws in, Edgar lies on the sofa talking with Kurt about the meaning of life and the finality of death.

The next morning, a rough sea is visible through the windows. Edgar is asleep; Kurt has stayed up with him all night and calls him 'the most arrogant person I've ever come across'. Alice tells Kurt about Edgar's childhood, and when he wakes up he says he wants to see his daughter Judith. But the junior officers of the garrison have sent him flowers to congratulate him on his illness, and Judith informs that she will not visit him. Edgar puts on his uniform and heads out into the cold, leaving Alice to warn Kurt: 'never let him into your family affairs, never let him get to know your friends, for he'll take them away from you and make them his . . .'

Kurt says Edgar has become 'another person, calm, reserved, considerate' since he gave up drinking, but Alice warns him that 'he's up to no good' and says that he will have turned his destructive power on to him. Edgar arrives, in full uniform, having been to town. He says he met Kurt's estranged son – a young cadet – and has arranged for him to be posted to the island, where he will be under his command. He also tears up his will (which would have left everything to Alice) and says he has filed a petition for divorce: 'I intend to unite my destiny with a woman who will bring my home not only devotion to her husband but also youth and – shall we say – a little beauty?' Alice throws her ring at him and tells Kurt that Edgar tried to kill her by pushing her into the sea. But Edgar has already spoken to Judith, Alice's only witness to this, and secured her silence. He goes, saying that Kurt has ten minutes to leave. Alice begs him not to go, and Kurt declares that 'Now that he wants to rob me of my son, he must die'. She begs him to blow up the fortress, and reveals that Edgar has been involved in embezzling funds. She fantasizes about his downfall ('Alice, are you a devil too?' asks Kurt) and flirts with Kurt: 'now I'm free, free, free!'

Later that evening, Edgar has lit dozens of candles and is 'making preparations to go': destroying cigars, whisky, love letters and pictures of his wife. He leaves and Alice and Kurt enter, having become involved in an erotic, sado-masochistic relationship. Kurt is both repulsed and attracted:

Since I saw you in all your horrible nakedness, since my passion blinded me, I know the full force of evil. What's ugly becomes beautiful and what's good seems ugly and weak!

It is clear that they are leaving together. Edgar returns and reveals that he invented everything that happened in town. When Alice calls Kurt her 'lover', Edgar draws his sabre, performs a 'dance of death' and collapses. To Alice's surprise,

Kurt leaves, saying 'Go to the hell from whence you came!' Husband and wife are left together again, wondering whether 'life is serious or just a hoax?', and, as the curtain falls, they agree, to our horror, to celebrate their silver wedding.

Part Two (which is a separate play but shares the same principal characters) opens in Kurt's house, where Judith ('a little flirt with plaits down her back and skirts that are too short') is teasing Kurt's son Allan. But Judith already has a fervent admirer – an unnamed Lieutenant – and there seems to be no future for Allan. When Kurt arrives, he talks about the pleasure of being reunited with his son, but Alice warns Kurt of Edgar's continued malice towards him.

Edgar soon undermines Kurt's quarantine methods and criticizes him for having pulled out of a savings scheme he has set up. He also tries to get Judith married off to an old colonel and Allan is in despair. Edgar tells Kurt that his investments have failed and that he is going to have to sell everything he has, and soon buys Kurt's house. Allan is about to be sent off to Lapland (having had his commission bought by Edgar) when Judith declares her love. Kurt realizes that his financial situation prevents him from entering parliament, and Edgar announces his intentions to do so himself. Kurt acknowledges that everything Edgar has done to destroy him is like 'an everyday transaction between fellow citizens'; but Judith has sent a message of rejection to the colonel and Edgar has a stroke when he hears the news. By the end, all he can do is 'slobber unintelligibly' while Alice curses his dying body, saying a 'garden would be too good a resting place for this barrowload of muck'. His last words are 'forgive them for they know what they do' and as the play ends, the others realize the strange, appalling grandeur behind Edgar's malevolence.

∞ About the play

The Dance of Death marks Strindberg's first significant return to the theatre after the 'inferno crisis'. It is influenced by the eighteenth-century mystic Emmanuel Swedenborg, whose writings gave a powerful image of marriage in hell, and of human life as purgatory. As Strindberg wrote in a note:

If this existence is already purgatory or an inferno for crimes we have previously committed, we are all demons, here to torment each other, and when we are driven against our will to do evil, we are only doing our duty, but suffer all the same from the fact that we have done wrong. This is the double curse of existence. No one has the opportunity of tormenting one another as thoroughly as a man and a woman who love [and hate] one another.

The play was also inspired by the real-life marriage of Strindberg's sister Anna and Hugo von Philps.

At the centre of *The Dance of Death* is Edgar and his wife Alice. She describes him as 'a bully with a slave's mentality', as a vampire:

[who] likes to sink his claws into other people's destinies, suck excitement out of other lives, batten on others, because his own life is so totally boring to him.

Edgar has a brutal sarcastic wit, and a strong sense of his own strength and independence:

When I come to die, I'll be able to say I don't owe any-body anything. I've never got anything for nothing. I've had nothing but enemies all my life, and they've helped me on my way, not harmed me.

But he also has a powerful sense of the finality of death:

Once the mechanism's done for, of course, there's hardly so much as a barrowload of muck to tip on the garden, but as long as it holds you have to kick and fight with your hands and feet for all your worth.

Despite all this, Edgar is capable of flashes of affection and wit ('I'm a very good husband, and this old lady's the best wife in the world'). Despite his misanthropy and control mania, and his paranoia and melodramatic self-pity, Edgar is touched by a strange kind of tragic grace. As Kurt says:

> He'd be comic if he weren't tragic, and for all his pettiness there's something grand about him.

Edgar's wife, Alice – like two out of three of Strindberg's own wives – used to be an actress ('All my friends are big stars now!'). Not surprisingly, she has a melodramatic sensibility: one minute playing the victim, the next a highly sexualized and vengeful Fury. Her hatred for her husband knows no bounds:

> What shall I say? That I have sat in this tower for a life-time, a prisoner, kept from life by a man I have always hated, and whom I now hate so boundlessly that the day he died I would laugh for joy!

But she is complicit in the disaster of their marriage, and is no innocent.

Kurt is the hapless witness to their desperately dark relationship. In some ways, he is presented as an innocent, the voice of normality in an increasingly abnormal situation. But he is in no sense a bland figure and Strindberg manages to suggest an inner sadness – above all in relationship to his failed marriage and his children – which is striking.

Part Two was almost certainly written to order for Strindberg's German publisher, who felt that *Part One* was too gloomy. It is greatly inferior, and does not provide new insights into the central couple. Both plays are very hard to pull off in the theatre, above all because the balance between morbid gloom and satirical wit is a fine one to strike. But they have a striking theatricality which, when acted and directed well, can be riveting to watch.

The Dance of Death is deeply flawed, aesthetically and dramatically as well as morally and spiritually. Many of its psychological motivations are left unexplained and it has an alarming tendency to loop back on itself or lurch forward uncontrollably. Yet its ferocious, desperate, almost comically macabre quality makes it an extraordinarily powerful image of the impossibility of marriage, and the dark, self-destructive hatred that can be the result:

> I'm already your slave, but you aren't content with that, your slave has to be tortured and thrown to the dogs.

∽ In performance

Part One of *The Dance of Death* was first performed in Cologne in 1905 and was seen with *Part Two* in Berlin later that year. The play received its Swedish première (in two parts on separate evenings) at Strindberg's Intimate Theatre in 1909. Strindberg told August Falck that it was his 'best play', and described the part of Edgar as:

> A refined demon! Evil shines out of his eyes, which sometimes flash with a glint of satanic humour. His face is bloated with liquor and corruption, and he so relishes saying evil things that he almost sucks them, tastes them, rolls them around his tongue before spitting them out. He thinks of course that he is cunning and superior, but like all stupid people he becomes at such moments a pitiful and petulant wretch.

Max Reinhardt staged both plays together at the Deutsches Theater in Berlin in 1912. This production was seen in Copenhagen in 1915. They were first performed in London in 1924 and subsequently in 1928, when the *Times* reviewer Charles Morgan wrote:

> Loose, tangled and contradictory as this play often is, it leaves an astonishing, an almost unaccountable, impression of genius. To the coldly regarding eye, it exhibits a crowd of faults – now of over-emphasis, now of forced movements towards a climax, now of rash inconsistency of structure, yet as a beggar's cloak full of holes may have a kind of majestic beauty when the wind fills it, so this

broken drama, having unmistakably the winds of vision in it, has beauty and dignity and power.

Despite this praise, it was not until Laurence Olivier and Geraldine McEwan performed both parts together in one evening in 1965 at the Old Vic that *The Dance Of Death* began to be widely recognized in the English-speaking theatre. It was produced by the RSC in 1978. In 2001, Ian McKellen and Helen Mirren played husband and wife on Broadway (*Part One* only), and McKellen reprised it in London with Frances de la Tour in 2003.

Ingmar Bergman attempted to produce the play twice: the first time (1976), he was interrupted when he was arrested by the tax authorities; the second attempt (1978) was aborted when his leading actor, Anders Ek, died.

Part One translated by Michael Robinson, Oxford, 1998; *Part Two* by Michael Meyer, Methuen, 1991

A Dream Play
(*Ett drömspel*)

1901

∾ Characters

The Voice of Indra and Indra's Daughter
Agnes
The Glazier, *her father*
The Officer
His Father and Mother
Lina
The Stage Door-Keeper and the Billposter
A Ballet Dancer
The Voice of Victoria
A Singer and a Prompter
A Policeman and a Lawyer
A One-Armed Clerk and a One-Eyed Clerk
Kristin
Three Doctoral Candidates
A Quarantine Master
A Dandy, A Coquette and her 'Friend'
A Poet
He and She
A Retired Man
Three Maids
Edith and her Mother
A Naval Officer
Alice
A Schoolmaster and a Schoolboy
A Newly Married Man and Wife
A Blind Man
Two Coal-Heavers
A Gentleman and his Wife
The Chancellor of the University

The Deans of Theology, Philosophy, Medicine and Law
Dancers, members of the opera chorus, children, schoolboys,
sailors, all 'Right-Thinking People, etc.

⌘ The story

The Prologue takes place in the atmosphere above earth.
Indra's Daughter has been travelling through the cosmos and
has lost her way. She asks her father about the world below.
She thinks it is beautiful, but he says it was once much more so.
She hears human speech and thinks 'it has not a joyful sound'.
She then hears cries of joy and tells her father that he judges
mankind 'too harshly'. He tells her to 'descend and see'.

Indra's Daughter, now a human called Agnes, asks her
father, a Glazier, about a nearby castle 'topped by a flower-
bud, resembling a crown' rising out of manure. She suggests
a prisoner is waiting for her to free him. They go inside and
find the Officer rocking in his chair, striking the table with
his sabre. Agnes says she has come to free him, and he
declares that life has been unfair to him. They watch as his
mother, convinced that she is dying, makes peace with her
husband. She instructs her son never to 'quarrel with God'
or feel that life has been unfair, and shows him a book that as
a child he tore up and hid, letting his brother take the blame.
She lends her servant, Lina, a cloak for a christening. Her
husband complains, as it was a recent present from him, but
she concludes: 'Help one person, and you hurt another. Oh
this life.'

Agnes finds herself in a theatre corridor. There is a door
with a hole shaped like a four-leaf clover. She asks the Stage
Door-keeper whether the shawl she is crocheting is ready yet.
The Old Woman tells her about her lover who abandoned
her thirty years previously. A Billposter tells Agnes that the
Old Woman was a great ballerina, and that he has achieved
his childhood dream of owning a green fishing chest and net.
They see the Officer, ecstatic because 'Miss Victoria' has
finally agreed to marry him. It grows dark, and the Officer

leaves to call the Glazier to put in double windows. He returns, with his roses withered. Victoria has still not appeared. Agnes tells the Stage Door-keeper that she will take her place and learn about the world. The Old Woman says she must not sleep, day or night, but can wear her shawl; if she finds it too heavy, she will relieve her.

It is now autumn. The Officer, grey-haired, is still waiting for his love. The Billposter returns from fishing, disappointed with his net. Spring arrives and the Officer, now white haired, holds only a few twigs from his bouquet. He sends for a locksmith to open the door. The Glazier arrives with a diamond: surrounded by opera singers and dancers, he is about to use it to open the door, when a Policeman stops him. The scene changes to a Lawyer's office. He asks Agnes for her shawl: he wants to burn it with all its 'griefs and sorrows', but she says it is not finished yet – she wants to add his grief to it. He says it would not be big enough. His hands are blackened and his clothes stink with the crimes and despair he is forced to hear. The worst are poor married couples who amass huge debts. 'Who shall pay?' he asks: 'He who feeds the birds,' she replies.

They go to a church where degrees are being conferred. The dancers from the theatre crown several men with laurel wreaths, but the Lawyer is turned away. He and Agnes, whose shawl is now washed white, are left alone. 'Why is he unworthy?' asks Agnes. Is it because he 'spoke up for the poor, said a good word for the criminal?' He tells her not to speak evil of mankind: he will plead their cause. She looks into a mirror and sees in it the 'world set to rights'. After criticizing the university faculties who help no one, she tells the Lawyer that she will give him a wreath that will suit him better. She plays the organ, from which human voices are heard, begging the Lord to be merciful. It transforms into Fingal's Cave, where the Lawyer hears weeping and moaning. He tells Agnes that a wife and home is the only joy available in the world, and they decide to get married, convinced that their poverty will not matter if they love each other.

Agnes and the Lawyer are in a simple room in his office. A servant, Kristin, pastes up the windows to cut down heating costs, but Agnes complains: 'You are shutting out the air. I'm suffocating.' They try to solve the problems marriage has brought them: poverty, dirt and their child's crying. Despite their best intentions, it is proving impossible. The Officer, now a doctor, arrives and persuades Agnes to go with him to Fairhaven, where it is summer. The Lawyer sees that he is going back to his 'first hell', and leaves through the door, saying: 'When I close it, I open the way out for you, Agnes!'

The Officer and Agnes arrive at Foulstrand, a quarantine station for Fairhaven. The Quarantine Master, with his face blackened, shows them around. Rich people who have over-indulged exercise on torture machines. Among them are an old Dandy, still in love with an old Coquette, who flirts with her Lover under his nose. They see ovens where cholera victims are disinfected. They meet a Poet who gazes at the sky but yearns for mud. Lina appears, now married with five children, ignored and unloved, her beauty and joy destroyed. Two lovers arrive in a white boat: one of them is Victoria. They have been contaminated by the 'petty dirt of life' and must stay in quarantine for 'forty days and forty nights'. The ovens are lit. The Officer cannot bear to see her suffer. Agnes cries: 'Human beings are to be pitied.'

In Fairhaven, everyone is at a holiday dance, except for the children who work as servants. Edith sits alone outside, starts to play Bach on the piano and the dancers all stop to listen. A Naval Officer leads his partner, Alice, away. The Officer is forced to learn mathematics, and finds that 'logic' is absurd. Agnes and he are told they must dance 'before the plague breaks out'. He shows her a newlywed couple: they are happy, but worried about their happiness dying, and walk into the sea to drown. They meet the richest and most envied man in Fairhaven – who is blind. His only wish is to be able to see his son the Naval Officer depart on his ship. Edith and Alice watch the boat depart: 'Parting and meeting. Meeting and parting. That is life.' The Lawyer tells Agnes that she has yet to experience the worst thing, 'repetition', and tells her to return to her duties. She says she would rather die, and wants to open the locked door. The Lawyer tells her she must retrace her steps. She agrees, but says she must first must go into the wilderness to find herself again. She hears the 'lost souls of Foulstrand' and wants to rescue them. The Lawyer tells her: 'Someone tried once, and they hanged him on a cross.' When she asks who, he tells her 'right thinking people' – the same who denied him his laurel wreath.

They find themselves by the Mediterranean. Agnes declares: 'This is Paradise', but two Coal-heavers say that it is 'hell'. They are forbidden to swim in the sea or eat the oranges that grow nearby. They do all the work for little food while the idle rich eat luxuries. Agnes is shocked at the Lawyer's explanations, while one of the Coal-heavers says that it is time to get violent.

Back at Fingal's Cave, Agnes tells the Poet that the cave is the 'ear of Indra' and recites the wind's song of human suffering. They see ships that have been destroyed by the waves, including the ship they saw leave Fairhaven. Agnes thinks she must have dreamed it all, but he says that he wrote it in poetry once. He hands her a petition to take to Indra: 'Why were you born in pain? Child of Man? Grief follows grief. So does the journey until your death.' They both watch as the waves rise and threaten the ship. The crew pray for 'Christ to have mercy!' and a figure walks across the water to save them. The crew jump overboard in fear. The ship becomes a house, a tower of Babel and then a training ground where soldiers attack a church.

Agnes returns to the theatre corridor and asks the Stage Door-keeper to open the door. The Officer appears, young again and in love. Several university Deans quarrel about opening the door, which may conceal 'dangerous truths'. Agnes accuses them of sowing doubt in the minds of the young and is threatened with death. The door is finally opened to reveal . . . nothing. Agnes is satisfied, but the chorus of 'All Right-Minded People' are confused and offer her threats. Agnes asks the Poet to accompany her to the wilderness, where she will explain everything. The Lawyer arrives and reminds Agnes of her child. She is stricken with conscience, but decides she has a higher duty to mankind.

Back at the castle, Agnes tells the Poet that she is soon to be consumed by fire and 'rise again into the ether'. Humans would not fear death, she argues, if they had faith in their prophets. The Poet asks her to explain the 'riddle' of man's suffering. She says life on earth is only a dream. In order for people to rid themselves of their earthly element, they must suffer. However, suffering conflicts with love and between the 'agony of the ecstasy and the ecstasy of the agony', mankind lives in strife. She will say no more, and shakes the dust off her feet by burning her shoes. Other characters join in: among them the Stage Door-keeper, who burns her shawl, the Officer his roses and the Lawyer a useless lawsuit. Agnes departs to set mankind's griefs before God's throne:

> Farewell! Tell your brothers and sisters I shall remember them,
> Where I now go, and their lament
> I shall bear in your name to the throne.
> For human beings are to be pitied!

The castle burns and on its roof a giant chrysanthemum bursts into flower.

↻ About the play

A Dream Play's exceptionally complex plot is an essential part of its nature. It is a piece of pure story-telling, a surreal journey through a dreamland. Strindberg wrote it with a growing interest in Hinduism, and the play echoes the important moment in *The Bhagavad Gita* when Krishna declares that the 'world is an illusion'.

Strindberg summarized his intentions in his preface:

> In this dream play, the author has . . . attempted to imitate
> the inconsequent yet transparently logical shape of a
> dream. Everything can happen, everything is possible and
> probable . . . and just as a dream is more often painful
> than happy, so an undertone of melancholy and of pity for
> all mortal beings accompanies this flickering tale.

As in dreams, this constantly shifting scenario is made up of highly realistic fragments – many taken directly from Strindberg's own life – peopled by characters caught in their own unique circumstances. The result is a dense parable of the pain of human life, rich with complex iconography, drawn from several different religions (Christianity, Buddhism, Hinduism) as well as a whole range of different literary genres. Its circular movement leads inexorably to a philosphical understanding of the role of suffering.

At the play's centre is the character of Agnes, a young girl discovering the hard truths of life. She encounters love and heartbreak, ambition and humiliation, hopes of a better life and despair. She is also confronted with the injustice of society and the impossibility of a happy marriage. Her pilgrimage is the emotional and philosophical heart of the play. The ritualized burning of worldly goods (and troubles) that she ini- titates at the end is the essential prerequisite to attaining the paradise and fulfillment that is finally glimpsed.

The people Agnes meets are all drawn with realism: the frustrated Officer who thinks that life has been unfair and is locked in expectation of the lover who will never join him; the Stage Door-keeper whose youth and glory days are gone, and who is crocheting a shawl as a record of the suffering of the world; the Billposter who is still locked in his childhood desires and disappointments; the Lawyer who has seen the desperate and wicked pass through his office, and has experi- enced unhappy marriage but is prepared to be involved in another one; the servant Kristin endlessly papering the cracks in the windows; and the Poet who has created a world in his writings but who cannot live in the real one. And there are dozens of other figures: the angry Coal-heavers on the brink of violent revolution; the rich Blind Man who is denied the one thing he wants; the hypocritical and foolish academics who squabble amongst themselves and fail to recognize true talent; the backstage world of the theatre; and the crew who jump overboard in fear when they see a figure walking on the water to save them – and dozens of others, all drawn with an extraordinary mixture of satire, humanity and tenderness.

A Dream Play has a powerful, almost hallucinatory sense of location, rich with detail and particularity, even as it continually shifts and changes. It also has an astounding theatricality, and reads more like a score for an ambitious piece of performance art than a conventional play. Strindberg had not read Freud (whose *Interpretation of Dreams* was published in 1900), but *A Dream Play* is like a dramatization of Freud's most profound observations. Utterly radical in conception, and dazzling well achieved, *A Dream Play* is one of Strindberg's consummate masterpieces.

∞ In performance

A Dream Play had to wait six years for its première at the Swedish Theatre on 17 April 1907.

As well as the recently added Prologue, Strindberg sent the director an introduction to be spoken to the audience. It is one of the most revealing things he wrote:

> Until recently the notion that life is a dream seemed to us only a figure of Calderon's. But when Shakespeare in *The Tempest* has Prospero say 'We are such stuff as dreams are made on' and employs Macbeth to comment on life as 'a tale, told by an idiot', we ought surely to give the matter some further thought.
>
> Whoever accompanies the author for these brief hours along the path of his sleepwalking will possibly discover a certain similarity between the apparent medley of the dream and the motley canvas of our disorderly life . . .

As far as the loose, disconnected form of the play is concerned, that, too, is only apparent. For on closer examination, the composition emerges as quite coherent – a symphony, polyphonic, now and then the manner for a fugue with a constantly recurring main theme, which is repeated and varied by the thirty odd parts in every key. There are no solos with accompaniments, that is, no bravura roles, no characters, or rather, no caricatures, no intrigues, no certain lines that invite applause. The vocal parts are strictly arranged, and in the sacrificial scene of the finale, everything that has happened passes in review, with the themes repeated once again, just as a man's life with all its incidents, is said to do at the moment of death. Yet another similarity!

Now it is time to see the play itself – and to hear it! With a little goodwill on your part, the battle is almost won. That is all we ask of you.

Curtain up!

Despite all this, however, Strindberg stayed at home:

It is 8pm . . . and the curtain is now rising on the *Dream Play*, while I sit at home as is my custom at premières. Last night I saw the dress rehearsal – and all my confidence in my most loved play, child of my greatest pain, vanished. I became gloomy, decided that it ought never to be performed – such things must not be said to people, and they must not murmur at their fate. I have been waiting for some catastrophe to intervene and prevent the performance . . . . 11pm. Telephone call that the *Dream Play* was a success.

It only played for twelve performances. Strindberg's second wife Harriet Bosse played Agnes.

Max Reinhardt's production at Dramaten, Stockholm in 1921 created a world which, according to Siegfried Jacobsohn, was full of:

A shivering, desperate, shrieking humanity . . . so distorted, so gloomy, so full of fantastic life and motion, that it might be Van Gogh's.

The great Swedish director Olaf Molander produced the play no less than seven times between 1935 and 1955 and, partly in reaction to Reinhardt's 'German expressionist' approach, refined his notion of 'fantastic realism'. Molander's protégé Ingmar Bergman was also obsessed with the play, and has directed it four times (1963, 1970, 1977 and 1986).

A Dream Play had its British première in 1930. It was performed at the Traverse Theatre in Edinburgh in a version for nine actors in 1974 and John Barton directed it at the RSC in 1985. It is rarely performed today.

Translated by Michael Robinson, Oxford, 1998

The Ghost Sonata
(Spöksonaten)

A Chamber Play

1907

ᴄᢒ Characters

Hummel, *a Company Director*
Arkenholz, *a student*
A Milkmaid, *a vision*
A Caretaker's Wife
A Caretaker
A Dead Man, *a Consul*
The Dark Lady, *the daughter of the Dead Man and the
    Caretaker's Wife*
A Colonel
The Mummy, *the Colonel's wife*
A Young Lady, *his daughter, but actually Hummel's daughter*
A Posh Man, *called Baron Skanskorg, engaged to the
    Caretaker's daughter*
Johannsson, *Hummel's servant*
Bengtsson, *the Colonel's manservant*
The Fiancée, *Hummel's former fiancée, a white-haired old
    lady*
The Cook
A Maid
Beggars

ᴄᢒ The story

It is Sunday morning in the street outside a fashionable
house. Through the windows of the drawing-room a marble
statue of a beautiful young woman can be seen. An old man,
Hummel, sits in a wheelchair reading the paper while a
Milkmaid washes her face in the fountain. A Student asks her

for a drink of water, and tells her that a nearby house collapsed the evening before: he was on the scene and helped rescue several victims. He asks her to bathe his eyes. Hummel says the student's heroism is in the papers, and recognizes him as the son of Arkenholz, a man he was accused of bankrupting. He tells him that in fact Arkenholz swindled *him* out of all his savings. In payment, he asks the Student to go to see *The Valkyrie* that night and sit next to a Colonel and his daughter. The Student accepts this 'strange adventure', and says that he would like to live in the house. He is told that the Colonel lives there with his wife, a wrinkled old 'Mummy', obsessed with the statue of herself as a young woman. It is revealed that the Student is a 'Sunday child', who can see things others cannot. Hummel tells him about the house's other inhabitants: the white-haired woman sitting in the window of the house was Hummel's fiancée sixty years ago, but no longer recognizes him, while the Dark-haired Lady, the daughter of the Caretaker's Wife, has a noble lover who is divorcing his wife in order to marry her. He is also the only son of the man lying dead upstairs. Hummel tells the student he is going to die soon and asks him to stay with him. He takes his hand, but his own is freezing cold and the Student asks him to let go. The Student sees the Colonel's daughter and cries in despair at her beauty. Hummel tells him: 'Serve me, and you shall have power'. The Student asks 'Is this a pact? Must I sell my soul?' Hummel asks him to be son and heir to him: 'Enjoy life and let me look on, at least from a distance.' They watch the house's inhabitants again and the Dead Man, unseen by Hummel, leaves the house to count the number of wreaths that have been left for him. Hummel's servant Johansson arrives and wheels him away, but returns to remind the Student about his evening's task. He warns the Student about his master's destructive power, adding that he is being blackmailed by him and works for no wages. He reveals that Hummel is only frightened of one thing – the Milkmaid. Hummel returns, surrounded by beggars, and says he once saved a girl from drowning; at which point, both he and the Student see the Milkmaid raising up her arms 'as if she were drowning'. Hummel is terrified.

The action moves to the round drawing-room inside the house, some days later. Bengtsson tells Johansson about the 'ghost supper' they are to serve that night. The Colonel has been holding these for twenty years with the same guests. Bengtsson shows Johansson the Mummy, who has been sitting in a dark closet for forty years. Bengtsson compares the statue to the old woman. He also shows Johansson the 'death screen' which they put up when someone in the house is going to die. Hummel appears on crutches. He has not been invited, but asks Bengtsson to announce him and tells Johansson to 'beat it'. He is startled by the Mummy, who calls him Jacob and says that she is his old lover, Amalia. He asks after the child – 'our child' – who is in the 'hyacinth room'. She says the Colonel still believes that she is his daughter, despite being told the opposite. Hummel tells her of his plans to marry his daughter to the Student, now his heir. She tells him that her old lover – the Baron – and Hummel's former Fiancée will join them at supper. The Mummy says they keep meeting because 'crimes and secrets and guilt bind us together', and leaves, asking Hummel to 'spare' her husband. Hummel confronts the Colonel with his debts, including the mortgage to the house which he – Hummel – owns. The Colonel agrees to tolerate him in his home and to dismiss Bengtsson. But Hummel has evidence that the Colonel is neither a nobleman nor an officer: indeed, he proves that he used to be a footman. The Colonel welcomes the Student and asks him to entertain his daughter. The guests gather and sit in ghastly silence as Hummel claims that the Young Lady is his daughter and that her illness was caused by the 'air that reeks of crime' in the house. He intends to 'root out the weeds, expose the crimes, settle past accounts, so that these young people may make a fresh start in this home, which I have given them!' He demands that the guests leave or he will have them arrested. The Mummy stops the clock's pendulum and tells them she intends to 'stop time in its course'. She identifies Hummel and accuses him of being a 'stealer of souls' and of having murdered the Dead Man. She also reveals that the Student's father never owed him a penny. She rings for Bengtsson, who announces that Hummel served in his kitchen, where he sucked 'all the goodness out of our home'. He accuses him of luring a young girl out on to the ice and drowning her because she had witnessed one of his crimes. Hummel hands the Colonel's debts to the Mummy. She leads Hummel to the cupboard where a rope hangs. Bengtsson erects the death screen, while in the 'hyacinth room' the Young Lady accompanies the Student on the harp as he sings the 'song of the sun'.

Days later, the Student and the Young Lady are in the 'hyacinth room', where there is a large Buddha, out of whose lap grows a flower. The Young Lady sits at her harp, and she and the Student talk about the hyacinths pointing up to the stars. He wants to marry her, but first, says the Young Lady, must come 'the waiting, the trials, the patience'. The fat Cook appears to ask what they want for dinner, but she cooks meals with no nourishment, draining the sustenance and eating it herself. When the Student asks why they do not dismiss her, he is told that it is 'ordained' that she stay. She also has a Maid who never does any work, and everything is imperfect in the house. The Student asks the Young Lady to sing for him, but she tells him he must wait ('First the toil, the toil of holding the dirt of life at bay') and warns him that he can never win her. The Student describes Hummel's funeral and tells the Young Lady that his father was sent to a madhouse for suddenly speaking the truth. He talks about the house and how he thought it was paradise, only to find it full of lies and hypocrisy: nothing fulfils its promise. He tries to play the harp but no sound comes from it. He curses the corrupt 'madhouse, this prison, this charnel house the earth' and calls on Christ to save them. The Young Lady collapses and tells Bengtsson to unfold the death screen. The Student welcomes death, which will deliver the innocent girl from the poison and guilt of others. As the room fills with white light, the harp's strings begin to rustle and the Student sings his song. As the Young Lady dies, the room disappears and Arnold Böcklin's painting *The Isle of the Dead* appears in the background: 'Music, soft, tranquil, and pleasantly melancholy is heard from the island.'

∽ About the play

Strindberg wrote *The Ghost Sonata* in considerable physical pain: the psoriasis which caused his hands to bleed was at its most virulent and the stomach cancer which killed him five years later was beginning to cause him discomfort. Furthermore, his relationship with Harriet Bosse had come to an end and he was living alone in the Blue Tower. To an extent, with *The Ghost Sonata*, Strindberg faced up to his imminent death.

The Ghost Sonata was not to be his last play – he was to write five more – but it was his last major piece. The title is in homage to Beethoven, whose music Strindberg always loved. The play is labelled 'Opus 3' and has a musical structure in three distinct movements, which lead towards an eventual harmony. Despite its extraordinary, surreal atmosphere, it is shot through with detailed realism, both psychological and scenic. It is a strange mixture of social satire, fairy-tale, ghost story and spiritual parable.

At its centre is Arkenholz, the young Student on a journey from naïvety through to understanding, and from youth to maturity. He accepts a Faustian bargain, and meets and falls in love with the Young Lady. As in a fairy-tale, he undergoes dangers and confronts an ogre in order to free the princess. He is blessed with certain skills, above all his clairvoyancy. By the end, he has gained the courage to express the truth. The Young Lady is beautiful, but she is also dying. She only comes to life in the beautiful last scene – in which she dies.

The catalyst for this action is the old man Hummel. He is deeply contradictory. On the one hand he says that he wants to do something good to the world:

> Listen, all my life, I've *taken*; now I've a longing to give! But no one will accept what I have – – – I'm rich, very rich, but I have no heirs except for one scoundrel, who plagues the life out of me – – – become my son, inherit me while I'm still alive, enjoy life and let me look on, at least from a distance.

But Hummel is also a monster, a satirical portrait of the corrupt capitalism that was emerging throughout Europe at the time. He is enormously wealthy, deceives the poor, tricks the police and destroys the Colonel's sense of self. Worse, he is a murderer.

The Colonel's wife is a grotesque creation: half-baby, half-parrot, embalmed like an Egyptian mummy and obsessed with the statue portraying her as a youth. She cannot stand sick people, including her own daughter. She is also capable of powerful intervention and her denunciation of Hummel towards the end of the second scene leads directly to his death:

> We are poor miserable creatures, all of us; we have erred and we have sinned, like everyone else; we are not what we seem, for at heart we are better than ourselves, since we hate our faults; but that you, Jacob Hummel with your false name, can sit here in judgement on us proves how much worse you are than us! You are also not who you seem to be! – You're a stealer of human souls – you stole me once with your false promises; you murdered the Consul who was buried here today, you strangled him with notes of hand; and you've stolen the student by binding him with an imaginary debt of his father's, who never owed you a penny . . .

This quartet is surrounded by various other figures, satirical portraits of the Swedish bourgeoisie. The Colonel lives in a world of dreams and denial, and Hummel's ruthlessly stripping him of his illusions is one of the play's most shocking sequences. The Colonel is joined by the elegant Baron Skanskorg and Miss Holsteinkrona, Hummel's fiancée. In the servants, Johannsen and Bengtsson, we see Strindberg's customary interest in the edginess of the working class: rebellious, virile and dangerously aggressive. Strindberg was apparently plagued by bad cooks and his portrait of the Cook is partly revenge. She is a vampire who sucks 'the life out of us, and we out of you, we take the blood and give you back the water'. Throughout, there is a powerful sense of ambivalence and illusion in which nothing is but what is not.

Despite its morbid gloominess, *The Ghost Sonata* offers glimpses of happiness, in the flashes of benevolence that are such a part of his most malevolent characters, in the Student's youthful optimism as he enters the house and in the Student's ecstatic embrace of the Young Lady's death:

> The deliverer is coming! Welcome, you pale and gentle one! – And you, you beautiful, unhappy, innocent creature who bear no blame for your suffering, sleep, sleep without dreams, and when you wake again . . . may you be greeted by a sun that does not burn, in a house without dust, by friends without faults, by a love without flaw.

Some detect irony in the Student's final song, but Strindberg's explicitly spiritual intentions are made all too clear in a letter to his publisher in 1907:

> It is horrible like life, when the veil falls from our eyes and we see things as they are. It has shape and content, the wisdom that comes with age, as our knowledge increases and we learn to understand. This is how 'the Weaver' weaves men's destinies; secrets like these are to be found in every home. People are too proud to admit it; most of them boast of their imagined luck, and hide their misery. The Colonel acts out his private comedy to the end; illusion (Maya) has become reality to him – the Mummy awakens first, one cannot wake the others . . . I have suffered as though in Kama-Loka [a dream world through which humans wander before they enter the kingdom of death] during the writing of it and my hands

have bled (literally). What has saved my soul from darkness during this work has been my religion . . . The hope of a better life to come; the firm conviction that we live in a world of madness and delusion (illusion) from which we must fight our way free. For me things have become brighter, and I have written with the feeling that this is my 'Last Sonata'.

☙ In performance

The Ghost Sonata was written specifically for the 161-seat Intimate Theatre which Strindberg had set up with the young actor August Falck. It was premièred on 21 January 1908 and was heavily criticized. Max Reinhardt directed a remarkable expressionist production of the play in Berlin in 1916, which was seen in Stockholm in 1917 and Copenhagen in 1920.

The play was not seen again in Stockholm until the young Ingmar Bergman directed the first of his four productions of the play in a children's theatre in 1941. The great Swedish director Olof Molander directed the first of his five productions in 1942; its quality caused Bergman to consider giving up directing altogether. Bergman's subsequent productions were presented in Malmo (1954) and Stockholm (1973 and 2000). He has called the play 'the most remarkable drama ever to be written in Swedish', and both he and Molander emphasized the play's human qualities over and above its expressionistic theatricality.

The Ghost Sonata received its English-language première by the Provincetown Players in New York in 1924, and its British première in Oxford in 1926. It is very rarely performed in Britain, but was seen at the Gate Theatre, Notting Hill in 1997. It has been televised by the BBC twice (in 1962 and 1980). The composer Aribert Reimann wrote an opera based on the play in 1984.

Translated by Michael Robinson, Oxford, 1998

The Legacy

The plays of Ibsen, Chekhov and Strindberg have had a profound influence on the subsequent development of twentieth-century drama, novels and films.

No work of Ibsen's has had more impact than *A Doll's House* and the thirty years after it was written saw a flurry of 'New Woman' plays, of which Florence Bell's and Elizabeth Robins's *Alan's Wife* (1894) and Ghita Sowerby's *Rutherford and Son* (1912) were the most remarkable. *A Doll's House* had a huge impact on discussions about the position of women in society and became one of the cardinal texts of feminism. Ibsen was also the great pioneer of naturalism in the theatre and many small 'club' theatres were opened in order to première his scandalous masterpiece *Ghosts*. 'Ibsenism' was a movement which swept across Europe and America in the 1890s and could hardly be ignored by anyone involved in the theatre.

Bernard Shaw was a devoted Ibsenite and his early plays, especially *Widowers' Houses* (1892), *Candida* (1895) and *Mrs Warren's Profession* (1902), all bear the marks of Ibsen's influence. Similarly, the plays of Harley Granville Barker and Sean O'Casey (in *Juno and the Paycock*, the educated young Mary is reading *A Doll's House*, *Ghosts* and *The Wild Duck* – 'buks only fit for chiselurs') are rich with the influence of Ibsen. Several important English-language novelists were inspired by him: Thomas Hardy, Henry James, James Joyce and D. H. Lawrence are the most eminent. With the reaction against naturalism in European theatre, Ibsen's influence began to wane: the expressionists preferred Strindberg, and Bertolt Brecht dismissed Ibsen as a bourgeois writer. In America, however, Tennessee Williams and Arthur Miller drew heavily on him, particularly the latter's *All My Sons* (1947).

Ibsen's insistence that drama should be about the real things in life – money, society, marriage, children, illness, sex and death – has had more impact than the particularities of his dramatic style. Not since Shakespeare had a playwright addressed the big questions with such skill and moral courage. His legacy is evident in the determination of twentieth-century playwrights to write about 'real life' in a way which is uncompromising and profound.

Chekhov's influence, meanwhile, has been, like his plays, subtle and pervasive. While there has been no such thing as an obvious successor, he often surfaces in the work of writers who appear to be his polar opposite. Tennessee Williams's emotional candour and full-blown poeticism might seem light years away from Chekhov's muted colours, but Williams, having found that reading Chekhov was an invaluable means of recovering from an early nervous breakdown, went on to write his own version of *The Seagull*, *The Notebook of Trigorin*. David Mamet's dynamically vernacular style might seem equally remote from Chekhov's ambiguities, but he has in fact written versions of *Uncle Vanya*, *The Cherry Orchard* and *Three Sisters*. Uniquely, too, Chekhov's influence has been retrospective: it has become a critical commonplace to describe certain productions of Shakespeare's comedies as 'Chekhovian' in atmosphere, though such a generic adjective has hardly attached itself to Ibsen, Strindberg or any other writer.

In England, Bernard Shaw, J. B. Priestley and the undervalued Rodney Ackland were all deeply affected by their first exposure to Chekhov, and it is at least arguable that Terence Rattigan and Alan Ayckbourn have been encouraged by Chekhov's sense of the absurd and of the pressures of repressed emotion. The connections between Chekhov and Harold Pinter – the unexpected weight of meaning behind a single phrase, the comic or oblique expression of strong feeling, the sense of a significant world beyond the immediate action – are evident.

More centrally, however, Chekhov has changed what we expect of the theatre. His characters seem close enough to us to apply to our lives, yet are so precisely rooted in their own time as to help a contemporary audience understand the history that lies between. His blending of comedy and tragedy within the same moment, his feeling for the discrepancy between limited abilities and high hopes and his unerring sense of human foible are such that few dramatists picking up a pen today are likely to escape him.

The forbidding nature of so much of Strindberg's work has meant that his influence has been more marginal. Many of his contemporaries found his misogyny unappealing, his despair unattractive and his energy alarming. His theatrical style was confusing – his naturalist plays shocked audiences and his later works baffled them – and it was the expressionist and symbolist dramatists of the years leading up to the First World War who most admired him: Franz Wedekind, Carl Sternheim, W. B. Yeats and Arthur Schnitzler. As Sean O'Casey was creating his own, non-naturalistic drama, he wrote approvingly that 'Ibsen can sit serenely in his *Doll's House*, while Strindberg is battling with his heaven and his hell.'

Strindberg's realistic plays became increasingly important after the Second World War, particularly with their merciless anatomy of the woes of marriage. Two of the greatest American plays of the twentieth century could hardly have been written without him: Eugene O'Neill's *Long Day's Journey's into Night* (1940) and Edward Albee's *Who's Afraid of Virginia Woolf?* (1962). In Britain, John Osborne touched the true Strindbergian vein in *Look Back in Anger* (1956):

> One day when I'm no longer running a sweet-stall, I may write a book about us all. It's all here. Written in flames a mile high. And it won't be recollected in tranquillity either, picking daffodils with Auntie Wordsworth. It'll be recollected in fire, and blood. My blood.

The dramatists of the 'absurd' – Jean-Paul Sartre, Eugene Ionesco, Samuel Beckett and Friedrich Durrenmatt – were also affected by Strindberg, and modern British writers such as Patrick Marber and Gregory Motton have acknowledged a debt. The great Swedish film director Ingmar Bergman has been obsessed by Strindberg his entire life, and many of his best films show this. Although Strindberg's feelings about the practicalities of the theatre were lukewarm, his notion of an 'intimate theatre' has been hugely influential: he is the spiritual father of the 'fringe' movement, which reached its height in the 1960s and 1970s and resulted in the opening of many small-scale, experimental auditoria.

These three great dramatists, all writing on the fringes of Europe, have changed our understanding of theatre's potential. Their themes are ours, their innovations have become our expectations, and they open a window onto both their times and our own. They are, quite simply, everywhere we look.

A Chronicle of Plays 1865–1914

1865
T. W. Robertson, *Society*
Bjørnstjerne Bjørnson, *The Newly Marrieds*

1866
Henrik Ibsen, *Brand*
T. W. Robertson, *Ours*

1867
Henrik Ibsen, *Peer Gynt*
T. W. Robertson, *Caste*

1869
Henrik Ibsen, *The League of Youth*

1870
Henry Becque, *Michel Pauper*

1871
Alexander Ostrovsky, *The Forest*

1873
Henrik Ibsen, *Emperor and Galilean*
Eugene Labiche, *The Wedding Guest*
Emile Zola, *Thérèse Raquin*

1874
Bjørnstjerne Bjørnson, *The Editor*
Dion Boucicault, *The Shaughraun*

1875
Alexander Ostrovsky, *Wolves and Sheep*
Bjørnstjerne Bjørnson, *The Bankrupt*

1877
Henrik Ibsen, *Pillars of Society*
Victorien Sardou, *Dora*

Bjørnstjerne Bjørnson, *The King*

1879
Henrik Ibsen, *A Doll's House*
Alexander Ostrovsky, *The Poor Bride*
Bjørnstjerne Bjørnson, *The New System*

1880
Anton Chekhov, *Platonov*
Victorien Sardou, *Divorçons*

1881
Henrik Ibsen, *Ghosts*

1882
Henrik Ibsen, *An Enemy of the People*
Victorien Sardou, *Fedora*
Henri Becque, *Les Corbeaux*

1883
Oscar Wilde, *The Duchess of Padua*
Bjørnstjerne Bjørnson, *A Gauntlet*
Sidney Grundy, *Glass of Fashion*

1884
Henrik Ibsen, *The Wild Duck*

1885
Arthur Wing Pinero, *The Magistrate*
Henri Becque, *La Parisienne*
Bjørnstjerne Bjørnson, *Love And Geography*

1886
Henrik Ibsen, *Rosmersholm*
Leo Tolstoy, *The Power Of Darkness*

1887
Anton Chekhov, *Ivanov*
August Strindberg, *The Father*
Arthur Wing Pinero, *Dandy Dick*
Victorien Sardou, *La Tosca*

1888
Henrik Ibsen, *The Lady from the Sea*
August Strindberg, *Miss Julie*
August Strindberg, *Creditors*
Arthur Wing Pinero, *Sweet Lavender*

1889
Arthur Wing Pinero, *The Weaker Sex*
Sidney Grundy, *White Lie*

1890
Henrik Ibsen, *Hedda Gabler*
Maurice Maeterlinck, *The Intruder*
Maurice Maeterlinck, *The Blind*

1891
Leo Tolstoy, *The Fruits of Enlightenment*

1892
Henrik Ibsen, *The Master Builder*
Oscar Wilde, *Lady Windermere's Fan*
George Bernard Shaw, *Widowers' Houses*
Eugène Labiche, *Haste To The Wedding*
Georges Feydeau, *Le Système Ribadier*

1893
Oscar Wilde, *A Woman of No Importance*
George Bernard Shaw, *Mrs Warren's Profession*
Arthur Wing Pinero, *The Second Mrs Tanqueray*
George Moore, *The Strike at Arlingford*
Elizabeth Robins and Florence Bell, *Alan's Wife*
Victorien Sardou, *Madame Sans-Gêne*
Maurice Maeterlinck, *Pelleas and Melisande*

1894
Henrik Ibsen, *Little Eyolf*
George Bernard Shaw, *You Never Can Tell*
George Bernard Shaw, *Arms and The Man*
Sidney Grundy, *The New Woman*

1895
Oscar Wilde, *An Ideal Husband*
Oscar Wilde, *The Importance of Being Earnest*
Henry James, *Guy Domville*

1896
Henrik Ibsen, *John Gabriel Borkman*
Anton Chekhov, *The Seagull*
Georges Feydeau, *Le Dindon*
Oscar Wilde, *Salome*

1897
George Bernard Shaw, *Candida*
George Bernard Shaw, *The Devil's Disciple*

1898
Arthur Wing Pinero, *Trelawney of the 'Wells'*
Eugène Brieux, *Les Trois Filles de Monsieur Dupont*

1899
Henrik Ibsen, *When We Dead Awaken*
Anton Chekhov, *Uncle Vanya*
George Feydeau, *La Dame de Chez Maxime*
George Feydeau, *L'hotel du Libre Echange*
Sidney Grundy, *The Degenerates*

1900
August Strindberg, *Easter*
Alfred Jarry, *Ubu in Chains*
Romain Rolland, *Danton*
George Bernard Shaw, *Captain Brassbound's Conversion*
Arthur Schnitzler, *La Ronde*
August Strindberg, *The Dance of Death Parts I and II*
Eugène Brieux, *La Robe Rouge*

1901
Anton Chekhov, *Three Sisters*
August Strindberg, *To Damascus Part III*
Harley Granville Barker, *The Marrying of Anne Leete*
J. M. Synge, *When The Moon Has Set*

Bjørnstjerne Bjørnson, *Laboremus*
St John Hankin, *Mr Punch's Dramatic Sequels*

1902
George Bernard Shaw, *Mrs Warren's Profession*
J. M. Barrie, *The Admirable Crichton*
Maxim Gorky, *The Lower Depths*
August Strindberg, *A Dream Play*
Lady Gregory and W. B. Yeats, *Cathleen Ni Houlihan*
Lady Gregory and W. B. Yeats, *The Pot Of Broth*
Romain Rolland, *14th July*
J. M Barrie, *Quality Street*
Sidney Grundy, *Frocks and Frills*
Eugène Brieux, *Les Avariés*

1903
George Bernard Shaw, *Man and Superman*
Somerset Maugham, *A Man of Honour*
J. M. Synge, *In the Shadow of the Glen*
St John Hankin, *The Two Mrs Wetherbys*

1904
Anton Chekhov, *The Cherry Orchard*
J. M. Barrie, *Peter Pan*
St John Hankin, *Lost Masterpieces*
George Bernard Shaw, *John Bull's Other Island*
Maxim Gorky, *Summerfolk*
J. M. Synge, *Riders to the Sea*
Franz Wedekind, *Pandora's Box*
Lady Gregory, *Spreading the News*
Arthur Schnitzler, *The Lonely Road*
W. B. Yeats, *On Bailie's Strand*
W. B. Yeats, *The King's Threshold*
(death of Anton Chekhov)

1905
George Bernard Shaw, *Major Barbara*
Harvey Granville Barker, *The Voysey Inheritance*
J. M. Synge, *The Well of the Saints*

David Belasco, *The Girl of the Golden West*
Maxim Gorky, *Children of the Sun*
St John Hankin, *The Return of the Prodigal*

1906
George Bernard Shaw, *The Doctor's Dilemma*
John Galsworthy, *The Silver Box*
Maxim Gorky, *Barbarians*
Maxim Gorky, *Enemies*
Arthur Wing Pinero, *His House in Order*
St John Hankin, *The Charity that Began at Home*
(death of Henrik Ibsen)

1907
Harley Granville Barker, *Waste*
J. M. Synge, *The Playboy of the Western World*
Paul Claudel, *Le Partage de Midi*
August Strindberg, *The Ghost Sonata*
W. B. Yeats, *Deirdre*
George Feydeau, *A Flea In Her Ear*
Lady Gregory, *The Rising of the Moon*
Elizabeth Robins, *Votes For Women*
St John Hankin, *The Cassilis Engagement*
J. M. Synge, *The Tinker's Wedding*
August Strindberg, *Storm*
August Strindberg, *The Burnt House*
August Strindberg, *The Pelican*
August Strindberg, *The Great Highway*

1908
J. M. Barrie, *What Every Woman Knows*
W. B. Yeats, *The Unicorn from the Stars*
St John Hankin, *The Last of the De Mullins*
Cicely Hamilton, *Diana of Dobson's*

1909
Maurice Maeterlinck, *The Blue Bird*
George Feydeau, *Look After Lulu*
John Galsworthy, *Strife*

D. H. Lawrence, *A Collier's Friday Night*
Carl Sternheim, *The Knickers*
Ferenc Molnár, *Liliom*
Arthur Wing Pinero, *Mid Channel*
Bjørnstjerne Bjørnson, *When the New Wine Blooms*
Stanley Houghton, *Independent Means*

1910
Rabindranath Tagore, *The King of the Dark Chamber*
J. M. Synge, *Deirdre of the Sorrows*
John Galsworthy, *Justice*
Harley Granville Barker, *The Madras House*
George Bernard Shaw, *Misalliance*
Ferenc Molnár, *The Guardsman*
Edmond Rostand, *Chantecleer*
Cicely Hamilton, *How The Vote Was Won*

1911
D. H. Lawrence, *The Widowing of Mrs Holroyd*
Arthur Schnitzler, *Undiscovered Country*
George Bernard Shaw, *Fanny's First Play*
Hugo Von Hofmannsthal, *Everyman*
Carl Sternheim, *The Money Box*
Cicely Hamilton, *Just To Get Married*

1912
D. H. Lawrence, *The Daughter-In-Law*
Eugene Brieux, *La Femme Seule*
Stanley Houghton, *Hindle Wakes*
Githa Sowerby, *Rutherford And Son*
John Galsworthy, *The Eldest Son*
Carl Sternheim, *Burger Schippel*
Arthur Schnitzler, *Professor Bernhardi*
Leo Tolstoy, *Redemption*
(death of August Strindberg)

1913
Somerset Maugham, *The Promised Land*
George Bernard Shaw, *Androcles and The Lion*

D. H. Lawrence, *The Merry-Go-Round*
John Galsworthy, *The Fugitive*
Georg Kaiser, *The Burghers of Calais*